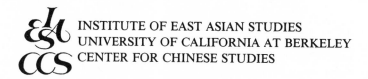

INSTITUTE OF EAST ASIAN STUDIES
UNIVERSITY OF CALIFORNIA AT BERKELEY
CENTER FOR CHINESE STUDIES

China's Education Reform in the 1980s

Policies, Issues, and Historical Perspectives

SUZANNE PEPPER

A publication of the Institute of East Asian Studies, University of California at Berkeley. Although the Institute of East Asian Studies is responsible for the selection and acceptance of manuscripts in this series, responsibility for the opinions expressed and for the accuracy of statements rests with their authors.

The China Research Monograph series, whose first title appeared in 1967, is one of several publications series sponsored by the Institute of East Asian Studies in conjunction with its constituent units. The others include the Japan Research Monograph series, the Korea Research Monograph series, the Indochina Research Monograph series, and the Research Papers and Policy Studies series. A list of recent publications appears at the back of the book.

Correspondence may be sent to:
Ms. Joanne Sandstrom, Managing Editor
Institute of East Asian Studies
University of California
Berkeley, California 94720

Contents

Acknowledgments

This monograph in its most recent incarnation was a paper presented to the International Conference on a Decade of Reform Under Deng Xiaoping, held at Brown University in November 1987. I would like to thank Professor Kau Ying-mao for permission to publish this revised and updated version separately before a final decision had been made on the publication of a conference volume.

In fact, what follows is the result of two conference assignments which together addressed two major questions being asked in the 1980s by students of Chinese politics and history about China's contemporary reform experience. Ironically, given the nature of the times, both assignments were "backward" looking in that they asked not just for an analysis of the reforms introduced in China since the death of Mao Zedong in 1976, but for the analysis to be made from the perspective of their past as well. The 1987 assignment called for an evaluation of reforms within the education sector and of their significance by comparison with policies in the preceding Maoist era. The earlier conference (To Reform the Chinese Political Order, June 1984, sponsored by the Joint Committee on Chinese Studies of the American Council of Learned Societies and the Social Science Research Council) with its "sweeping themes of history" approach was even more ambitious. The request in that instance was to assess the post-Mao reforms within the context of China's education reform tradition, extending back to the abolition of the imperial civil service examinations and the introduction of a modern school system during the early years of the twentieth century!

However presumptuous it may have appeared at first glance, the latter approach added an important dimension that until recently has been lacking in much work, including my own, on China's educational development both in the Maoist past and the post-Mao present. This perspective makes it possible to trace the origin of the contradictions between pre- and post-1976 education policies to the ambivalent relationship between China's modern school system and its critics of all political persuasions that is almost as old as the system itself. The nature of the ambivalence has evolved from one decade to the next. But certain basic concerns, plus the tensions and arguments surrounding them, remain clearly identifiable over time. They also now seem destined to span in one form or another the entire twentieth century from its first decade through its last. The presentation here thus "pre-dates" and "post-dates" the sections on education in the *Cambridge History of China*, volumes 14 and 15, which concentrate more specifically on the 1949–79 period.

Concerning the student protests of the late 1980s, however, the reader should not expect to find in the issues of educational reform and development with which this essay is primarily concerned, the primary reasons for student dissent. The two are inevitably linked and some of the issues may have played a necessary contributing role, but they did not in themselves constitute sufficient cause. For that, as suggested in the postscript on the student protests, it is necessary to look beyond the education sector to the economic and political reform movement as a whole and the general crisis of confidence that its cumulative failings precipitated in 1988–89.

Inevitably, more debts are accumulated in writing and producing a study such as this than can be acknowledged individually. In this respect, I would like to thank the conference participants collectively since many of their ideas have been incorporated at various points along the way. Christine Wong, Joyce Kallgren, and Deborah Davis also read through the entire manuscript at different stages of its evolution and contributed numerous helpful comments and criticisms. Given the events of 1989, that evolution of necessity continued well into the production stage during which editor Joanne Sandstrom presided with patience over a seemingly endless series of corrections, revisions, and updates.

As usual, however, I am most deeply indebted to the staff of the Universities Service Centre, which has provided the support system necessary to sustain my research in Hong Kong for many years. Special acknowledgment is due the former director, John Dolfin, who did much to keep the Centre going in the 1980s and who built its library into a major contemporary China research collection. The early drafts of this monograph were written at the "old" Centre where librarian Liu Huiling and my research assistant Wen Yenxia bore the brunt of my tedious search for references with unfailing tolerance and good humor. Revisions were completed at the "new" Centre, now part of the Chinese University of Hong Kong, where old friends Jean Xiong and Lau Yee-fui have been especially helpful in introducing the new venue for the old materials. Hopefully, there will never be any need to invoke the traditional disclaimer about responsibility but, given the political climate of early 1990, nothing is certain. In any case, it goes without saying that no one but myself should be held responsible for the way the materials have been used here, including any errors remaining and all matters of emphasis and interpretation.

Hong Kong
May 1990

Suzanne Pepper is a Berkeley Ph.D. (political science, 1972) and long-time resident of Hong Kong. Her publications on post-1949 Chinese education include the relevant chapters in the *Cambridge History of China*, vols. 14 and 15. She lectured on Chinese politics as the East Asia associate of the American-based Universities Field Staff International during 1985–87.

The Problems Defined

For those trying to steer a more-or-less steady course through the shifting currents of Chinese educational policies during the past twenty years, a few fixed landmarks can help to guide the way. Different people use different reference points. Mine are a certain common denominator of problems that virtually all countries, whether socialist or otherwise, have been found to encounter when they embark upon the path of educational development in the contemporary world. These problems inevitably take on political dimensions, because education is now commonly accepted to be a public as well as a private resource. Solutions thus depend ultimately on the decisions of governments and the makers of public policy. When formulated at that level, moreover, these concerns are not specifically professional or academic in nature. Although questions such as how students are taught, what they are taught, and what facilities are to be made available for learning are conventionally left to professional educators to answer, they do so on the basis of policy directives and within parameters that are rarely fixed by them alone. Each country's policies and parameters actually derive from a range of considerations, including its historical traditions, level of economic development, and the nature of its political system, together with the priorities adopted and the changing demands of its citizens.

Nevertheless, the problems with which policy makers must cope are remarkably similar everywhere. Nor are they recent discoveries. Virtually all can be traced in the international literature on educational development at least as far back as the 1920s and 1930s. Neither are they confined to the countries of what, in the latter half of the twentieth century, came to be called the Third World. But they do tend to take on somewhat different dimensions once national economies begin to move out of the low income range and governments no longer have to worry about large, basi-

cally illiterate populations living primarily in the countryside. A
common denominator of policy problems that have been associated
with educational development over time can be summarized as follows.

The most basic is usually expressed in quantitative terms. A
proclaimed goal just about everywhere is a system of universal mass
education capable of eliminating the stigma of illiteracy and providing everyone with at least an elementary education. Hence, the
measures of success are the proportion of the elementary school age
group actually in attendance and the proportion that completes the
course. But the costs of building and maintaining such a system for
the ever-increasing numbers of the school-aged population are often
more than low-income economies can afford. The costs of sending
youngsters to school are also greater than many working-class families can afford. It is not just a matter of tuition and fees, but also
of income forgone, since it is a commonplace in such societies that
the labor of all the family's members is often necessary to maintain
the economic survival of the unit as a whole. This is particularly
true of blue-collar families and especially of those within the agricultural sector. As a result, high drop-out rates are a typical feature
of Third World elementary schools. Wherever universal elementary
education has been adopted as a goal, therefore, the first practical
problem has been to find ways of getting everyone into school and
keeping them there for about five years, which is generally considered the time needed to achieve basic literacy and sustain it over
time. A supplementary goal, to devise ways of imparting a similar
degree of literacy to the existing adult population, is usually treated
as a secondary task after that of beginning to educate the younger
generation.

A second major problem concerns the need to coordinate education with employment opportunities. This problem, too, is regularly expressed in quantitative terms, especially when it translates into
"brain drains" and large numbers of educated but unemployed or
underemployed young people. Even though the demand for education tends to outstrip the supply, the latter seems to produce more
graduates and school leavers than economies can at certain stages of
development readily absorb. It has often proven easier to build
new schools than to provide commensurate opportunities on the
job market. If the associated dislocations continue long enough,
they can produce increasingly demoralized and alienated generations of young people, unable to find the jobs and salaries they have
been led to expect given their academic qualifications. Such dislo-

cations can also appear at any educational level. They are often exacerbated, where mass education has not yet become the established norm, by traditional distinctions between mental and manual labor. In such societies, disdain for manual labor can be acquired along with even the most rudimentary education, which thus inadvertently produces unrealistic expectations immediately it is introduced.

Furthermore, educated young people inevitably seem destined to leave less well endowed districts, regions, and countries, where the need for their talents may be greatest in objective terms. But the opportunities are rarely as attractive there as in the "First World" or in less backward sectors of countries everywhere, which have become the pools into which the brain drains flow. Naturally, these are not problems that education systems can solve on their own. Nevertheless, the problems are conventionally thought to be more manageable if there can be some coordination between the needs of the economy, on the one hand, and, on the other, the content and quality of education provided together with the expectations aroused in the process.

A third area of concern thus moves from questions of quantity into the realms of quality and content. These issues are complex and educators have built several theories concerning them, most of which perhaps can be traced to the fact that Third World education systems tend not to have undergone the practical "education for life" impact of the Dewey revolution. In other words, these education systems are often found to be narrowly academic in content, formalistic in teaching methods, restricted by examinations, and remote from the daily lives of the students and their communities.

A fourth set of problems is in many ways the most difficult of solution because all of the foregoing combine to create them, reformulated around the issue of equality. Hence this is an issue with many dimensions, which constantly shift and change. It has, very simply, to do with who gets how much of what kind of schooling. A proposition that appears to hold true cross-culturally, albeit with some important variations, is that people with less education want their children to receive more and people with more want to preserve the family's intellectual inheritance for its succeeding generations. When resources are scarce, as they always are, conflicts of interest necessarily develop between and among the various competing private and public demands.

The issue of equality, moreover, can be seen as existing on two levels: one international, the other domestic. The first manifestations of the former became apparent long ago when local elites began to denounce the efforts of colonial administrators to adapt schooling to local needs as an attempt to inflict a second-rate education on the colonized population. The demand of tribal leaders in New Guinea to have the study of Greek and Latin included in the curricula of their secondary schools used to be cited in the literature as a favorite example of this dilemma. The problem has since passed through many evolutions, but it still exists today, as education systems strive to attain "international standards." In the process, many generations of young people have been educated to the standards of societies other than their own, in ways that have often ill prepared them for the lives that most must continue to live in their own communities. It has been found, furthermore, that the more and the better young people have been educated, the greater has been the brain drain or outward migration rates from countryside to city, where such young people are also more likely to swell the ranks of the urban unemployed.

Thus the desire for equality on an international level, in terms of creating schools that are equal to advanced world standards, may be easy enough to achieve. But that achievement came most easily in small or at least narrowly based colonial-style education systems with their accepted ties of economic and cultural dependency to the dominant countries of Europe and America. Such standards are more difficult to maintain once twentieth century demands for mass education gain popular acceptance, as they now have to some degree or other in most countries of the world. Such standards are also more difficult to sustain if and when local elites begin to challenge the legitimacy of the dependent ties with the countries that determine the standards.

The same kind of problem also exists internally. A curriculum that caters specifically to the needs of the countryside, for example, will not be able to meet those of the cities. Hence the demand for education that is "relevant" to all, depending on its degree of specificity, might result in two different tracks or kinds of education. But until the means can be found to make urban and rural life equally attractive, such a dual education system might also be seen as an instrument for perpetuating the inequalities inherent in the existing division of labor between town and countryside. As expectations rise, people often conclude that it is unfair to maintain separate tracks and demand access to alternatives.

At the secondary level, the equality problem hinges on the need to provide education that will be college preparatory for some but terminal for the majority. The dilemma here revolves around questions of whether and when to begin channeling young people into academic and vocational streams so as to maximize opportunities for them in a way they will accept as fair, but also in ways that are appropriate for what their societies need and their economies can afford.

These questions are complicated further by the matter of cultural inheritance or the close connection between academic achievement and social background. Everywhere, city people are better educated than people in the countryside. The same is true of children from white collar families, by comparison with those of working class parents, and men by comparison with women. And everywhere these advantages and disadvantages tend to be passed on from one generation to the next.

Such inequalities obviously do not originate with education, nor can education systems be expected to solve them. But since people usually perceive education as the intervening variable that stands between them and social advancement, they often resent forms of schooling that seem to obstruct the route outward and upward—especially when the path appears to be more difficult to negotiate for some people's children than for others.

Clearly, there are no ideal solutions. Since these problems all interact and compete with one another for the scarce resources necessary to solve them, the most that any government can do is try to work out strategies that balance the costs and benefits of particular kinds of education, in different proportions, for different kinds of students, at any given time and place. Acceptable and affordable strategies also tend to change as ruling coalitions shift and as the dynamic of development itself produces changing interests, expectations, and demands among different sectors of the population.[1]

---

[1] The literature on educational development is voluminous. Although it is possible to extract a common denominator of issues, analysis and interpretation have varied, sometimes dramatically, over the years. The following are a selection of key references. For an early formulation with specific reference to China: The League of Nations' Mission of Educational Experts (C. H. Becker, M. Falski, P. Langevin, R. H. Tawney), *The Reorganization of Education in China* (Paris: League of Nations' Institute of Intellectual Cooperation, 1932); For the 1960s: C. Arnold Anderson and Mary Jean Bowman, eds., *Education and Economic Development* (Chicago: Aldine, 1965); James S. Coleman, ed., *Education and Political Development* (Princeton, N.J.: Princeton University Press, 1965); Adam Curle, *Educational Strategy for Developing Societies* (London: Tavistock, 1963). For the 1970s: Martin Carnoy, *Education as Cultural Imperialism* (New York: David McKay, 1974); Samuel Bowles and Herbert Gintis, *Schooling in Capitalist America: Educational Reform and the Contradictions of Economic Life* (London: Routledge and Kegan Paul, 1976); Ronald Dore, *The Di-*

Chinese policy makers, like their counterparts in most other countries, are grappling with this same combination of problems. What has made China fairly unusual, however, is that its leaders gradually articulated different and competing strategies for solving them. These strategies were many decades in the making and did not actually emerge as such until the late 1960s. They can trace their ancestry in direct lines of descent back to the education reform debates of the early twentieth century. But it was not until Mao Zedong's 1966–76 Cultural Revolution and the subsequent backlash against it led by Deng Xiaoping, that distinct approaches could be seen clearly in competition with each other. In fact, they had crystallized around differing conceptions of what form China's socialist modernization should take, tying them in the process to one of the most destructive of all political power struggles, namely, that for control of the Chinese Communist Party (CCP). As a result of this political dimension, educational development has probably been the subject of greater controversy in China than in any other country.

The following essay seeks to evaluate the educational reforms of the post-1976 Deng Xiaoping administration within the context of its historical antecedents and political parameters. From this exercise emerges a fascinating outline of arguments that have spanned close to a century of China's educational history. Patterns of development from the past have been recreated in the present, reproducing policy issues that will certainly continue well into the 1990s.

---

ploma Disease: Education, Qualification, and Development (London: George Allen and Unwin, 1976); Jerome Karabel and A. H. Halsey, eds., *Power and Ideology in Education* (New York: Oxford University Press, 1977); John W. Meyer and Michael T. Hannan, eds., *National Development and the World System: Educational, Economic, and Political Change, 1950–1970* (Chicago: University of Chicago Press, 1979). Also: John Simmons (The World Bank), ed., *The Education Dilemma: Policy Issues for Developing Countries in the 1980's* (New York: Pergamon, 1980); Ingemar Fagerlind and Lawrence J. Saha, *Education and National Development* (New York: Pergamon, 1983); and George Timmons, *Education, Industrialization, and Selection* (London and New York: Routledge, 1988).

PART ONE

The "Two-Line Struggle" in Chinese Education: Origins and Development

CHAPTER ONE

The Antiestablishment Backlash
of the 1920s

Following official Chinese discourse, it became fashionable during the late 1960s to associate differences over education policy with the all-encompassing "two-line struggle" said to be rooted in the Yan'an period (1935–47) of the CCP's history. In fact, the volumes of old documents recently reprinted in China verify that a relevant dichotomy did develop in the CCP's education policy between 1938 and 1944—although not in any such clear-cut form with Mao on one side and his enemies on the other, as was later suggested.[1] What the documents do reveal, however, is that the same controversies that existed in Chinese education circles generally at that time were reproduced in Yan'an as well, after the CCP's political and intellectual leaders made it their capital in the mid-1930s. As refugees from the Guomindang and Japanese-occupied areas, the new arrivals brought with them all of their conflicting assumptions and commitments. These then formed the basis of the "new" education policies devised for the Communist-led border region governments established in the north China hinterland from the mid-1930s.

---

[1] The fullest collection of such documents is the three-volume series Zhongyang jiaoyu kexue yanjiusuo (Central Education Research Institute), ed., *Laojiefangqu jiaoyu ziliao* (Education Materials from the Old Liberated Areas) (Beijing: Jiaoyu kexue chubanshe, 1981, 1986). The documents add much new detail but no startling revelations to the educational history of the CCP base areas. See, for example, Peter J. Seybolt, "The Yenan Revolution in Mass Education," *China Quarterly*, no. 48 (Oct.–Dec. 1971); Michael Lindsay, *Notes on Educational Problems in Communist China, 1941–47* (New York: Institute of Pacific Relations, 1950); Mark Selden, *The Yenan Way in Revolutionary China* (Cambridge: Harvard University Press, 1971), pp. 267–74.

The conflicting commitments had developed during the early 1920s as part of an overall critical backlash against the sudden rush to learn from the West that swept through China during the first two decades of the century. The decisive shift in favor of Western learning had not occurred until after the shock of defeat in the Sino-Japanese War of 1894–95. Thereafter China could no longer maintain even the pretense of its ancient superiority as the center of the East Asian world. After having clung so tenaciously to its past against the nineteenth century Western intrusion, China's educated elite suddenly abandoned Confucian learning, the ancient civil service examinations, and finally in 1911 the imperial system itself—all with unprecedented revolutionary haste. China's wealth and power would now have to be reconstructed in a different sort of world, where Western ways and means predominated.[2]

A key date in the process was 1905, the year the examinations were abolished. Thereafter, the elite sent their children to modern schools at home, and education abroad became de rigueur for all who could afford it. Indeed, these ends had constituted the ultimate argument for ending the centuries-old examination system. Once the need for Western learning was acknowledged by influential Qing dynasty officials, they soon recognized that the examinations were an obstacle to its general acceptance. So long as the examinations remained the principal route to public office, itself the principal career objective of all who pursued a higher education, students would not enroll in the new schools in large numbers. Nor would sufficient incentives exist to encourage the private financial support necessary for the widespread expansion of modern schools, since the state claimed not to have sufficient resources to assume full responsibility itself.[3] For the educated elite, then, the practical function of a classical Confucian education ceased to exist as of 1905. The abolition of the civil service examinations did not sever the direct route between learning and public office, of course, be-

---

[2] On this shift, see Mary Claubaugh Wright, "Introduction: The Rising Tide of Change," in Mary Claubaugh Wright, ed., *China in Revolution: The First Phase, 1900–1913* (New Haven: Yale University Press, 1968); William Ayers, *Chang Chih-tung and Educational Reform in China* (Cambridge: Harvard University Press, 1971), pp. 251–54.

[3] Ayers, *Chang Chih-tung*, pp. 237–44; Wolfgang Franke, *The Reform and Abolition of the Traditional Chinese Examination System* (Cambridge: East Asian Research Center, Harvard University, 1972), pp. 56, 59–65; Knight Biggerstaff, *The Earliest Modern Government Schools in China* (Ithaca: Cornell University Press, 1961), p. 88.

cause the plan was initially to recruit government officials from among the new school graduates. That formal break with the ancient link between intellectual and political power did not occur until the 1911 revolution overthrew the imperial system itself.

Beginning in 1905, however, the rush to study abroad commenced. Japan was the earliest destination of most because of cultural similarities, geographic proximity, lower costs, and because Japan had already mastered enough of the new science and technology to defeat the Chinese in battle. Sources differ on the numbers involved, but according to one, some 15,000 Chinese students went to Japan in 1906, whereas only 1,300 had gone in 1904 and 2,400 in 1905. The great majority were seeking diplomas from short-term courses as the quickest route to official positions back home. Only a small number were actually engaged in tertiary-level studies.[4] Large numbers continued to study in Japan, but that country's popularity declined as its aggressive designs against China grew after 1910. The United States then became the most popular destination, although the greater costs and difficulties involved in studying there limited numbers. In 1910, about 600 were studying in the United States, including those supported by public and private funds. By 1924, the number had climbed to 2,200.[5]

In this way, then, the precedents of attraction and reaction were set. Chinese officialdom may initially have needed to be dragged forcefully into the twentieth century. But once there, the tendency was to rush forward without pausing to contemplate the personal and social dislocations likely to ensue from shifting gears so abruptly. Modernizing officials at the end of the nineteenth century had sought to overcome conservative resistance by preserving "Chinese learning for the foundation," while promoting "Western learning for practical use" (*Zhongxue wei ti; Xixue wei yong*), to cite the most famous motto of that era. But within a few years, the "new" intellectuals and students returning from abroad had raced far ahead, dismissing the formula altogether in their eagerness to be rid of the foundation as well. Successive waves of "returned students" established a modern school system for China and then imposed successive waves of reform upon it, all patterned on those they had

[4] Y.C. Wang, *Chinese Intellectuals and the West, 1872–1949* (Chapel Hill: University of North Carolina Press, 1966), p. 64.

[5] According to Chinese Ministry of Education statistics, cited in Theodore E. Hsiao, *The History of Modern Education in China* (Shanghai: Commercial Press: 1935), p. 102.

observed abroad, especially in Japan and the United States.

It was in reaction to that initial rush to create a completely new China and a completely modern education system that the post-1919 reappraisal of foreign learning and foreign models developed. The countervailing backlash that set in during the late 1910s appeared to draw strength from a number of sources in the years following the May Fourth Incident of 1919. These sources included an underlying cultural conservatism that was, as it turned out, only submerged but not extinguished by the rush to modernize during the first two decades of the century; newly critical perspectives that returning students brought back from the West itself in the aftermath of World War I; the victory via the Russian Revolution of Marxism, as the most self-critical Western perspective of all; and the growing nationalism of the post–May Fourth years.

By dramatizing these shifting currents, the May Fourth incident itself—when Chinese students protested the decision by the victorious Western powers at the end of World War I to transfer Germany's special concessions in Shandong province to the Japanese—emerged as a historic turning point. Preceding it there had been an idealistic faith in the power of Western democracy and science to save China. Afterward came the consequences of disillusionment and skepticism, as the diverse currents hardened into competing political commitments and ideologies. The CCP was founded and grew rapidly in this climate. It was also at this juncture that the backlash developed among Chinese educators and erstwhile education reformers against the uncritical imitation of Western ideas and models in China's schools. This backlash was not the monopoly of any particular political inclination. Instead it seemed to draw inspiration from the range of ideas that marked the era.

Students returning home with their privileged status as possessors of the most advanced foreign learning suddenly found themselves the objects of satire. In 1921, the "returned student" was immortalized as the "false foreign devil" by twentieth century China's most famous writer, Lu Xun, in the most famous of all his creations, "The True Story of Ah Q." It was this returned student who prevented Ah Q, the illiterate Chinese Everyman, from joining the 1911 Revolution, which overthrew the last dynasty and established the Republic.

Meanwhile, the skepticism was spreading quickly even among those most receptive to foreign ideas. Jiang Menglin, a returned student from the United States, leader of the movement for a "new education," and a sponsor of John Dewey's 1919–21 lecture tour in China, lashed out at the uncritical imitation of foreign ideas in China's schools at that time.[6] Dewey himself responded to the growing climate of skepticism during his tour by cautioning against uniform prescriptions and detailed foreign borrowing. In 1923, Tao Xingzhi summarized the confused odyssey they were all embarked upon: "At first she [China] sacrificed everything old for the new. Gradually she came to a realization that the old is not necessarily bad and the new is not necessarily good. Thus our schoolmen have become much more critical than in former years."[7]

Tao Xingzhi had been educated at Columbia University Teachers' College in New York, was a liberal disciple of John Dewey, and headed the pro-American Chinese National Association for the Advancement of Education. He was already sensitive to the problems of cultural borrowing when, in 1922, he and Dewey helped draft resolutions that became part of the Americanized School Reform Decree promulgated that year. Tao claimed that his own personal awakening did not actually occur until the next year, however, when he decided to buy a change of cotton peasant clothes and "rushed back to the way of the common people." Thereafter he devoted himself increasingly to mass education and non-formal schooling, eventually turning away from the formal education system altogether in order to concentrate on the vast numbers who never entered it.

Reflecting its diverse intellectual and political origins, the backlash against Western influence found adherents all across the developing political spectrum. Their interests and inclinations were already taking them in many different directions. But by the mid-1920s, a common denominator of agreement had crystallized, which then hardened during the following decade into a critical consensus against the new established school system. The consensus was such that budding Marxist Mao Zedong and cultural conservative Liang Shuming as well as pro-American liberals could all share it. By the 1930s, the critique was so popular that virtually everyone was at least paying lip service to it, including the Guomindang government, League of Nations experts, American missionaries, and the Rockefeller Foundation.[8] The argument was

---

[6] Barry Keenan, *The Dewey Experiment in China: Educational Reform and Political Power in the Early Republic* (Cambridge: Harvard University Press, 1977), p. 78.

[7] Quoted in ibid., p. 91.

[8] Mao Zedong, "Hunan zixiu daxue chuangli xuanyan" (The Founding Announcement of the Hunan Self-Study University), Aug. 1921, *Mao Zedong ji* (Mao

based on the following points:

- The new schools, study abroad, and foreign-run missionary education at home had all combined to foster an urban-oriented elite divorced by its learning and life style from the practical needs of Chinese society.

- The new intellectuals were estranged from the rest of society in part because they were inclined to accept uncritically and apply mechanically the Western ideas and educational models to which they were indebted for their new learning.

- Those models then acquired an impractical and elitist nature, which they did not necessarily have in their original settings, when transplanted into the alien Chinese environment where many traditional values still held sway. Chief among these were the social status and self-perceptions of the intellectuals including their disdain for practical work and manual labor.

- New and more appropriate forms had to be designed, and the necessary sources of teachers and money had to be found in order (1) to promote mass education, especially rural mass education since the great majority of China's people lived in the countryside, and (2) to promote learning at all levels that would be more relevant to China's most pressing needs.

A few additional quotations serve to illustrate these points. The Hunan Self-Study University in Changsha was founded in August 1921 by Mao Zedong and his friends, very much in the spirit of the times. Mao explained their motives in the university's founding announcement. This was to be a new kind of institution combining the best of modern and traditional schools, while avoiding the defects of both. Mao began with a statement almost identical in spirit

---

Zedong's Works) (Hong Kong, 1975), 1:81–84; Mao Zedong, "Hunan nongmin yundong kaocha baogao" (Report on an Investigation of the Peasant Movement in Hunan), March 28, 1927, *Mao Zedong ji* 1:246–47; Guy S. Alitto, *The Last Confucian: Liang Shu-ming and the Chinese Dilemma of Modernity* (Berkeley and Los Angeles: University of California Press, 1979); James C. Thomson, Jr., *While China Faced West: American Reformers in Nationalist China, 1928–1937* (Cambridge: Harvard University Press, 1969); Mary Brown Bullock, *An American Transplant: The Rockefeller Foundation and Peking Union Medical College* (Berkeley and Los Angeles: University of California Press, 1980); League of Nations' Mission of Educational Experts (C. H. Becker, M. Falski, P. Langevin, R. H. Tawney), *The Reorganization of Education in China* (Paris: League of Nations' Institute of Intellectual Cooperation, 1932).

to that which liberal educator Tao Xingzhi would make two years later (quoted above). Mao noted that the old Confucian academies had been replaced by modern schools as everyone "rushed to condemn the academies and praise the schools." "In fact," he continued, "both the academies and the schools have things to censure and praise."

The good points of the old academies, wrote Mao, included minimal supervision and a simple curriculum as well as the sincere human feelings they fostered between teachers and students. Modern schools could boast correctly of their new subjects and scientific teaching methods. But their greatest fault was their mechanical, uniform teaching and management styles. Their curriculum was also too heavy, allowing students to gain little knowledge of the outside world. And they treated education like a commercial transaction that only the rich could afford since fees were so high. The bad points shared by both traditional and modern schools were their strict requirements and regulations, which served to exclude all but a "few special people." The new Self-Study University therefore aimed to combine the *form* of the old academy with the *content* of modern learning to create an institution of genuinely popular learning.[9] Unfortunately, Mao and his friends found themselves on the losing side of Hunanese provincial politics; the victorious local warlord put an end to their experiment after only two years of life.[10]

Presently Mao, like many other political activists at the time, turned his attention to the countryside. There they discovered, among other things, that rural people shared their ambivalence about modern education. The results of everyone's social investigations told essentially the same story. For example, Mao noted in his 1927 "Report on an Investigation of the Peasant Movement in Hunan" that a dispute had arisen between the county education boards and the developing peasant movement. The former demanded that education funds be used to establish modern schools; the latter wanted to use the money to support their own evening classes and "peasant schools." As a result, the funds had to be split between the two.

---

[9] Mao Zedong, "Hunan zixiu daxue."

[10] Angus W. McDonald, Jr., *The Urban Origins of Rural Revolution: Elites and the Masses in Hunan Province, China, 1911–1927* (Berkeley and Los Angeles: University of California Press, 1978), pp. 116–20.

"Modern" schools by definition were those which used a Westernized curriculum and teaching methods. The new curriculum included Chinese language, arithmetic, history, nature study, science, music, and athletics. By contrast, in the "peasant schools" the principal subject was still Chinese—often taught in the old-fashioned way using the traditional Confucian primers—plus some practical use knowledge. Rote memorization and recitation were the standard learning techniques. Students progressed individually and so could drop out according to the dictates of farm work and family responsibilities, reappearing later to pick up where they had left off. The new schools were less flexible in their teaching routines with the students, strictly classified into grades, progressing together through fixed terms from year to year.

Mao reported that at the mass level, for basic elementary schooling, rural people preferred the old fashioned classes. Peasants rejected the education provided by the modern primary schools referring to it as "foreign." They regarded it as inappropriate for the needs of village life because the subjects taught were all about urban things. Nor were the new-style teachers sympathetic toward the peasants' old-fashioned attitudes, as Mao admitted he also had not been until 1925, after he became a Marxist.[11]

The villagers' continuing preference for traditional schooling was reflected in John Lossing Buck's early 1930s survey of rural China. Of the 87,000 persons surveyed on this question, 45.2 percent of the males and 2.2 percent of the females reported receiving some schooling. Of the males, 66.5 percent reported that the education they received had been in the traditional style, for an average of four years.[12]

Traveling a route very different from both the Marxists and pro-American liberals, cultural conservative Liang Shuming nevertheless reached conclusions similar to those of Mao Zedong and Tao Xingzhi. It is not recorded that Liang ever exchanged his scholar's gown for a peasant's cotton tunic. But by the early 1920s,

---

[11] Mao Zedong, "Hunan nongmin yundong." Mao's authorship of the passage on education has recently been questioned, but its content remains unchallenged. For other reports on the rural dislike of modern schools see Evelyn Sakakida Rawski, *Education and Popular Literacy in Ch'ing China* (Ann Arbor: University of Michigan Press, 1979), pp. 162–67; Sally Borthwick, *Education and Social Change in China: the Beginnings of the Modern Era* (Stanford, Calif.: Hoover Institution, 1983), pp. 80–83.

[12] John Lossing Buck, *Land Utilization in China* (London: Oxford University Press, 1937), pp. 373–75.

he had begun to explore the causes of China's demoralization and concluded that it was due to Western influence. Previous reform efforts had been led by intellectuals in imitation of the West, to gain wealth and power. They failed to achieve their objective and were extracting China's cultural roots in the process. Wealth and education were concentrating in the cities, and the countryside was being destroyed. In particular, Liang blamed the new Western-style education, which was "educating people for another society" but inadequate to meet China's own needs.

In Liang's view, the new system actually contained the worst of both worlds. The defects of traditional education were still present, whereas its good points had been jettisoned and those of the West lost somewhere in between. The authority of the old educated class, argued Liang, had derived from its dual role as political leader and transmitter of moral standards. The new education ignored the old values, and intellectuals had become self-serving, luxury loving, and profit seeking as a result. They retained their privileged elite status without any sense of moral responsibility. In addition, he anticipated that Chinese society, like societies in the West, would soon divide into permanent hereditary classes since the new education was so costly that only the rich could afford it. Unlike Western intellectuals, on the other hand, their Chinese counterparts still generally aspired to become officials and retained the traditional Chinese scholar's disdain for manual labor. He concluded that the new education was serving only to alienate further the elite from the masses and the cities from the countryside.

Liang's critique, moreover, extended to all levels of education. Rural children, once educated in modern primary schools, were lost to the countryside thereafter, looking down on the life and work that continued there unchanged. Like the peasants in everyone's rural surveys, Liang criticized the curriculum of the new schools for its urban orientation, irrelevance to practical needs, and the impersonal style of the Westernized teachers within them. But he went a step further, declaring that the new education was actually of no use to anyone. He criticized secondary schools and the higher technical institutes as largely pointless. Students in the former acquired no practical skills, and those in the latter were not given the kind of education ostensibly intended. Even the agricultural colleges produced graduates who may have been drawn to rural problems at the start of their careers but who invariably moved into city jobs unrelated to the fields in which they were trained. Liang ultimately criticized all of China's higher education as "irrelevant." He called for students to stop relying on foreign books that could not contribute to China's immediate needs and for the reorientation of research to concentrate on the applied sciences.[13]

In 1931, the European "education experts" who made up the League of Nations' Mission expressed similar views, although from very different perspectives.[14] The new Guomindang (GMD) government that emerged from the violent break of the GMD-CCP alliance in 1927 invited the League to collaborate in preparing a grand plan for comprehensive education reform. Despite evidence of good intentions on many points, only a few of the recommendations were introduced before history again intervened in the form of full-scale Japanese invasion (1937–45) and the subsequent GMD-CCP civil war (1945–49).

The League's report endorsed all the principles inherent in the previous decade's critique of education. Instead of devising solutions that could be tested only piecemeal outside the system, however, the experts' recommendations aimed to transform the system itself. Indeed, they were critical of the very tradition the individualistic reformers were perpetuating with their uncoordinated experiments and pilot projects. The report referred to China's schools as "independent organisms modelled on the forms and ideology of private education instead of being included in an organised system of public education related to immediate social problems."[15]

The authors blamed, first, the Chinese tradition of family, clan, and village schools confined by narrow private interests and private sources of financial support. Second, they blamed the import of foreign models and the inordinate influence exercised by the returned students, who introduced the new models of life and learning firm in the belief that they were the best means to the desired end. Many richly endowed schools and colleges had been set up, but no initiative had yet been taken to integrate them into a coherent mechanism for promoting public education. The imitation of foreign educational institutions, including the use of their curricula, textbooks, and methods, had many adverse consequences. The net result, a disjointed system emphasizing schools of higher standard while mass education was neglected, created an "enormous abyss between the masses of the Chinese people, plunged in illiteracy, and not understanding the needs of their country, and the

---

[13] Alitto, *The Last Confucian*, pp. 140–44, 150–51, 160–66, 200, 212.
[14] League of Nations' Mission, *Reorganization of Education in China*.
[15] Ibid., p. 19.

intelligentsia educated in luxurious schools and indifferent to the wants of the masses."[16]

The mission concluded that the gap between elites and masses, partly an unavoidable consequence of the new Western learning, was being deliberately perpetuated in many ways. These included preferential enrollment practices, high fees, and the regional distribution of schools. Universalizing elementary education should have been among the highest national priorities. But in practice, it could only be achieved with more efficient administration and resource use, as well as a more reliable tax system to ensure adequate funding, and the rational distribution of facilities. The education system was overstaffed and buildings underutilized at all levels. The ratio between the cost of educating primary and college students was 1:200. Comparable ratios in European countries at the time did not exceed 1:10. Similarly, the difference between primary and college teachers' salaries was 1:20 or more in China, by comparison with no more than 1:4 in Europe, indicating "extraordinary neglect" of basic level mass education in China. The mission estimated that, given the existing resources, both human and material, at least twice the number of students could have been accommodated in the existing schools at all levels.[17]

At the secondary level, the most urgent problem was not expanding supply but improving quality. Secondary schools were organized essentially to perform the college-preparatory function rather than to provide a general education that would be complete in itself. The instruction provided was thus too literary and academic while the interests of the majority were being slighted in deference to the minority. The experts cautioned explicitly against the creation of two separate education systems, one vocational and the other general college preparatory. Rather, curriculum reform was recommended for all secondary schools to orient them more closely to the realities of life including the principles of agriculture, industry, and commerce.[18]

At the tertiary level, the mission concluded that the Chinese had not yet understood the function of a university. Its task was supposed to be not the passive supply of knowledge but training individuals to acquire it for themselves. Yet lectures predominated, with textbooks and lecture notes constituting the students' main

---

[16] Ibid., p. 21.
[17] Ibid., pp. 45, 50–52, 62–64, 76–79, 80–84, 90–92.
[18] Ibid., pp. 98–138 passim.

reading matter. Seminars and independent study were rare. Most books used were in foreign languages, and most examples given were of foreign origin. This last reinforced tendencies, inherited from traditional teaching methods of the past, to memorize prepared texts without questioning or application.

The experts also found much to criticize in the structure of higher education, which then comprised more than 50 institutions all established within less than 25 years. Too many institutions were concentrated in the same area (Beijing and Shanghai) and did almost the same work without any rational division of labor between them. The system was further criticized for the "hypertrophy of legal, political and literary studies" to the neglect of science and technology. Just over 59 percent of all students enrolled in full degree programs were studying law, politics, and the liberal arts, with another 6 percent in education. Just under 10 percent were studying in the natural sciences, 11.5 percent in engineering, and only 3 percent in agriculture. Without actually acknowledging the ancient tradition that was reproducing itself in modern guise, the report noted regretfully that "the ambition of most Chinese university students is a career in the public service, central or local, and failing that, a post as a teacher."[19]

The mission did, however, reserve harsh words for the elitism being perpetuated by teachers and students. The aura of the past, when scholars were exempt from manual labor and granted the privileges of official position, still surrounded them, heightened now by their possession of the new Western learning. Their "superficiality and self-conceit" was being passed on from one student generation to the next, contributing to the demoralization of academic life. The experts tried to distinguish between the (acceptable) political activities of the students as articulators of a wider public opinion and their (anti-social) contempt for authority. This latter was manifested, for example, in demands to attend fewer lectures than given credit for, to dictate the nature of examinations, and to dismiss teachers or administrators. Life in schools where such demands erupted was distorted by "dreary intrigue and humourless exasperation." Such behavior was judged a symptom of larger problems arising from the almost total lack of contact between teachers and students and the passive nature of the learn-

---

[19] Ibid., p. 151, and pp. 139–58 passim.

ing process itself—thus perpetuating the cycle of social irresponsibility.[20]

Finally, the mission expressed skepticism about the general desire to go abroad for study since the objective was usually only the prestige of a foreign degree. The returned students' well-known problems of adjusting to work in China and the dislocations they were creating caused the mission to recommend that only advanced scholars be permitted to study abroad and only in fields for which there were no adequate facilities yet existing in China itself.[21]

In conclusion, one additional point must be emphasized which concerns the ambivalence inspired by the critique as a whole during the 1920s and 1930s. This ambivalence was most evident in the unwillingness to correct the defects that everyone willingly acknowledged. Those defects were, to reiterate: the formalistic imitation of Western learning; promoted and sustained by the influence of those educated abroad; the failure to adapt the new learning to the needs of Chinese society; and the consequent growing disparities between education for elites and masses, especially between urbanized elites and rural masses.

Despite its prevalence, however, this critique never succeeded in generating anything more than experimental challenges to the modern school system. This remained by and large impervious to the kinds of reforms that would have solved the problems everyone acknowledged. Exactly why this should have been so remains unclear. But the burden of responsibility probably rested most heavily with the professional educators who staffed the system, since they seemed overwhelmingly committed to it despite its defects. Nor should such a conclusion be overshadowed by two countervailing considerations, namely, that so many of the critics were themselves prominent members of the intellectual establishment; and that their most immediate adversaries were usually from the political rather than the intellectual arena.

A genuine contradiction appears to have developed, in other words, between the widely perceived need for change and the willingness to undertake the measures necessary to realize it for the system as a whole. Similarly, this contradiction existed not only between people of different persuasions but even within individuals themselves. Like most everything else in unreconstructed

---

[20] Ibid., pp. 158–60, 167–72.

[21] Ibid., pp. 173–74.

twentieth-century Chinese society following the collapse of the old order, the argument over education reform seemed to reflect a people at war with themselves. They harbored conflicts of interest and opinion so great that only some master adjudicator would have been able to break the impasse and enforce a reconciliation.

One apparent example of such conflict at the personal level can be found in the writing of American-educated Theodore Hsiao (Yale-in-China; Columbia, M.A.; Princeton; New York University, Ph.D.). Reflecting the climate of the early 1930s, he sympathized with the renewed upsurge of anti-Christian sentiment which was also a part of that era. He was thus appropriately critical of Christian mission schools for their opportunistic motives, the socially detached education they provided, their racist treatment of Chinese colleagues, and the pretexts they provided for foreign intervention in China. Yet without addressing directly or explaining the ambivalence reflected in his comments, he went on to laud the Christian missionary, his converts, the mission press, and the vernacular Bible as pioneers and forerunners of China's twentieth-century "intellectual awakening." On the question of continuing to send students abroad, he agreed with the critics that Chinese youth should be educated at home. But for the transformation of economic and social life then underway, he gave credit to Western science. And he had special praise for the thousands of students educated abroad who brought back Western learning. They had become "a new class" sought after by government and society "to direct, or to assist in the realization of, the potentialities of the nation."[22]

As for the reform experiments that derived from the critique during the 1920s and 1930s, they were almost as numerous as the people contributing to it, ranging from Mao's Self-Study University to Liang Shuming's rural reconstruction efforts. But their experiments were disparate, uncoordinated, and implemented outside the formal school system. Nor did they ever progress much beyond the pilot project stage. In an era of military governments, warring parties, and foreign invaders, the immediate cause of failure could almost always be traced to a hostile or at best nonprotective political environment. Those who thought they could succeed by working against the official power structure, or at least outside it soon discovered the futility of their efforts. Political intervention may have been tagged as the chief enemy by liberal reformers in particu-

---

[22] Hsiao, *History of Modern Education in China*, pp. 104, 117–24.

lar. But once they embarked upon a public undertaking, even one so unpretentious as an education reform experiment, the initiators found that local political sponsorship was the minimum prerequisite. Without it they had neither the protection necessary for survival nor the cooperation essential for success.

Yet the reform efforts also demonstrated that however crucial the political variable in any given instance, it was not the sole culprit and probably not even the principal one underlying the reform failures. Politicians and militarists may have been to blame for the demise of individual projects. But their lack of protection outside the established school system only widened the base of responsibility by pointing to the failure of the system as a whole to respond to demands for reform. And that system, including the Ministry of Education which presided over it, was the creation of the intellectuals and returned students. They led and staffed the government education bureaucracy and in that capacity enjoyed the political support necessary to build the formal school establishment more or less as they wished.

In fact, successive governments, far from being hostile to "reform," were perhaps too receptive to the idea—indicating at least that a predilection for change was not the monopoly of the antiestablishment opposition. These governments sponsored repeated reorganizations of the national education system during the first three decades of the century. The League of Nations' Mission was to have set the stage for another in the 1930s. But each reorganization was carried out in accordance with the views of successive generations returning from abroad, and each reproduced essentially the same combination of defects as its predecessors.

The first modern school system, set up in 1903, was patterned on that of Japan and introduced by returned students from that country. A reorganization was carried out in 1912, under the influence of the early wave of Chinese students returning from the United States. The 1912 system was something of a compromise between the two national influences. By 1922, the influence of those returning from the United States predominated, and yet another reorganization occurred. The School Reform Decree of that year marked the high point of American influence on Chinese education. Individual schools were given the right to develop their own curricula; elective courses were permitted at the secondary level; social studies was introduced into the recommended standard secondary school curriculum; the credit system was adopted; so too was the American division of six-year elementary schools and six-year secondary, the latter divided further into junior and senior levels of three years each. In place of the Japanese-style multitrack system with separate schools for academic, vocational, technical, and teacher training, all courses were to be taught within individual secondary schools following the model of the American comprehensive high school.

Modifications on the 1922 system were then made in 1928, under the new Guomindang government. These were generally aimed at giving the government more powers over education, after a short-lived attempt in 1927–28 at radical decentralization based on the French system. The leading promoter of this latter experiment was Cai Yuanpei. Famous as chancellor of Beijing University during the May Fourth period, Cai served briefly as chief education administrator under the new government with the aim of giving educators primary influence over education policy. Additionally, his goals were to promote scientific research, art, and the habit of physical labor among intellectual's. Cai's experience as an education reformer at this time was unusual in that he was actually able to devise an experiment for the system as a whole, but typical in that his plans were soon aborted by overriding political pressures. In this case, the pressures came from demands within the GMD leadership to restore the centralized Education Ministry system in order to bring education under the control of the national government and party organization. Measures were also presently introduced aimed at bringing all private and missionary schools under Chinese government control and transferring leadership of foreign schools to Chinese churches and Chinese management bodies.[23]

Throughout the 1920s and especially after the GMD government was established, however, the "returned students" monopolized the leading administrative and academic positions in the central government's Ministry of Education, the provincial education bureaus, and the top universities. Invariably the most prestigious positions in government administration and academia went to the

23 Ping Wen Kuo, *The Chinese System of Public Education* (New York: Teachers College, Columbia University, 1915), pp. 78–135; Hsiao, *History of Modern Education in China*, pp. 50–65; Keenan, *Dewey Experiment*, pp. 65–66; William J. Duiker, *Ts'ai Yuan-p'ei: Educator of Modern China* (University Park: The Pennsylvania State University Press, 1977), pp. 86–92; Zhongyang jiaoyu kexue yanjiusuo, ed., *Zhongguo xiandai jiaoyu dashiji, 1919–1949* (Chronicle of Events in China's Modern Education, 1919–1949) (Beijing: Jiaoyu kexue chubanshe, 1988), pp. 61, 138, 164, 190.

returned students rather than graduates of the new Chinese colleges. The former, on their return to China, tended to congregate near the centers of national power, in Beijing before 1927 and in the Shanghai-Nanjing area after the GMD government moved the national capital to the latter city. They were responsible for the disproportionate number of new colleges in those two urban areas. Between 1916 and 1922, the number of colleges in Beijing rose from 17 to 40, and then fell back to 17 by 1932. Between 1922 and 1932, the number in Shanghai rose from 13 to 25. Virtually all of the new Shanghai schools were either government-run or private non-missionary, and both types were controlled by foreign-educated Chinese.[24]

Meanwhile, the returned students and professional educators continued to preside over a system that was hopelessly inadequate for the needs of Chinese society in modern terms. Official statistics never claimed more than 25 percent of the school-age children to be in attendance at the elementary level during the pre-1949 era. Secondary and tertiary education was even more abbreviated. In 1949, China's secondary schools had an enrollment of only 1.3 million, or about 2 percent of the relevant age group. Only 120,000 students were enrolled at the college level (0.3 percent of the age group) in a population that was then about 540 million.[25]

In a sense, then, China's newly modern education system and the Western-trained professional educators who maintained it were reproducing one of the Chinese intellectual tradition's greatest ironies. For that tradition, too, was maintained by a small, highly educated elite that perpetuated itself over millennia within a population the majority of which remained either totally unschooled or at best semiliterate. By contrast, the critique that developed during the 1920s and 1930s, despite the "traditional" and "conservative" strains also contained within it, was in effect a modern populist protest against that continuing contradiction between the elite and mass levels of China's intellectual life.

That a "critical consensus" was developing throughout the 1920s, that the sharpest critics included some of the returned students themselves, and that the failure of individual reform projects could usually be traced to some immediate political cause should not therefore be allowed to obscure the full context of the contro-

---

[24] Wang, *Chinese Intellectuals and the West*, pp. 365–68.
[25] *China: Socialist Economic Development* (Washington, D.C.: The World Bank, 1983), 3:134.

versy. Tao Xingzhi and James Yen were acclaimed because they were *exceptions* to the rule, not representatives of it.[26] And they had to set up their experiments *outside* the formal education system, because there was no tolerance for them within it. Thus their success was undermined not only by politicians and warlords, but also by their own fellow intellectuals. Because of such resistance, the system as a whole could not have been reformed in accordance with the prevailing critique even had there been a politics-free environment in which to proceed.

Nor is it sufficient to draw the line of distinction between reform-minded intellectuals outside the government bureaucracy and reform-resistant individuals within, although such "ideal types" could be found in both places. But the contradictions persisted generally even within the former group, and the critique had adherents even among those most firmly committed to the conventions of the new learning. These inherent contradictions were highlighted in the League of Nations' report. The authors were careful to note that most of their criticisms had already been formulated by Chinese educators. But the authors' most basic reservations were directed against those same educators for perpetuating the prevailing and fundamental "misconception of the function of a university" and advancing the "false argument" that modern Europe and America were the products of science and technology instead of the other way around. Hence, the belief still prevailed that China had only to acquire Western science and technology in order to become similarly advanced. Both misconceptions lay at the heart of the system these educators had created and were responsible for many of the defects they themselves acknowledged.[27]

The conflict that had emerged in pre-1949 China, then, was not just between right and left or tradition and modernity. Nor was it

---

26 Among interested foreigners, James Yen was the best known of the education reformers, particularly for his rural education and reconstruction work in Ding County, Hebei. See, for example, Sidney D. Gamble, *Ting Hsien: A North China Rural Community* (New York: Institute of Pacific Relations, 1954); Thomson, *While China Faced West*, pp. 48–58; Shirley S. Garrett, *Social Reformers in Urban China: The Chinese YMCA, 1895–1926* (Cambridge: Harvard University Press, 1970), pp. 154–63; Charles Hayford, "Rural Reconstruction in China: Y.C. James Yen and the Mass Education Movement" (Ph.D. dissertation, Harvard University, 1973).

27 For different perspectives from the 1980s on China's twentieth century educational history see Ruth Hayhoe and Marianne Bastid, eds., *China's Education and the Industrialized World: Studies in Cultural Transfer* (Armonk, N.Y.: M.E. Sharpe, 1987).

a contradiction between rural and urban interests or between politicized amateurs and academic professionals. The conflict cut across all of those dimensions and persisted as a highly ambivalent controversy even among establishment intellectuals themselves over the flawed structure of the education system they had created but were incapable of correcting. The dichotomy that developed in Yan'an over education policy arose directly from that ambivalence.

CHAPTER TWO

The Yan'an Decade

In an interesting example of social reproduction, China's new generation of intellectuals—and the most left-leaning among them at that—then tried to build in the Communists' new Shaanxi-Gansu-Ningxia Border Region a replica of the much-maligned education system they had left behind in the Guomindang areas. The Shaan-Gan-Ning region, whence the CCP fled after being driven from its rural Jiangxi base in 1934, lay at the nether end of the "enormous abyss" educationally and in most other ways as well. It was predominantly rural, poor, and sparsely populated. Towns were small provincial backwaters and social customs outmoded even by the standards of rural China at that time. The literacy rate was the lowest reported for any region. When the CCP established its capital there in the mid-1930s, there was no modern school system to speak of and therefore no interests to defend—not at least until the new arrivals began creating them. By the end of the 1930s, many thousands of intellectuals (in those days the term was used for anyone with a secondary school education or above) had congregated in the region to join the Communist-led anti-Japanese resistance movement.

Xu Teli, Mao's old teacher from Changsha, was initially assigned to head the Shaan-Gan-Ning government's education office. Xu began immediately to promote mass education as he had done in the Jiangxi Soviet in the early 1930s. The number of elementary schools in northern Shaanxi grew rapidly from just over 100 in 1935 to 1,341 in early 1940. Most were three-year junior primary schools, which were easiest to set up and maintain at the village level. Student enrollment increased from about 2,000 to 41,458.[1]

---

[1] "Bianqu sinianlai xuexiao jiaoyu menglie zengjia" (The Vigorous Increase of Schooling in the Border Region During the Past Four Years), *Jiefang ribao* (Liberation Daily), June 5, 1941, reprinted in *Shaan-Gan-Ning geming genjudi shiliao xuanji* (Selection of Historical Materials from the Shaan-Gan-Ning Revolutionary Base)

By 1940, however, such statistics were being publicized to bolster the argument that primary schooling had been too precipitous in its growth. It was probably no mere coincidence that Xu Teli was transferred to other work in 1938. From that year, concern began to mount, at least as reflected in education department documents, over the low quality of the education being provided. Xu was succeeded as head of the department by Zhou Yang, a Communist cultural luminary recently arrived from Shanghai. What, if anything, Zhou had to do with the mundane details of elementary schooling has yet to be revealed. By the time this new concern for quality peaked in 1942, he too had been transferred to other work. But his arrival in the border region and its education department coincided with the onset of the "regularization" drive that would dominate border region education during the next four years.

Low standards became the chief preoccupation. The newly arrived educators now responsible for the burgeoning system considered this defect to be the result of setting up schools too quickly. The "ruralness" of the system also bothered them. Many of the new schools were little different from the old style *sishu,* or private Chinese classes, with a teacher and four or five students. As noted, rural people seemed to prefer this type of instruction, which modern educators dismissed as backward and old-fashioned.

Initially, in 1938, the education department cautioned that the method of "merging" or closing schools should be avoided in the drive to improve quality. This was because past experience had already proven that there would be a direct trade-off, sacrificing quantity for quality since parents did not like sending young children the longer distances to schools in other villages. If the number of schools declined, therefore, the number of students could not increase.[2] This precaution was soon abandoned, however, as the

---

(Lanzhou: Gansu renmin chubanshe, 1985), 4:451. These figures were for the Shaan-Gan-Ning region only. During 1935–40, this Communist-led border region grew in size from a population of about one-half million concentrated primarily in northern Shaanxi, to an estimated 1.5 million in the larger Shaan-Gan-Ning region. The Communist-led base areas throughout north China shrank markedly during the early 1940s Japanese offensives against them, but the Shaan-Gan-Ning region lay beyond the reach of the Japanese advance. On the history of this period, see, for example, references cited in chap. 1, n. 1.

[2] "Jiaoyuting guanyu gaijin yu fazhan xiaoxue de zhishi" (Education Department Directive on Improving and Developing Primary Schools), *Xin Zhonghua bao* (New China News), April 25, 1938, reprinted in *Shaan-Gan-Ning geming genjudi shiliao xuanji,* 4:61–65.

movement to "regularize" (*zhengguihua*) the system escalated. In 1940, each county was authorized to close up to 10 ordinary junior primary schools. The closure of schools that could not muster between 20 and 30 students was also authorized.[3] By the time this trend culminated during the 1942–43 school year, the number of schools had been reduced by almost half, to 752; enrollments were down to 26,816.[4] Those remaining were ordered to follow the rules and regulations. Elementary education could not be improved unless all the "necessary systems" were established with unified texts, teaching materials, fixed standards, uniform teaching plans, regular schedules, and students divided properly into grades and classes.[5]

Improved quality also required the "concentration of strength to run complete primary schools and create their central function of being model schools." Here was the innocent enough formulation of an idea that, when eventually institutionalized nationwide, would become the controversial "keypoint" school system. In 1940–41, the Shaan-Gan-Ning Border Region could boast only 47 complete five-year primary schools and perhaps another 50 central (*zhongxin*) three-year junior primaries. These added up to 100 model schools, although some of the five-year institutions were "very deficient" and therefore unable to perform their "model functions" as guides and pacesetters in their districts. The education department instructed the counties to concentrate their resources in a few good schools, ensuring that they had more funds, the best teachers and administrators, complete furnishings, and followed all the rules. Some people will say this is just putting on a show, said an education department official, and "it is just that," namely, to show everyone how schools should be run.[6]

---

[3] Liu Songtao, "Ban xiaoxue de liangtiao luxian" (The Two Lines for Running Primary Schools), *Renmin jiaoyu* (People's Education), June 1957, reprinted in *Lao jiefang qu jiaoyu gongzuo jingyan pianduan* (Selections on Education Work Experience in the Old Liberated Areas) (Shanghai: Shanghai jiaoyu chubanshe, 1979), p. 185.

[4] Jiang Longji, "Guanyu minban gongzhu zhengce de chubu zongjie" (A Preliminary Summary of the People-Manage-Public-Help Policy), n.d., mimeo, reprinted in Zhongyang jiaoyu kexue yanjiusuo (Central Education Research Institute), ed., *Lao-jiefangqu jiaoyu ziliao* (Educational Materials from the Old Liberated Areas) (Beijing: Jiaoyu kexue chubanshe, 1986), 2:xia:376.

[5] Wen Jize, "Zenyang gaijin bianqu de xiaoxue jiaoyu" (How to Improve Primary School Education in the Border Region), Sept. 7, 1940, *Xin Zhonghua bao* (New China News), Sept. 22, 1940, reprinted in *Shaan-Gan-Ning geming genjudi shiliao xuanji*, 4:383–85.

[6] Ding Haochuan, "Jinnian jiaoyu gongzuo de zhongxin" (Central Tasks of This Year's Education Work), Jan. 17, 1941, originally in *Xin Zhonghua bao* (New China

The net effect of these efforts would have been to reproduce in the border region the same education system that existed in the rest of the country. Just as the critique of that system had adherents all along the political spectrum, so the instincts of professional Chinese educators were also essentially the same whatever their political inclinations. Economic considerations were mentioned scarcely at all as a justification for the school mergers, even though the border regions were experiencing financial difficulties at this time. Rather, the rationale was drawn strictly on academic grounds, appealing to the conventional view among Chinese educators that quality of necessity meant a concentration of resources both human and material; that mass education should be sacrificed to achieve it; and that no school was preferable to a low-quality school.

The shift came in the spring of 1944. The documents remain silent on who actually made which decisions. At the time, the 1944 changes were attributed simply to the overall reorientation and radicalization that occurred in many sectors of border region public life following the 1942 Party rectification campaign that Mao dominated. Thus the later claim that the 1944 educational reforms represented "Mao's line" has some basis in fact, although there is no direct evidence linking him to the specific policy changes implemented at that time. These essentially reversed the regularization drive that had overtaken the education system between 1938 and 1942.

Two sources of inspiration were officially cited for the new direction.[7] One was the "new education" introduced around the turn of the century or, more specifically, the ongoing debate it had

---

News), Feb. 2, 1941, reprinted in *Shaan-Gan-Ning geming genjudi shiliao xuanji* 4:417–20. For a chronicle of documents and directives from the 1938–42 period, see *Zhongguo geming genjudi jiaoyu jishi, 1927.8–1949.9* (A Record of Education in China's Revolutionary Bases, August 1927 to September 1949) (Beijing: Jiaoyu kexue chubanshe, 1989), pp. 133–238, passim.

[7] In two widely reprinted editorials from *Jiefang ribao* (Liberation Daily), which circulated with the reform directives. The following discussion of the rationale for the 1944 reforms is based on these two articles: "Genjudi putong jiaoyu de gaige wenti" (Problems of Reforming Ordinary Education in the Base Areas), April 7, 1944, and "Lun putong jiaoyu zhongde xuezhi yu kecheng" (On the System and Curriculum of Ordinary Education), May 27, 1944, reprinted in *Shaan-Gan-Ning bianqu jiaoyu fangzhen* (The Educational Policy of the Shaanxi-Gansu-Ningxia Border Region) (Shaan-Gan-Ning bianqu zhengu bangongting, July 1944), pp. 31–53; translated in Michael Lindsay, *Notes on Educational Problems in Communist China, 1941–47* (New York: Institute of Pacific Relations, 1950), pp. 51–63; also in *Chinese Education* 4:3 (Fall 1971):183–204.

generated. The second was Marxist teachings on the role of education in society. Marxists advocated combining production with knowledge, and Lenin had put that idea into practice. The border regions did not aim to transplant the practical proposals of Marx and Lenin, but only "to translate them into proper Chinese." The result should be a kind of education joined together with the people. Yet the border regions in the 1940s were dominated by war, economic difficulties, and revolution. Education remained largely divorced from those realities.

The main reason for this failing was the influence of the conventional system. It had an international background and was linked with the whole of human knowledge. Hence, "no matter how much it is criticized and attacked, to substitute another system for it is not something that can be done overnight." Yet its weaknesses for China lay in its very foreignness. It was the product of peacetime, city life, and a high stage of capitalist mechanized production. It was characterized in its European, American, and Japanese variants by a long period of study from first grade through college, with every grade rigidly demarcated and linked, dozens of compulsory subjects, and hundreds of technical courses. In Guomindang China, there had been a general copying of this "international" education system, and although many intellectuals had opinions against it, their efforts to reform the system had borne little fruit. Naturally, if it was inappropriate for China's cities, it was even less suited to the rural Communist-led border regions. Yet they had made the same mistake of trying to develop that conventional education system—even though most people in the regions were living in sparsely populated agricultural villages with backward production techniques and an underdeveloped social division of labor. In the words of the *Liberation Daily,*

> Because the old education system (after the abolition of the imperial examinations) wanted to study foreign countries, so the returned students became its guiding spirit. Education in China was almost all of a kind to prepare students for study abroad. Foreign countries were everywhere taken as the model. So its base was not in its feet, but in its head. The returned students system has had its progressive functions in China. We should not in general deny that, like those false patriots who the more they talk about restoring the classics, the more they cannot leave the foreign. But we definitely must cause the base of education to be rooted in the needs of the broadest mass of the people.[8]

---

8 "Genjudi putong jiaoyu de gaige wenti," p. 41.

Concrete examples were provided to illustrate what this meant in terms of people's lives. For instance, most young people in the border regions had three "career" options. They could return home and work with their families; become cadres, that is, work in some public capacity at the local level; or continue their schooling. Yet the border region's developing education system, with its new academic orientation and emphasis on quality, was not adequately preparing students for any of these options. After finishing elementary school, young graduates usually had no inclination to return home. Nor were they able to take up a cadre position. As for continuing their studies, although the curriculum was now designed for that end, only a minority could continue on to secondary school, and the border regions had no real universities. The higher-level cadres' schools were not linked to the regular system in any way, while the people actually responsible for leading the war effort and economic production had nothing to do with that system or vice versa.

The future, on the other hand, was something else again. In the future, every worker would be able to study math, physics, and chemistry. A system where students passed on from one grade and level to the next was also one for the future but not the present. "To forget the future because of the present is incorrect; to forget the present because of the future is especially incorrect." The most urgent needs were for mass education and education for the cadres who were working for the people. Both would be very different from the old system. Both would have their own objectives rooted in life and work. They would be neither preparatory nor attached to the level above. The mass elementary level should focus on the life of home and village. For the cadres, although their schools might still be called middle schools, teacher training schools, universities, or training classes, all should base their courses on the armed struggle and production. People with actual experience in those areas should be taken on as teachers to replace those without interest or experience in such subjects.[9]

The new slogans were "oppose the old-style uniformity" and "oppose regularity in education." At the secondary level, the earlier goal of transforming the border region's six middle schools into college-preparatory institutions was reversed. The recently standardized curriculum and enrollment procedures were revised to pro-

---

[9] Ibid., pp. 42–43.

vide terminal education for students who could then fill the urgent
personnel needs of the government, military, and production units
in the region. The curriculum was redesigned with an eye to practical relevance given the war effort and economic needs. The 19
courses that had formed the standardized curriculum were reduced
to only 8. Flexibility was the hallmark of the new system. "In-
equality of standards" was unavoidable and nothing to worry
about.[10]

The school "run by the people" (*minban xuexiao*) was the
answer to the problem of promoting universal mass education at
the village level. These schools, financially supported and managed
by the grass-roots localities themselves, were essentially an adaptation of the old *sishu* or privately run village classes. The difference
was that the collective or village as a whole, rather than just an individual within it, had to assume responsibility for administration
and finance. Another more important difference was reflected in
the full designation: *minban gongzhu*, that is, run by the people
with public assistance. The latter meant higher-level government
help with finances, printing educational materials, introducing and
training teachers as well as administrative and academic guidance.
Where necessary, for example, villagers were to be persuaded that
the old Confucian primers were no longer very useful. Many of the
rules and regulations were revised, such as the one that fixed a
minimum number of students as a condition for keeping a school in
operation.[11] Under the new formula, most of the quantitative losses
at the elementary level were regained. By the spring semester,

---

10 "Shaan-Gan-Ning bianqu de zhongdeng jiaoyu gaikuang" (General Survey of
Secondary Education in the Shaanxi-Gansu-Ningxia Border Region), June 1944, reprinted in *Laojiefangqu jiaoyu ziliao,* 2:shang:444–45, 448–49; Peter J. Seybolt,
"The Yenan Revolution in Mass Education," *China Quarterly,* no. 48 (Oct.–Dec.
1971), pp. 659–60.

11 "Bianqu zhengfu guanyu tichang yanjiu fanli ji shixing minban xiaoxue de
zhishixin" (Border Region Government's Directive on Promoting the Study of
Models and Experimentally Running Popularly Managed Primary Schools), in
Shaan-Gan-Ning bianqu jiaoyu fangzhen, pp. 4–9; Jiang Longji, "Guanyu minban
gongzhu zhengce de chubu zongjie," passim. Apparently just prior to the Communist evacuation of Yan'an before the advancing Guomindang troops in March 1947,
Jiang Longji, a deputy director of the Shaan-Gan-Ning Border Region Education
Department, prepared this report, which survived only in undated mimeographed
form. It summarizes the pros and cons of *minban* schools with unusual candor—as
though the military emergency had saved the report for posterity from the ministra-
tions of official editors. For a chronicle of the 1944 education reforms, see *Zhongguo geming genjudi jiaoyu jishi,* pp. 259–80, passim.

1945, the number of primary schools in Shaan-Gan-Ning had grown to 1,377 (more than 1,000 of which were of the new *minban* variety), with a total enrollment of 34,000 students (see table 1).

The Yan'an experience is important to our story for several reasons. First, it provided a sort of controlled experiment that showed how instinctively committed Chinese educators were to the forms and structures of the established system. Given the opportunity, they immediately proceeded to replicate that same system regardless of its acknowledged defects and however inappropriate to the time and place.

Second, the Yan'an experience played an adaptive function between past and future. This role was developed in the course of carrying out Mao's brief for the Party's rectification movement as a whole, namely, to "sinicize Marxism" or "translate it into proper Chinese." The then sympathetic observer Michael Lindsay wrote of the 1944 reforms that they "show Chinese Communist theory at its best, combining Marxist principles with strong common sense and concern for practical problems."[12] He might more accurately have said that while Marxist principles were being applied to the task of education reform, at the same time the decades-old critique of China's modern education system was being incorporated within the theory and practice of Chinese communism. This integration proved an important step in the growing status of the antiestablishment critique. Previously, it had always remained outside the system, and individual reforms had rarely progressed beyond the experimental stage. With the 1944 Yan'an experience, by contrast, the antiestablishment critique acquired a stronger foundation. Its adherents managed to win enough backing to create a policy-making precedent within a new political establishment that was in turn about to win national power.

A third point to emphasize, however, is that the official recognition accorded the old critique in rural wartime Yan'an was not by any means sufficient to establish its preeminence either within the CCP or the wider academic community responsible for running the education system on a nationwide basis. The *Liberation Daily* editorials cited above suggest that even in 1944 Yan'an, the ambivalence between reform and regularization remained very much alive. Especially, references to the education of the future betrayed the continuing pull of the established system.

[12] Lindsay, *Notes on Educational Problems,* p. 39.

Table 1

Shaanxi-Gansu-Ningxia Border Region Government-run and
Minban Elementary Schools, Students

(parentheses show *minban* schools, students, included in total figures)

Date	Schools	Students
1940	1,341	41,458
1942	1,198	40,366
1943	752	26,816
Oct. 1944	1,090 (574)	33,636
End 1944	1,181	34,202
Spring semester 1945	1,377 (1,057)	34,004 (16,797)
Fall semester 1946	1,249 (940)	34,063 (15,373)

SOURCES: For 1940, "Bianqu sinianlai xuexiao jiaoyu menglie zengjia" (The Vigorous Increase of Schooling in the Border Region During the Past Four Years), *Jiefang ribao* (Liberation Daily), June 5, 1941, in *Shaan-Gan-Ning geming genjudi shiliao xuanji* (Selection of Historical Materials from the Shaan-Gan-Ning Revolutionary Base) (Lanzhou: Gansu renmin chubanshe, 1985), 4:451; for all other years, Jiang Longji, "Guanyu minban gongzhu zhengce de chubu zongjie" (A Preliminary Summary of the People-Manage-Public-Help Policy), n.d., mimeo, in *Laojiefangqu jiaooyu ziliao* (Educational Materials from the Old Liberated Areas), Zhongyang jiaoyu kexue yanjiusuo, ed. (Beijing: Jiaoyu kexue chubanshe, 1986), 2:*xia*:376.

Finally, the 1944 Yan'an reforms like so many others elsewhere also did not enjoy a very long life. The civil war, the loss of Yan'an itself in early 1947, and the simultaneous escalation of land reform throughout the Communist-led areas all combined to disrupt the implementation of education policy. As soon as civilian life and social order began to resume in north China in the late 1940s, the forces of regularization took up where they left off in 1942, leaving the 1944 reform effort to lapse like all of its predecessors. Thus, the CCP inherited in 1949 the same conventional system that had stood for thirty years impervious to all the reformers' efforts.

Nevertheless, as we shall see below, the contest between pro- and antiestablishment orientations has waxed and waned ever since. That persistence might be due to the Chinese penchant for creating new traditions and then trying to use them ever after as authoritative precedents. Or perhaps the contest persists because the basic social and economic distinctions that gave birth to the controversy so long ago also still exist. But whatever the underlying causes, the regularization drive that followed Mao's last great effort between 1966 and 1976 to change China's entire education system in conformity with the old reformers' goals has recreated, in turn, patterns and practices in the post-Mao era that would have been entirely familiar to Yan'an educators during the 1938–42 regularization drive. Seemingly independent of direct economic concerns, assumptions about what is necessary to promote a modern school system have endured essentially unchanged among professional Chinese educators since the 1930s, regardless of their political inclinations.

The ideas that have thus been passed on from one generation to the next include: an identification of quality with modernity, which in turn means fixed uniform standards, emulating those of the West; the assumption that in order to guarantee such standards resources must be concentrated in a few centers of strength; a further assumption that the children of existing elites constitute a quality resource that should be educated in such centers regardless of the social implications; a willingness to sacrifice quantity for quality even to the extent of closing down schools and sending children home; and a related tolerance for investment priorities that disproportionately emphasize tertiary and elite education at the expense of the lower and mass levels.

CHAPTER THREE

Reinforcements from the Soviet Union: Regularization and Cultural Revolution

The basic challenges of educational development had already been clearly articulated in China by 1949, when the new CCP government was established. They were how to provide elementary schooling at the mass level, tertiary education for the elite few, and intermediate secondary schooling—all in ways that the economy could afford and the interested public would accept as equitable and appropriate to the nation's needs. The historical foundations of the educational controversies surrounding these tasks were also well established. The new ingredients in the early 1950s came from the Soviet Union as ally and advisor; and from the escalating imperatives of socioeconomic revolution, which was the newly victorious CCP's ultimate reason for existence. Finally, the Party's power now extended nationwide to encompass not just an isolated northern rural hinterland, but the cities, the coastal areas, and the South as well.

Although no documents have yet come to light that might reveal more fully the nature of the CCP's debts to Stalin and the Soviet Union, Soviet influence appears in retrospect to have been used selectively by the Chinese over the years and incorporated into both sides of their education debate. Initially, during the early 1950s, that influence reinforced "regularization" with an intensity that overwhelmed even the professional educators. But the end result of that first phase, once the rush of enthusiasm had passed, was a Sino-Soviet compromise that Chinese educators could live with and eventually come to accept more or less as their own.

Learning from the Soviet Union

The ambivalence inherent in the pre-1949 controversy over the established education system and foreign borrowing undoubtedly helps explain how the CCP's leaders could have embarked upon a course similar in so many respects to the one they themselves had so forcefully criticized. The future that Yan'an editorial writers could temporarily not worry about had now arrived. In any event, the CCP government propelled the country into a "learn from the Soviet Union" movement that took on all the hallmarks of the rush to learn from the West during the early decades of the century—except that this time the tide of enthusiasm lasted less than ten years (from 1950 to 1956 at most). According to the official rationale, since the best of Western science and technology had already been absorbed by China's new political ally, the most logical course would be to learn directly from the Soviet Union. The objective was to achieve under socialism the goal of "national reconstruction" that had eluded China for half a century, and in 1949, the Soviet Union still seemed to offer a credible alternative formula for achieving that end. Whether such exuberant deference to the Soviet "elder brother" (an officially encouraged term of endearment) was also justified is another matter. The political and intellectual costs of such dependency were registered almost immediately.

The most widely publicized features of the new formula for education were the restructuring of the system in accordance with the then "Soviet model" and the concurrent campaign for "thought reform" among the intellectuals. Both were most intensively implemented at the tertiary level. Thought reform laid down the parameters within which everyone would henceforth have to live their lives and pursue their careers. The new orthodoxy would be based on the canons of Marx, Lenin, and Mao Zedong, while authority for interpretation would be monopolized by the central leadership of the CCP. But contributing to the campaign as well were many, although not all, of the charges that had kept the critique of Chinese education alive for thirty years. The issues selected for the first thought reform campaign were those that dovetailed with the concurrent drive to learn from the Soviet model, with its emphasis on central planning and heavy industry.

Specifically, the themes from the recent Chinese past that gave added dimension to the Soviet-inspired thought reform exercise were: the Western, and especially the American, orientation of China's intellectuals; Western and missionary-run education in China itself; the inherited Chinese disdain for practical application, which was responsible for the education system's deficiencies in science and technology; and the intellectual community's perception of itself as the modern successor of China's traditional ruling elite.[1]

Thought reform peaked in 1951–52 and university reorganization in 1952–53. In an authoritative statement marking the start of the former, Deputy Education Minister Qian Junrui said that thought reform was a prerequisite for reorganization, because resistance within the academic community was obstructing tertiary-level reform.[2] The system was divided into distinct kinds of institutions each with its own specialized function. American-style liberal arts colleges were abolished, with arts and science faculties being split off from the larger universities to form the core of Soviet-style comprehensive (*zonghexing*) universities. About a dozen of these were formed, in more or less even distribution around the country, with only one each in Beijing and Shanghai. The remaining disciplines of the old universities were reorganized into separate technical colleges or merged with existing specialized institutes.

As a result of this reorganization and the accompanying new national student enrollment and job assignment plans, also modeled on Soviet practice, those majoring in technical and engineering fields rose from about 20 percent in the late 1940s to 35 percent of the total number of students in 1952. By 1953, the percentage enrolled in engineering, science, medicine, and agriculture had reached approximately 60 percent of all college students at that time.[3]

In conventional development parlance, the education system had been redesigned to produce fewer hard-to-employ liberal arts graduates and more of those trained to move directly into the technical jobs needed for economic construction. In the 1930s, in-

---

[1] The story of early-1950s thought reform has been told many times. See, for example, Theodore H.E. Chen, *Thought Reform of the Chinese Intellectuals* (Hong Kong: Hong Kong University Press, 1960); Merle Goldman, *Literary Dissent in Communist China* (Cambridge: Harvard University Press, 1967), pp. 87–157; Robert Jay Lifton, *Thought Reform and the Psychology of Totalism: A Study of "Brainwashing" in China* (New York: W.W. Norton, 1963); Mu Fu-sheng, *The Wilting of the Hundred Flowers* (New York: Praeger, 1962).

[2] Qian Junrui, "Gaodeng jiaoyu gaige de guanjian" (The Key to Reforming Higher Education), *Xuexi* (Study) (Beijing), 5:1 (Nov. 1, 1951):10–11.

[3] *Renmin ribao,* Sept. 24 and 26, 1952; July 6, 1953; Dec. 17, 1953, *Guangming ribao,* Dec. 17, 1953; May 25, 1954; "Quanguo geji xuexiao xuesheng renshu de fazhan jiyu jiefangqian de bijiao" (The Development of National Student Enrollments at the Various Levels of Schooling and a Comparison with Before Liberation), figures compiled jointly by the Ministries of Education and Higher Education, dated Sept. 1954, in *Renmin jiaoyu* (People's Education) (Beijing), no. 10 (Oct. 1954), pp. 34–36.

vestigators in China had found that a majority of college students still aspired to a career in government service. Now, ready or not—and many were not—China's young intellectuals were being channeled into the fields of learning decreed by the national enrollment and job assignment plans. These, in turn, were designed to meet the needs decreed by Soviet-style centralized economic planning and the priorities for heavy industrial development. These priorities were articulated in China's First Five-Year Plan (FFYP), which began in 1953.

Also following the Soviet example, nationally unified teaching plans, syllabuses, materials, and textbooks were introduced for every academic specialty or major. The content was based on translations of Soviet equivalents, which were sometimes simply reproduced verbatim. In this manner, the earlier much-criticized practice of relying wholly on unrevised Western teaching materials reproduced itself in the early 1950s. Now, however, even the precise methods of instruction for each course were prescribed from Soviet practice.

The teaching plans specified the aims, requirements, and contents of each major, including the courses to be taught within it. The syllabus for each course was so detailed as to include the items to be taught, their sequence, the time to be spent on each item, and the exact material to be covered during each hour of instruction. All institutions were directed to adopt these uniform teaching plans and syllabuses as they were prepared by the central authorities. Only through such a totally planned system, it was said, could the required numbers of people be trained to the specifications of each grade and level in all the various technical specialties required for the country's economic development. The declared intent was to achieve "standardization and uniformity" in teaching methods and content throughout the country's tertiary level institutions.

The basic unit within this new structure of learning was the teaching-research group (*jiaoxue yanjiu zu*). All faculty members were organized into these groups or offices, formed on the basis of the subjects taught for the purposes of collective course preparation, practice teaching, and mutual supervision. A specific aim was to ensure that the faculty actually taught according to the study plans prescribed for each specialty. Group members prepared outlines and lecture notes together as a team, dividing up the work in different ways and attending one another's classes as a basis for group evaluations afterward. An editorial in the CCP's official newspaper, the *People's Daily,* summarized the new relationships:

"Since all teaching work is carried out under a unified aim and plan, each subject taught by each teacher is, both qualitatively and quantitatively, essential for the realization of the general aim and plan. If teaching work is not carried out through the guided, organized, and collective activity of the teaching-research office, it will be difficult to achieve the desired result."[4]

Also in deference to such concerns, the worker-peasant accelerated middle (secondary) school experiment was declared a failure and abandoned in 1955. These schools had been introduced with much fanfare in the early 1950s, before the education system locked into "the plan." Combining new revolutionary aims with Yan'an-style irregularity, the accelerated middle schools tried to compress the six-year regular secondary school curriculum into three or four years. The experiment was promoted with the aim of preparing students for college and producing quickly a new kind of intellectual drawn directly from working-class ranks. Students were recruited from among adult workers and peasants, especially those already serving as cadres, and cadres whether or not of working-class origins who had "joined the revolution" as many did in the 1940s rather than continue their schooling. Despite much publicity about the "splendid job" they were doing, the 1955 announcement said that these schools were impossible to popularize, did not "ensure quality," and could not compete with the regular method of progress in "proper sequence." Many students in such schools had been held back in the same grade from year to year and ultimately dropped out because they could not keep up. Among the students promoted to the tertiary level, the "majority" did not produce good academic records.[5]

---

[4] *Renmin ribao,* April 24, 1954. Many contemporary press accounts described these new plans and practices. On the teaching-research group, see also *Renmin ribao,* Sept. 16, 1953; and Tseng Chao-lun, "Higher Education in New China," *People's China* (Beijing), no. 12 (June 16, 1953), pp. 6–10. Other sources include: Chu-yuan Cheng, *Scientific and Engineering Manpower in Communist China, 1949–1963* (Washington, D.C.: National Science Foundation, 1965), pp. 186–217; Theodore Hsi-en Chen, *Chinese Education Since 1949* (New York: Pergamon, 1981), pp. 34–43; Ronald F. Price, *Marx and Education in Russia and China* (London: Croom Helm, 1977), passim; Leo A. Orleans, "Soviet Influence on China's Higher Education," in Ruth Hayhoe and Marianne Bastid, eds., *China's Education and the Industrialized World: Studies in Culture Transfer* (Armonk, N.Y.: M.E. Sharpe, 1987), pp. 184–94.

[5] *Renmin ribao,* June 23, 1955; *Guangming ribao* March 21, 1954.

The accelerated middle school experiment demonstrated the continuing clash of interests in the post-1949 system between regular and irregular modes of schooling. The 1955 announcement suspending enrollment for these schools noted that, in the future, all workers and peasants, including cadres, should take the same entrance exams and study in the same schools as regular students. Spare-time education became the preferred alternative to gradually raise the cultural level of those who, for whatever reason, could not compete within the regular system. The accelerated middle schools thus met the same fate as all the other "irregular" experiments in China's recent educational history. The regular system rejected them, as it always had, this time in the name of Soviet-style planned modernization.

Blooming and Contending

No sooner had China begun to rebuild itself in accordance with the Soviet model, however, than the model itself began to change. Joseph Stalin died in 1953, preparing the way for important changes within the Soviet bloc. Even prior to Khrushchev's report criticizing Stalin at the Soviet Union's Twentieth Communist Party Congress in February 1956, the rigidities of Soviet intellectual life had begun to ease, and China followed suit accordingly. These events held potentially embarrassing political consequences for the CCP, and nowhere more so than in its relationship with the intellectuals among whom the initial resistance to Soviet influence was well known. As Professor Fu Ying of Beijing University noted with but thinly veiled sarcasm, previously it had been impossible to disagree with Lysenko's theories. More recently, after those theories began to be criticized in the Soviet Union, it had become impossible not to disagree with them.[6]

Appropriately, therefore, one of the first public steps taken by the leadership to distance itself from its Soviet mentor was announced at a special Party conference convened to discuss "the question of the intellectuals." Said Premier Zhou Enlai in his keynote speech at the meeting, "China's science and technology are still very backward. We are also still unable to acquire and put into use many of the latest scientific achievements of the world. We are also still unable to solve independently of the Soviet experts many of the complex technical questions now arising in our construction

---

[6] *Guangming ribao,* May 25, 1956.

work." China would henceforth reduce its intellectual dependence
on the Soviet Union. "We must first discard all servile thinking,
which shows a lack of national self-confidence," Zhou continued. It
was true that Soviet aid was still needed to overcome China's
scientific backwardness. But there was a right and a wrong way to
accept such aid. The latter was "to seek a solution from the Soviet
Union to every question, large and small, that arises and to send
mostly secondary school graduates rather than scientists, to study in
the Soviet Union. The result would be to remain forever in a state
of dependence and imitation." The correct way was "to make an
overall plan that distinguishes between what is essential and urgent
and what is not... and to systematically use the latest achievements
of Soviet science so as to bring ourselves abreast of Soviet levels as
quickly as possible."[7]

Following Khrushchev's report, the CCP issued its own statement in April 1956, similarly criticizing Stalin's errors. With regard to their implications for China's intellectual life, the Chinese
report noted that "many of our research workers still have the dog-
matic habit of thinking by rote without independence of mind or
creative spirit, and are influenced to a certain degree by the individual worship of Stalin."[8]

China's new line was launched in May under the slogan "let a
hundred flowers bloom and a hundred schools of thought contend"
(*baihua qifang, baijia zhengming*). Lu Dingyi, head of the CCP's
Propaganda Department, provided the authoritative public elabora-
tion. If China was to become rich and powerful, said Lu, the arts
and sciences must prosper. The prerequisite was freedom of
thought, debate and creativity. The question he addressed was how
much freedom for whom. While Lu's guidelines for literature, art,
philosophy, and the social sciences raised as many questions as they
answered, his prescription for the natural sciences was clear and the
change significant. "Natural sciences including medicine have no
class character," he said. "They have their own laws of
development....Therefore, it is wrong to put class labels such as
'feudal,' 'capitalist,' 'socialist,' 'proletarian,' or 'bourgeois' on cer-

---

[7] Zhou Enlai, "Guanyu zhishi fenzi wenti de baogao" (Report on the Question of
Intellectuals), delivered Jan. 14, 1956, *Renmin ribao,* Jan. 30, 1956, translated in
Robert R. Bowie and John K. Fairbank, eds., *Communist China, 1955–1959: Policy
Documents with Analysis* (Cambridge: Harvard University Press, 1962), pp. 128–44.

[8] *Renmin ribao,* April 5, 1956, translated in Bowie and Fairbank, eds., *Communist China, 1955–1959,* pp. 144–51.

tain medical theories, or those in biology or other natural sciences.... Some fall victim to this fallacy unconsciously because they want to give undue stress to the need to learn from the advanced sciences of the Soviet Union." This prescription, adapted from changes under way in the Soviet Union itself, nevertheless reopened some doors to the West. Whereas before there had been no need because the Soviet Union had already absorbed all that was of value from the capitalist West, now all of its intellectual merits should be "studied critically."[9]

In the months of blooming and contending that followed, China's academic community elaborated the officially anointed critique of over-dependency and mechanical copying into an attack against many basic features of the planned Soviet education system. In the process, educators revealed their continuing commitment to pre-1949 patterns and practices. The old commitments surfaced readily at a Beijing symposium of university leaders convened in August to discuss the changing academic environment. The officially recognized defect of the education system, in keeping with the new "hundred flowers" theme, was the students' inability to think and work independently. In debating why and what to do about it, however, the assembled educators revived the old dichotomy between quantity and quality. According to the official press accounts of the conference, "many" participants held that the "fundamental cause" of the problem was too many students. More college graduates had been produced since 1949 than during the entire period between the 1911 Revolution and 1949. As a result, tertiary-level institutions were enrolling students of "uneven attainment," unlike in pre-Liberation days when they could pick and choose one from among every twenty candidates. Participants requested that the authorities "study thoroughly" whether such a large number of college-trained people was really necessary for national construction.

Another major complaint at the August symposium was the inadequate attention paid not just to China's economic, physical, and social conditions, but more specifically to the "original historical legacy" of Chinese higher education. This included its experience and achievements as well as the nature of its teachers, students, and material equipment. A related complaint concerned the

---

[9] *Renmin ribao,* June 13, 1956, translated in ibid., pp. 151–63. Lu Dingyi's speech was given on May 26, 1956.

emphasis on "overall development" in Soviet pedagogical practice, as opposed to the Chinese preference for favoring individual ability and special talent. Acknowledging this tradition, the majority criticized excessive leveling and demanded greater concern for the individual character and preference of each student. Conference participants also demanded a relaxation of the controls exercised by the Ministry of Higher Education. Individual schools should be allowed to adjust teaching plans and drop courses to suit their own conditions, and students should be given the freedom to do what they liked with their after-class time.[10]

The quantity-versus-quality argument was dismissed without even the courtesy of a rebuttal. The 1956 freshman class was the largest in China's history. But provisional regulations issued for the fall semester, incorporated some of the educators' demands. No sooner had the measures been introduced, however, than the authorities retreated in dismay at the "obvious mistake" they had made. Independent study seemed the last thing students wanted to do with their new free time, political lessons were neglected, and attendance at various organized extracurricular activities dropped.[11] "By now," reported Shanghai educational authorities in late October, "many leadership cadres have learned that although the past practice of rigorous control and interference was wrong, the present attitude of shrinking from leadership and letting things go their own way is also an obvious mistake."[12]

A speech by Jiang Nanxiang given during the summer was published twice in October as an authoritative rebuttal and reminder of the limits beyond which official tolerance was not prepared to go. Jiang was the president of Qinghua University, on a career track that would lead to ministerial posts, and had long been associated with the central leadership of the Youth League. After the CCP's Central Committee had introduced the new policy of promoting free discussion, said Jiang, "some comrades" began to question the correctness of learning from the Soviet Union at all. He acknowl-

---

[10] On the Beijing symposium and a similar gathering in Shanghai, see *Renmin ribao,* Aug. 2, 17, and 18, 1956; also, Zhongyang jiaoyu kexue yanjiusuo, ed., *Zhonghua renmin gongheguo jiaoyu dashiji, 1949–1982* (Chronicle of Events in Education in the People's Republic of China, 1949–1982) (Beijing: Jiaoyu kexue chubanshe, 1983), pp. 175–76. On these issues, see also *Guangming ribao,* July 29, 30, and 31, 1956; Aug. 1, 1956.

[11] *Renmin ribao,* Oct. 28, 1956.

[12] *Guangming ribao,* Oct. 29, 1956.

edged that the exercise had initially been pushed to excess but asserted that "we must definitely not deny the need for learning from the Soviet Union" because of such mistakes nor "abandon the new socialist education policy—the policy of thoroughly realizing overall development."[13]

"Overall development" had also become a catch-phrase used to describe Soviet-style pedagogical planning and thus served as the antithesis of "independent thinking" in the 1956 debates. The policy of overall development, he reiterated, was embodied in the teaching plan with its requirements for politics, physical education, basic knowledge, specialization courses coordinated with field work, extra-curricular activities, and so on. Individual capacities could only develop on the basis of such a rational foundation of learning. Yet, "some people consider that the pedagogical plan in the schools today obstructs the development of individuality and special talent. They maintain that the schools in old China allowed completely free development and some scientists were fostered, but the pedagogical plans today have provided too concrete, too rigid rules for the students, and talent cannot be fostered." Jiang dismissed the old system as costly and wasteful, unsuitable for producing the large numbers of people needed for national development. Nor can we allow students to study what they want, he declared, because if we do the state's manpower needs will not be met. "Objective needs come first, individual wishes and special capabilities are born and developed on this objective foundation, and individual wishes are not immutable."[14]

CCP leaders subsequently pushed the blooming and contending far beyond the bounds of academic controversy when they called, in 1957, for general criticism to help the Party rectify its work style.

---

[13] Jiang Nanxiang, "Lüelun gaodeng xuexiao de quanmian fazhan de jiaoyu fangzhen" (A Brief Discussion of the Educational Policy of Overall Development for Institutions of Higher Learning), *Zhongguo qingnian* (China Youth) (Beijing), no. 20 (Oct. 16, 1956), pp. 9–12.

[14] Ibid. A revised version of this article appeared in *Zhongguo qingnian bao* (China Youth News), Beijing, Oct. 18, 1956. Despite the authoritative nature of Jiang's statement, it was publicized as part of the officially encouraged 1956 blooming and contending and was thus subjected to appropriate rebuttal ("Quanmian fazhan jiaoyu wenti taolun: he Jiang Nanxiang tongzhi shangque jiaoyu fangzhen wenti" [Discussing the Problems of Overall Development Education: Deliberating with Comrade Jiang Nanxiang on Questions of Educational Policy], *Renmin jiaoyu*, no. 12 [Dec. 1956], pp. 5–9). On the controversy over the educational policy of overall development, see, for example, *Renmin jiaoyu*, September through December, 1956.

These larger political implications need not detain us here, even though the academic community emerged into the forefront of the regime's critics and later bore the brunt of the Party's wrath during the "anti-rightist" campaign that followed.[15] In fact, the academic controversy of 1956 together with the more widely publicized political events of 1957 created an impression, correct to be sure, of continuing resistance among university intellectuals to the Soviet import. But that impression tended to obscure the extent to which they could, at the same time, find common academic cause with the Soviet model and also adapt it to their own aims.

The pressures they exerted for such adaptation were evident throughout. Those that were successful included the rejection of irregular education within the regular system, as exemplified by the accelerated middle school experiment. The demand to train "special talents" would also soon be at least partially exonerated. Meanwhile, Soviet-style centralization and uniformity—of standards, curricula, teaching plans, schedules, textbooks, materials, and the teaching-research group that ensured the uniform application of all the rest—became standard features of the post-1949 Chinese education system. But in retrospect, and especially given the regularization patterns of the pre-1949 past, many features of the Soviet import must have been well received. This would help explain why they were all restored immediately the threat of cultural revolution was lifted in the late 1970s and why they remain so difficult to change even after a decade of countervailing influences from the West throughout the 1980s. Indeed, we should probably question just how many of the 1950s Soviet "innovations" were actually imports and which were Chinese variations of same or outright Chinese designs proliferating in the newly compatible climate.[16]

This question is reinforced by the case of the national unified college entrance examinations introduced in 1952. The examinations dovetailed nicely with the new Soviet-style manpower-planning and state job assignment systems, also introduced at this time. But the national unified examinations were never part of the

15 Roderick MacFarquhar, ed., *The Hundred Flowers Campaign and the Chinese Intellectuals* (New York: Praeger, 1960); Roderick MacFarquhar, *The Origins of the Cultural Revolution: Contradictions Among the People, 1956–1957* (New York: Columbia University Press, 1974).

16 Ronald Price asks a similar question in his essay "Convergence or Copying: China and the Soviet Union," in Hayhoe and Bastid, eds., *China's Education and the Industrialized World*, pp. 158–83.

Soviet repertoire. Rather, they bore marked resemblance both in form and function to the old imperial examinations.

The initial aim in the early 1950s was to give individual schools responsibility for examining and enrolling candidates in accordance with centrally determined standards and procedures following Soviet practice.[17] In pre-1949 China, enrollment was also carried out by the schools themselves. That aim was never achieved under the regular post-1949 system, however, because the new curriculum, designed as it was to meet the unfamiliar needs of Soviet-style modernization, could not have been implemented and the relevant jobs subsequently filled without some more centralized enforcement mechanism. Year after year in the early 1950s, official statements explained the reasons. There was still a "wide gap" between the personal desires of the students and the enrollment plans, which were formulated to meet the overall needs of national construction. Most candidates were still flocking to enroll in a few popular departments, courses, and institutions in the largest cities. Without assigned enrollment, the others would have been unable to obtain enough students. The fields that never seemed to receive enough voluntary or first preference applications in the early 1950s included geography, mining, civil and military engineering, teacher training, mathematics, finance, economics, politics, law, and physical education.[18] While some of the preferences were new and some old, the concentration in a few popular fields and locations was a holdover from the pre-1949 past. Structures had been changed in the interests of an objectively accepted goal, namely, modernization. But the subjective values and patterns of behavior necessary to achieve it lagged well behind.

Faced with this dilemma, Chinese decision makers looked back into Chinese history for an allocation formula that would at least be accepted as more-or-less fair by all concerned. The result was the

---

[17] *Guangming ribao,* June 23, 1955; *Renmin ribao,* June 30, 1955. Soviet tertiary-level admissions procedures have remained essentially the same since the mid-1930s. For a good description, see Nicholas De Witt, *Education and Professional Employment in the U.S.S.R.* (Washington, D.C.: National Science Foundation, 1961), pp. 242–74.

[18] See, for example, *Renmin ribao,* Sept. 25, 1953, and May 25, 1954; and in particular on the unwillingness to become teachers inherited from the past, *Renmin ribao,* July 11, 1952, and Oct. 23, 1953: Chen Xuanshan, "Banianlai gaodeng shifan jiaoyu de juda chengjiu burong mosha" (The Great Achievements in Tertiary Level Teacher Training Education During the Past Eight Years Must Not Be Obliterated), *Renmin jiaoyu,* no. 10 (Oct. 1957), p. 12.

national unified college entrance examinations, which candidates throughout the country took on the same days, at the same time, and in the same sequence. Examination scores and the candidates' individual preferences—plus political and personal criteria that varied over time—were then used to allocate all freshmen in accordance with the national enrollment plan. The plan, coordinated and carefully balanced between the national and regional levels, stipulated the number of students to be enrolled from each region, into each institution of higher learning, and each specialty within it. From 1952 to the present, except for two disruptions during Mao Zedong's cultural revolutions and despite more recent attempts at reform in the late 1980s, this unified examination system remains the basic means of enrollment at the tertiary level. The reasons for its existence also remain essentially the same today as in the early 1950s.[19] In the process, they underline the question raised above about the extent to which Soviet-style innovations could find common ground with regularization modes inherited by Chinese educators from their own past and combine to form a genuine Sino-Soviet compromise model.

Cultural Revolution I, 1958

After the blooming and contending was brought to an abrupt halt in June 1957, Premier Zhou Enlai announced the new official line for education in his "Government Work Report" that same month. Those who wanted the education system to return to its pre-1949 state were wrong. But errors had been made in implementing the Soviet-style reforms. The errors included rejecting some rational features of the old pre-1949 system, failing to carry forward the experience gained in the pre-1949 liberated base areas, and failing to adapt the Soviet model more carefully to China's particular conditions.[20]

---

[19] For the general similarities between China's post-1976 enrollment system and the old imperial examinations, compare Suzanne Pepper, *China's Universities: Post-Mao Enrollment Policies* (Ann Arbor: Center for Chinese Studies Monograph No. 46, University of Michigan, 1984); and, for example, Ichisada Miyazaki, *China's Examination Hell: The Civil Service Examinations of Imperial China,* translated by Conrad Schirokauer (New Haven: Yale University Press, 1981). Reforms in the 1980s are discussed below.

[20] From Premier Zhou's report made to the Fourth Session of the First National People's Congress, June 26, 1957, *Renmin ribao,* June 27, 1957, translated in Bowie and Fairbank, eds., *Communist China, 1955–1959,* pp. 299–329.

The failure to apply the lessons of the CCP's own pre-1949 rural experience was a concern that featured only marginally in the intellectual and political debates of 1956–57. To explain this new official concern, it is necessary to consider instead the CCP's widely proclaimed goals when its new government was established in 1949. It had been announced, for example, that "tens of thousands" of workers and peasants would soon be educated and able to stand beside intellectuals from other family backgrounds.[21]

Toward that end, institutions of higher learning were directed to lower their admissions standards for working-class candidates; the accelerated secondary schools mentioned above were set up; and at the elementary level, the *minban,* or people's schools, were promoted as a means of popularizing basic-level education in the countryside. Also, at the elementary level the regular six-year primary school, based long before on the American system, was reduced to five years, in order "to enable the overwhelming majority of the working people to receive a complete elementary education."[22] The customary pre-1949 division into three or four years of junior primary and two or three years of senior primary school was abolished because it encouraged dropouts after the junior level.[23] Even the most conservative computations recorded a doubling of the national elementary school enrollment figure between 1949 and 1953, from 24.4 million in 1949–50 to 49.7 million in 1952–53.[24]

The advent of the First Five-Year Plan (FFYP) in 1953, however, had brought a sudden reappraisal. The State Statistical Bureau reported that, during the 1949–52 period, many defects had occurred in education work. The criticisms echoed those heard during the Yan'an regularization drive a decade earlier: lack of planning and foresight, insufficient coordination with economic development, blind and rash advance, and giving importance to quantity but not quality in anti-illiteracy work as well as elementary educa-

[21] Lu Ting-yi, "Education and Culture in New China," *People's China,* no. 8 (April 16, 1950), reprinted in Stewart Fraser, ed., *Chinese Communist Education: Records of the First Decade* (New York: John Wiley and Sons, 1965), p. 89.

[22] From a report on education work by Guo Moruo in his capacity as chairman of the Culture and Education Affairs Committee of the central government on Oct. 25, 1951, in *Renmin ribao,* Nov. 5, 1951.

[23] The five-year elementary system was stipulated in the central government's "Decision on the Reform of the School System," promulgated on Oct. 1, 1951 (printed in *Renmin ribao,* Oct. 3, 1951). The short-course middle schools were established by central government directive in 1950 (*Renmin ribao,* Dec. 20, 1950).

[24] "Quanguo geji xuexiao xuesheng renshu de fazhan," pp. 34–36.

tion.[25] The new aim was to purge these holdovers from the CCP's rural revolutionary past. It was as if the necessity of regularizing the tertiary sector in order to meet the demands of central planning, industrialization, and the FFYP automatically revived the old familiar patterns in the rest of the system as well.

Perhaps because the imperatives seemed greater at the tertiary level, however, the regularization effort there continued throughout the FFYP period whereas at the mass level the effort lasted only half that long. According to the State Statistical Bureau's figures, elementary school enrollments declined from 55 million in 1952 to 51.2 million in 1954.[26] Different sources offered different figures, with those cited above from the education ministries being the most conservative. But all pointed to a quantitative decline at the elementary level for the regularization years 1953–55. During that phase, six-year elementary schooling was reinstated as the regular norm together with the old division into junior and senior levels.[27] The goal of a *minban* school in every village was allowed to lapse. No one was inclined to promote so "irregular" a form of schooling, and the regular system could not continue to expand so quickly.[28]

Enrollment quotas for secondary-level normal schools, which trained elementary school teachers, were reduced, and some of the schools were closed.[29] The idea of lowering college admissions stan-

[25] From the State Statistical Bureau's "Report on the Restoration and Development of the National Economy, Culture, and Education for 1952," *Renmin ribao,* Sept. 30, 1953. This became the new verdict on educational development for the early post-liberation years (see also, for example Guo Moruo's report in *Renmin ribao,* Oct. 1, 1953).

[26] State Statistical Bureau, "Report on the Restoration and Development of the National Economy, Culture, and Education for 1952"; idem, "Report on National Economic Development and the Results of Implementing the National Plan for 1954," *Renmin ribao,* Sept. 23, 1955.

[27] "Zhengwuyuan guanyu zhengdun he gaijin xiaoxue jiaoyu de zhishi" (Government Administration Council Directive on Rectifying and Improving Elementary Education), Nov. 26, 1953, in *Zhongguo jiaoyu nianjian, 1949–1981* (China Education Yearbook, 1949–1981) (Beijing: Zongguo dabaike quanshu chubanshe, 1984), p. 733. Also, *Jiaoyu dashiji, 1949–1982,* pp. 79, 88.

[28] *Renmin ribao,* June 23, 1955; *Guangming ribao,* July 21, 1955, and Aug. 12, 1955. For a general survey of the *minban* schools over time, see Jean C. Robinson, "Decentralization, Money, and Power: The Case of People-run Schools in China," *Comparative Education Review,* Feb. 1986, pp. 73–88.

[29] On the "Directive Concerning the Work of Developing and Consolidating Normal Schools" from the Ministry of Education, see *Renmin ribao,* June 20, 1954. On Minister of Education Zhang Xiruo's later admission of error in this regard, see his report in *Renmin ribao,* June 21, 1956.

dards for working-class candidates was also abandoned together with the accelerated middle school experiment. The annual enrollment regulations stipulated that such candidates were to be granted preference in admission only when their entrance examinations scores were otherwise competitive.

That a stable equilibrium had not been achieved along this line, however, became apparent in 1955. During the last two years of the FFYP, a sort of hybrid system began to develop that drew upon the CCP's past rural experience for popular use, while maintaining the regular system at the higher level. Thus a new 12-year plan for science was developed during those years, which carefully delineated priorities and projects in the most urgently needed fields, as anticipated by Zhou Enlai in his January 1956 speech on intellectuals. By contrast, the new 12-year plan for agriculture adopted in January 1956 proclaimed the goal of universal compulsory primary schooling in the rural areas within 12 years and the elimination of illiteracy within 7. The village *minban* schools were once again designated as the medium that would make this possible. Now, however, the "people" responsible for running them were the agricultural producers cooperatives, the new work units being formed at the village level as the tide for agricultural collectivization swept the country. Local people themselves would have to be pressed into service as teachers.[30] The Ministry of Education criticized itself for having so recently suppressed the development of teacher-training schools. Primary school enrollments resumed their rapid upward movement once more.

In effect, the CCP's most basic problem at this point was that it could neither reconcile nor was it willing to ignore the conflicting demands created by Soviet-style economic development, the realities of Chinese society, and the CCP's own revolutionary commitments. Thus China's education system at the end of the FFYP still bore marked similarities to its pre-1949 predecessor. The "regular" Sino-Soviet model at the elite level still rested on a base of mass illiteracy, which it could offer little hope of eliminating in the foreseeable future. In 1956, only about 52 percent of all school-age children were attending primary school. Similarly, in 1957–58, there were some 64 million children in elementary schools and only

---

[30] From article 29 of the "Draft Program for National Agricultural Development, 1956–1967," promulgated Jan. 23, 1956, *Renmin ribao,* Jan. 26, 1956. On the educational implications specifically, see *Guangming ribao,* Feb. 22, 1956; and *Renmin ribao,* Feb. 27, 1956.

7 million enrolled at the secondary level. Yet at that time, there were an estimated 150–200 million young people in the elementary and secondary school age groups.[31]

The demand to improve quality through uniformity and standardization, as conceived by professional Chinese educators, could only be achieved at the cost of reducing numbers and the rate at which teachers were trained to teach them. The goal of universal primary schooling would thus recede even further into the future under a rigorous application of the Soviet model. The only way there could be a school in every village was by reverting to the Yan'an philosophy of not worrying too much about equalizing standards since this could only be achieved in a regular state-supported system staffed by properly trained teachers.

Tensions were also mounting at other points within the system. The development of primary and secondary schooling that had occurred was producing growing proportions of graduates for whom there were no places available at the next higher level because it was impossible to provide enough schools for everyone everywhere all at once. In accordance with the classic development dilemma, providing new places at the elementary level was easier than expanding secondary schooling. Similarly, it was easier to increase secondary school enrollments than to provide appropriate opportunities on the job market once the new students graduated. The Chinese government was therefore anticipating in 1957, another potentially disruptive symptom of development in the form of growing numbers of young people whose expectations for more schooling and/or employment commensurate with their new education could not immediately be met. Zhou Enlai had highlighted this dilemma in his 1957 government work report when he emphasized the need to devise forms of secondary schooling that would be college preparatory for some but terminal and work-oriented for the majority—at the same time that recent rapid growth had created a corresponding rise in expectations. Because of the great need for development personnel, Zhou noted, most secondary school graduates since 1949 had been able to continue on to college. But expansion at the tertiary level could not continue to match that at the secondary. Henceforth, an increasing number of primary and

---

[31] *Renmin ribao,* June 21, 1956; *Guangming ribao,* March 23, 1959; State Statistical Bureau, ed., *Ten Great Years* (Peking: Foreign Languages Press, 1960), p. 192; Robert D. Barendsen, *Half-work Half-study Schools in Communist China* (Washington, D.C.: Dept. of Health, Education, and Welfare, 1964), pp. 1, 7.

secondary school graduates would have to reconcile themselves to "productive labor" in agriculture and industry.

At the same time, however, the demands for national construction and intellectual independence from the Soviet Union made quality an issue of increasing concern. The need for quality meant that the existing educated elite would perpetuate itself into the indefinite future, especially after it became apparent that the Party's early hopes for higher worker-peasant college enrollments could not be realized if academic plans and standards were to be met. Yet the existing educated elite was not only bourgeois by reason of its birth, but if the hundred flowers episode was any indication, remained unchanged in many of its concerns and commitments, which were being passed on to the younger generation as well.

From the 1957–58 academic year, therefore, class and political background became increasingly important criteria both for admission to higher education and for access to other benefits. And in 1958, the "Great Leap Forward" for economic development included extensive education reforms, which were introduced at the time as a "cultural revolution." According to conventional periodization, this episode marked the end of direct Soviet influence and the start of a new Chinese road to socialism. But in education, ironically, the reform ideas still seem to have been based on Soviet inspiration. Although never formally acknowledged as such, the particular Soviet inspiration was Khrushchev's education reforms of 1958. The Chinese were already discussing openly in 1957 the preliminary version of these Soviet reforms in relation to the need for similar changes in their own system.[32] The 1958 reforms were announced simultaneously in both countries at the start of the academic year. The Chinese version included in substance or spirit all the main features of the Khrushchev innovations, except that the Chinese went on to implement the provision for "special schools." This proposal, whereby the nation's brightest youth would receive education appropriate to their talents, proved too controversial in the Soviet Union because of its elitist implications and was dropped from the final package of reform proposals there.[33]

---

[32] Zhang Jian, "Xuexi Sulian jingyan de chengji bushi zhuyao de me?" (Are Not the Achievements in Studying the Soviet Experience Essential?), *Renmin jiaoyu*, no. 8 (Aug. 1957), pp. 16–18.

[33] On the Khrushchev education reforms, see Nigel Grant, *Soviet Education* (New York: Penguin, fourth ed., 1979), pp. 102–4, 109–17; Mervyn Matthews, *Education in the Soviet Union: Policies and Institutions Since Stalin* (London: George Allen and Unwin, 1982), pp. 15–33; idem, *Privilege in the Soviet Union: A Study of Elite Life-*

Whatever their origins, however, the reforms took on a rather different significance in Chinese practice, where they could just as easily be interpreted as a derivation of the Yan'an experience. For they reflected the Chinese environment, which was still predominantly rural and where the general availability of education was still much lower than in the Soviet Union. Also, unlike the Soviet Union, it was not the privileged status of the new intellectual elite that needed reforming in China, but the continuing influence of the old that had yet to be broken. Finally, the Chinese reforms were introduced via the comprehensive new strategy of mass mobilization for economic reorganization and development, code-named the "Great Leap Forward."

The opposition in 1958 was, allegedly, "some bourgeois educators" and "some of our comrades" who agreed with them in proposing to restrict the extent and speed of education development. They also advocated one type of school system only—state-run and state-funded, with regular schools, teachers, and methods of instruction. These "erroneous suggestions" were opposed, and Mao's strategy of "walking on two legs" was adopted as the only means of popularizing education among the worker-peasant masses within a reasonable period of time, given the huge burden of state expenditure that would otherwise be necessary.[34]

The directive of September 19, 1958, which launched the education reforms, called for a "cultural revolution" and criticized education work for the errors of neglecting politics, Party leadership, and productive labor. The directive demanded an end to the old notions that education could only be "led by experts" and that mental and manual labor were two mutually exclusive endeavors.[35] Quantitative goals were as extravagant for education as for the economy. Now illiteracy was to be eradicated and primary schooling universalized within just 5 years, and there would be a secondary school in every agricultural producers cooperative. Within 15 years, college education would be available for everyone with the necessary qualifications who wanted it; quality could be pursued during the 15 years thereafter. Many different forms of schooling would be

---

Styles Under Communism (London: George Allen and Unwin, 1978), pp. 114–17, 126–30; George Z. F. Bereday, William W. Brickman, and Gerald H. Read, eds., *The Changing Soviet School* (Boston: Houghton Mifflin, 1960), pp. 86–100, 290–91.

[34] Lu Dingyi, "Jiaoyu bixu yu shengchan laodong xiangjiehe" (Education Must Be Combined with Productive Labor), *Hongqi* (Red Flag), Sept. 1, 1958, pp. 1–12.

[35] *Renmin ribao*, Sept. 20, 1958.

used to create this system of mass education: schools run by the state and by collectives; general education and vocational training; education for children and for adults; full-day schools, work-study schools, and spare-time schools.

The task of rapidly universalizing education for the masses and raising the technical level of industry and agriculture was given specifically to the half-work half-study and spare-time schools. These could be run on a self-supporting basis without financial aid from the state. They also did not require a professional staff but could rely on "whoever could teach." In the Chinese equivalent of Khrushchev's "special schools" proposal, however, the September 1958 directive also stipulated that some of the already established regular schools should have the responsibility of raising the quality of education. Such schools were to maintain a complete curriculum and pay attention to raising the quality of their own academic work.[36]

The Great Leap Forward soon collapsed, of course, and the forces of regularization inevitably reasserted themselves once more. But this time they did so in a deliberately disjointed fashion. Again it was Zhou Enlai who indicated the course education policy would take. The full-time regular schools at all levels should make it their task to raise quality, he noted in his 1959 government work report. But beyond that, "we should first concentrate relatively more strength to run well a group of keypoint schools (*zhongdian xuexiao*), so as to train specialized personnel of even higher quality for the state and bring about a rapid rise in our country's scientific and cultural level."[37] The decision to systematize the development of keypoint schools is generally traced to Zhou's 1959 statement, although the formal directive was not issued until 1962.[38] The line

---

[36] Ibid.

[37] Report made to the First Session of the Second National People's Congress, April 18, 1959, *Renmin ribao*, April 19, 1959.

[38] "Jiaoyubu guanyu you zhongdiandi banhao yipi quanrizhi zhong, xiao xuexiao de tongzhi" (Education Ministry Circular on Having a Group of Full-Day System Secondary and Primary Schools Run Well in a Keypoint Manner), Dec. 21, 1962, in *Zhongguo jiaoyu nianjian, 1949–1981*, pp. 736–37. Concentrated or "keypoint" development was followed at all educational levels throughout the FFYP period, but apparently in a form similar to the central school concept adopted in Yan'an. The extension of the concept to mean also a deliberate concentration of all human and material resources including the "best" students was debated in 1956, but appears not to have been authorized as national policy and applied systematically throughout the education system until the immediate post–Great Leap years. Hence both contemporary and later references to pre-1958 keypoint schools do not mention what

of unequal development between mass and elite education, soon to be excoriated in the 1966–76 Cultural Revolution, was thus clearly articulated. But it followed directly from the otherwise "revolutionary" directive of September 1958 and Mao's own policy of "walking on two legs." Ironically, CCP-led decision makers in these 1958–59 directives had finally succumbed to pressures from professional educators against the leveling principle imposed by the Soviet model and in favor of the inherited "Chinese" custom of education for "special talent."

When the high tide of enthusiasm for the Great Leap receded, experiments aimed at shortening the curriculum and increasing the productive labor component within it for the full-day schools were curtailed. By the mid-1960s, Mao's "walking on two legs" slogan (*liangtiaotui zoulu*) had been reformulated in practice as "two tracks" or two kinds of education (*liangzhong jiaoyu zhidu*). The two main tracks were (1) vocational and work-study schooling for the masses while (2) the regular full-day system and especially the keypoint schools within it were strengthened to provide college preparatory education for the few. These latter, by reason of the entrance criteria (examination scores plus class/political background and personal connections) were the children mainly of intellectuals and cadres, that is, the existing educated and political elites. This remained true generally during the early 1960s, despite the varying degrees of discrimination applied against and access granted to the families of rightists, landlords, counterrevolutionaries, and other "enemy" categories.[39] It was this two-track system, or rather the regular stream within it, that Mao's final 1966–76 Cultural Revolution was designed to break. Only this time, "cultural revolution" was redefined to mean not just radical education reform as in 1958, but a systematic confrontation with all the perceived enemies, both old and new, of the Chinese Communist revolution.

---

subsequently became their most controversial characteristic, namely, the streaming or concentration of the most advantaged students within them (see, for example, ibid., pp. 167–70).

[39] On the developments between the Great Leap of 1958 and the advent of the Cultural Revolution in 1966, see especially Barendsen, *Half-work Half-study Schools in Communist China;* Stanley Rosen, *Red Guard Factionalism and the Cultural Revolution in Guangzhou* (Boulder, Colo.: Westview Press, 1982); Susan L. Shirk, *Competitive Comrades: Career Incentives and Student Strategies in China* (Berkeley and Los Angeles: University of California Press, 1982); Jonathan Unger, *Education Under Mao: Class and Competition in Canton Schools, 1960–1980* (New York: Columbia University Press, 1982).

Cultural Revolution II, 1966–76

The rationale underlying the second cultural revolution was that socialist transformation of the economy was not sufficient; the realm of the superstructure had to be revolutionized as well. To accomplish this aim, bourgeois ideas and the people who espoused them had to be changed. Otherwise, they might threaten the continuing existence of the revolution itself. As with Khrushchev's education reforms of 1958, however, it now appears that Mao was indebted to the Soviet experience for this redefinition of cultural revolution as well. It was as if, looking back over the progress that had been made in revolutionizing Chinese society to date, Mao decided that China had skipped a stage in rushing immediately to impose the postrevolutionary "classless" Stalin model on a society as yet unreconstructed along revolutionary lines. It was as if Mao was looking back to a stage that Stalin had created briefly in Russia as a prerequisite for the postrevolutionary order he would then create. Whether Mao actually knew about Stalin's 1928–31 cultural revolution is another secret of China's political history, but the similarities seem too great to be purely coincidental. Thus, either there is some such functional necessity built into Communist-led revolutions, or Mao knew about the earlier Soviet episode and used it as a precedent—translating it into "proper Chinese"—in order to break the impasse he perceived developing within his own revolution forty years later. In any event, the aim in both instances was to reinforce the destruction of bourgeois economic power by attacking bourgeois influence in the political and cultural realms as well. That brief Soviet experience is instructive, moreover, for the perspective it adds to Mao's grand design.

To summarize the Soviet experience briefly, the reinterpretation of "cultural revolution" to include class conflict occurred between 1928 and 1931.[40] The change seemed to derive from Stalin's disagreement with his "rightist" opposition over the speed of industrialization and agricultural collectivization. The rightists were also held to be conciliators of the bourgeois intellectuals, among whom support for the revolution was not overly enthusiastic. Hence, the campaign to discredit the rightist opposition was linked with the

---

[40] The following discussion is taken from Sheila Fitzpatrick, *Education and Social Mobility in the Soviet Union, 1921–1934* (Cambridge: Cambridge University Press, 1979); Sheila Fitzpatrick, ed., *Cultural Revolution in Russia, 1928–1931* (Bloomington: Indiana University Press, 1978).

effort to create a new proletarian intelligentsia and break the authority of the old. Public vigilance was aroused against intellectual saboteurs and wreckers in industry. The proletariat was called upon to resist the "influence, traditions and customs of the old society." Simultaneously, large numbers of adult workers were recruited into higher education and then promoted into the new jobs created by the program of rapid industrialization.

The process was also characterized by local initiative and popular mass mobilization. In this manner, dismissals and expulsions of faculty and students occurred at all levels. The targets in government offices were "corrupt and incompetent bureaucrats." These were purged "spontaneously" by militant workers, peasants, youth groups, and local Party organizations. Workers were even invited to participate in the tenure confirmation of university professors. Youth League (Komsomol) participants appeared the most enthusiastic in attempting to recreate the spirit of the October Revolution and the civil war with their cultural "armies" and "ambushes" (used for assaulting illiteracy and defending against bourgeois counterattacks). Suspicious of the government education bureaucracy, the militants initially developed their movement outside of it in an attempt to reorganize the basis of the education system.

Since it was a time for attacking conservative ideas as well as bureaucratic methods, radical alternatives flourished. The perceived enemy was rightist dangers in scholarship and art. Utopian plans and proposals comprised the solutions. One such new pedagogical concept was "the withering away of the school." The "bourgeois" secondary school was given over to vocational training. Gradual expansion gave way to enlarged enrollments and accelerated courses to meet the immediate demands of the economy, developing via forced marches and crash programs. It was also at this time that Soviet universities were reorganized into specialized technical institutes.

Besides linking education more closely with production, the new education principles demanded that students engage in "socially useful work" as part of their schooling. This work included participation in the adult world of political campaigns and manual labor. Schools were often emptied of students, who were sent out on work assignments to help fulfill the state economic plan. All schools had to attach themselves to production enterprises, as society itself became the school—breaking down the "authoritarianism" of the teacher and the formal classroom environment. There was even a plan to make the entire education system self-supporting by relying on student labor.

Expanded enrollments at the tertiary level included a deliberate effort to recruit large numbers of adults and workers, which led to an increase in the working-class composition of all college students from about 25 percent in 1927–28 to more than half in 1932–33. When the policy changed about that time and class or social status ceased to be a criterion for enrollment, the new students were not purged from the system but went on to become the foundation of the Soviet Union's new educated and political elite. It was on this basis that the new proletarian and old bourgeois intellectuals merged. But the adventure in radicalism to which the former owed their rise was soon repudiated and then "lost" by Soviet and Western historians, each for their own reasons. The militants who implemented the adventure became a "lost generation" of political activists. This left the regimented industrial model with its "class-less" new elite to stand alone as the sole legacy of the Stalin era. And it was this model that the newly victorious CCP set out to emulate in the early 1950s.

The similarities with the aims and means of Mao's Cultural Revolution are, of course, striking.[41] A chief difference, however, was that Mao presumably did not intend his Cultural Revolution to be only a brief interlude. Following the high tide of Red Guard attacks against their targets, the objective thereafter was to rebuild the superstructure with a new, or at least chastened, set of leaders who would institutionalize the Cultural Revolution's objectives on a more permanent basis. Stalin himself had ended his adventure in mass radicalism and class struggle, but he did so without exonerating its chief political targets or discrediting the new proletarian intellectual beneficiaries. These latter went on to become the pillars of his new *postrevolutionary* establishment. Mao, by contrast, tried to create a new *revolutionary* establishment and an education system that would help to reproduce it among the generations to follow him. In order to translate this goal into Chinese practice, he simply reached back to update the Yan'an tradition and the old education critique incorporated within it, added the class struggle component, and attempted to restructure the nation's entire education system on that basis.

---

[41] For some comparisons, see Gail Warshofsky Lapidus, "Educational Strategies and Cultural Revolution," in Fitzpatrick, ed., *Cultural Revolution in Russia, 1928–31,* pp. 79–104.

The aim, therefore, was not so much to promote equality as to reduce the old lines of distinction and all their intermediate variations: urban versus rural; regular versus irregular; the regular mode for urban elites, irregular education for rural masses, and so on. Quantitatively, enrollments soared at the mass elementary and secondary levels in the early 1970s. The keypoint college preparatory stream was abolished in favor of a neighborhood school system. Quality and the concern to compete with advanced international standards were deliberately downgraded in favor of practical relevance. Locally devised, albeit centrally orchestrated and heavily politicized, work-oriented curricula became the new norm throughout from the most prestigious university to the village primary school.[42]

Mao's Education Revolution in Historical Perspective

The most basic aims of Mao's "education revolution," as it was called, were thus twofold, reflecting its dual origins. These were the radical critique of China's new Western-style education and the class-based superstructural concerns of a newly victorious Communist-led revolution. Both traditions had their roots in the early decades of the century and both, far from being abandoned along the way, had reinforced each other over time coopting and incorporating the Soviet experience until they merged finally in the 1966–76 Cultural Revolution.

On the issue of foreign borrowing and cultural dependency, the League of Nations' Mission had advised the Chinese in 1931 not to imitate any foreign model but to borrow instead that "spirit of originality with which Americans have succeeded in adapting the culture of Europe to American conditions." Once the early post-1949 rush to learn from the Soviet Union had evolved into a genuine Sino-Soviet compromise, subsequent efforts to adapt the experience of the Russian revolution to Chinese conditions would undoubtedly have met the mission's criteria for originality, if nothing else. The assumption here is that the similarities between the Russian and

---

[42] On the "education revolution" component of the Cultural Revolution, see, for example, Theodore Hsi-en Chen, *The Maoist Educational Revolution* (New York: Praeger, 1974); idem, *Chinese Education Since 1949: Academic and Revolutionary Models* (New York: Pergamon, 1981); Ruth Gamberg, *Red and Expert: Education in the People's Republic of China* (New York: Schocken Books, 1977); Jonathan Unger, *Education Under Mao*, part 2.

Chinese "cultural revolutions" were not purely coincidental and that the former did serve as inspiration for the latter. Hence, Mao's cultural revolution was probably not an original creation, and China's twentieth century search for solutions based on authoritative foreign precedents was still operative. But overt mechanical imitation had given way to creative adaptation, since Mao's effort was clearly different from China's past exercises in emulating foreign models. His cultural revolutions bore the marks especially of the Chinese Communist movement's rural past and the indigenous critique of China's pre-1949 modernization efforts.

Concerning the debate over strategies of educational development, when the effort to raise the quality of border region schools was halted in 1944, Yan'an editorial writers had suggested that concern about uniform standards and pass rates would have to wait until the war was won and the Party's domain included the cities as well as the countryside. But once those conditions had been met, Mao would grow impatient with the inability of the "regular" education system to bridge the continuing urban-rural and elite-mass disparities that the CCP had inherited from the pre-1949 past. Hence, his 1966–76 Cultural Revolution included an attempt to reintegrate the entire education system in accordance with the antielitist, work-oriented norms that had been the Chinese reformers' long-cherished ideal.

Along with the ideals from the old reformers' critique, however, the 1966–76 experience shared the weaknesses that were responsible for the failure of their experiments as well. In the pre-1949 era, the education system as a whole had defied reform presumably because the criticism conflicted with the interests and commitments of the academic professionals within it. Hence individual reformers regularly moved outside the sytem to set up their various experiments. But there they fell victim to another danger, namely, lack of political protection and support.

The Communists initially seemed to represent a potential for success on this score since they both accepted the logic of the old reformers' arguments and understood the importance of political leadership. Yet in the end, Mao's formula rendered antiestablishment educational reform as politically vulnerable as it had always been. If the leadership had remained united, a viable solution incorporating the old critique might have evolved. But the leadership polarized, particularly after the Great Leap Forward, and the issue of education reform was one of many that divided it. Even then compromises might have been worked out. But once Mao decided he could only achieve his aims by escalating the conflict into open political warfare after 1966, policy differences of necessity hardened into two distinct lines. Indeed, his objective was to articulate his line clearly by contrast with its opposite. But in so doing, he both reified and defined the nature of his opposition. He thus ensured that his line would prevail only so long as he was able to retain power. When power was lost at his death in 1976, the enemies Mao had targeted, including both the "capitalist roaders" within the Party and the "bourgeois intellectuals" in academia, gave no quarter. They united in repudiating both his line and those who had helped to implement it.

Such is the political context, then within which post-Mao policies must also be assessed. For they represent not only the alternative strategy of socialist development that the "two-line struggle" ultimately brought into being, but also an explicit political repudiation of the Cultural Revolution experiment. This, in turn, defined the new political parameters that the post-Mao administration drew around itself, determining its choices and limiting its options. Everything criticized during the preceding decade had to be exonerated, while whatever was promoted then had to be discredited and dismantled. The entire Cultural Revolution episode was formally negated by the CCP in 1984, which meant that theoretically and politically, there could be no compromises.[43] But by 1980, the two-line policy struggle had already disappeared. Officially there was only one line, now restored to its rightful status after the intervening 1966–76 "decade of disaster." The process of restoring that line in every sector of Chinese life was designated as "reform"; the people who promoted it were the "reformers"; those who opposed them for whatever reason were rechristened "conservatives"; and the Maoist or Cultural Revolution orientation formally ceased to exist.

The post-Mao education reforms thus entailed the restoration of pre–Cultural Revolution policies, structures, names, and symbols— even on points the educational value and social consequences of which had long been debatable. Among such latter points were, of course, those inherited from the pre-1949 critique related to foreign borrowing, urban-rural disparities, and elite-mass distinctions. Ironically, the logic of the political struggle removed them more effectively from the field of educational controversy than at any

---

[43] *Renmin ribao,* April 23, 1984.

time since they were first raised more than half a century earlier. They were essentially banned not only from the realm of official policy but from public discourse as well. From the perspective of Chinese history, then, the "regular" education system, recreated after 1976, would have appeared curiously disembodied were it not for evidence that those issues had not disappeared but only retreated inward. Hence the attempt to negate such long-standing concerns raised questions from the start about the political wisdom and stability of the course adopted by post-Mao leaders. Had those concerns actually been eliminated or solved with the passage of time, they could have been safely consigned to the pages of history. Instead, it was only the public controversy over them that was more or less effectively suppressed, while the policies implemented in fact served to intensify related tensions at many points—tensions that were apparent well before the events of May and June 1989.

PART TWO

Education Reform in the 1980s:
Two Lines Become One

CHAPTER FOUR

Regularization in the Name of Reform

Deng Xiaoping claimed to be in charge of science and education in the late 1970s, and his writings were cited repeatedly as the source of authority for the policy changes occurring in that sector.[1] The imperatives he cited were similar to those of official reformers at the end of the nineteenth century. The key to modernization lay in science and technology, while education was the key to both. Japan had succeeded because it began paying attention to all three during the Meiji Restoration. China was now twenty years behind the developed countries. The United States had 1.2 million scientists and technicians; the Soviet Union had 900,000; but China had only 200,000, few of whom could still work. China had to catch up with international standards. The first priority was economic development, and the education system had to be geared to meet that aim. The social consequences and political implications need not be acknowledged. Hence, the most outstanding persons should be concentrated together in keypoint secondary schools and universities. Scientists and teachers must be given both spiritual and material encouragement. The effort to break down distinctions between mental and manual labor was not necessary. Growing crops in the experimental fields of an agricultural college counted the same as labor done in the countryside.[2]

Deng Xiaoping also proclaimed himself the layman leading experts, and the CCP similarly remained the leading authority in the realm of science and education. But the changes of the late 1970s meant that such leadership would be exercised in a very different

---

[1] Deng Xiaoping, "Guanyu kexue he jiaoyu gongzuo de jidian yijian" (A Few Opinions on Science and Education Work), Aug. 8, 1977, in *Deng Xiaoping wenxuan* (Deng Xiaoping's Selected Works) (Beijing: Renmin chubanshe, 1983), p. 45.

[2] Ibid.; and idem, "Zunzhong zhishi, zunzhong rencai" (Respect Knowledge, Respect Talent), May 24, 1977, in *Deng Xiaoping wenxuan*, pp. 37–38, 45–55.

way than in the early 1970s. Administrative procedures then had been deliberately designed to give substance to radical demands aimed at breaking the power of the academic authorities and the formal education bureaucracy. Those procedures could be summarized as *decentralization* within the education bureaucracy; *deprofessionalization,* with the inclusion of outsiders on school leadership committees; and the strengthening of *local Party control* over education. Such administrative changes did, in fact, break the authority of the professionals over education, displacing the impediment to radical reform they had always represented.

After 1976, these changes were all reversed, and the professionals regained leadership within the academic realm. Power was recentralized within the state education bureaucracy, from the county education bureaus up through the Ministry of Education. But under the new rules, the education establishment was allowed to reassert control over itself through the state education bureaucracy. Thus, during the late 1970s and early 1980s, outside political and nonprofessional interference was reduced, not absolutely but probably to a greater degree than at any time since 1949.

Deng Xiaoping's ideas in all the above respects had already been circulating in written form (underground and internally for purposes of criticism) even before Mao's death in September 1976. Hence, the implications of the arrests that followed soon after were registered at once within the academic community. Those arrested at that time included Mao's closest supporters, the Gang of Four; the CCP secretary of Chaoyang Agricultural College, which was then a radical model experimenting with "open door" education; and Zhang Tiesheng, who had been elevated to celebrity status after protesting the modified restoration of the college entrance exams in 1973.[3] Professional educators knew what they had to do and began at once in the autumn of 1976 to purge the system of its "irregular" features. The first to go were manual labor and open-door or work-study education for college students. Foreign students in Bei-

---

[3] The latter two arrests were not announced publicly, but the information was widely known among Chinese academics from whom I heard it in 1980, on the research trip mentioned below in chap. 7, n. 1. News of Zhang Tiesheng surfaced in November 1988, when a prison interview with him by Chinese reporters revealed that he had been sentenced to fifteen years' imprisonment by the Liaoning Intermediate Court in 1982 for "counterrevolutionary propaganda and instigation, and attempting to subvert the government." According to Zhongguo tongxun she (China News Agency), Hong Kong, Nov. 22, 1988, translated in Foreign Broadcast Information Service, *Daily Report: China,* Nov. 28, 1988, p. 35.

jing at the time reported that Chinese colleagues who had only just set out on the semester's work-study projects returned to campuses immediately. Rumors that the restoration of the unified college entrance examinations was imminent began circulating shortly thereafter, and book learning resumed accordingly.

Changes in the education sector thus did not need to await the Third Plenum of the Eleventh Central Committee in December 1978, which officially inaugurated Deng Xiaoping's reform administration. By that time, almost all the decisions necessary to recreate the regular education system in its pre-1966 state had already been announced, and implementation was well under way. In addition, heralding changes equally profound, U.S. Liaison Office personnel in Beijing were startled to learn in the fall of 1978 that Deng Xiaoping himself had ordered the Ministry of Education to send 10,000 students to America as soon as possible. By 1980–81, the formal education system had been reconstituted in as close an approximation of its pre–Cultural Revolution format as conditions would allow, considering the changes in personnel and student bodies that had occurred during the 1966–76 decade.[4] And despite all that had happened in the much longer interim, the restored system was also clearly a successor in form and philosophy to the one professional educators had tried to develop in the Shaan-Gan-Ning Border Region between 1938 and 1942. The characteristic features still included "regular" systems for everything; a preoccupation with fixed, uniform standards; concentration of resources in a few elite schools; school closures to promote quality; relegating "irregular" solutions to a separate status; and all the rest. The rest included the "new" component of learning again directly from the experience of the capitalist West. Such an orientation would have been entirely familiar to professional Chinese educators in 1938 but had not been permitted in so overt a manner since 1949.

Educators, when given the opportunity in Yan'an, had proceeded instinctively to reproduce for the rural wartime border regions a system based on these principles despite their widely acknowledged defects. Educators in the late 1970s reacted much the same way, as soon as Mao's successors handed the education sector back to them to run more or less as they saw fit. Hence, not only did "Maoist" antecedents stretch back in a direct line of succession to the radical-

---

[4] These changes are recorded in some detail in Suzanne Pepper, "Chinese Education after Mao: Two Steps Forward, Two Steps Back and Begin Again?" *China Quarterly,* no. 81 (March 1980), pp. 1–65.

ism of the 1920s. The proponents of "regularization" also retain direct links with a past extending back at least as far. Since these two orientations have existed in antithetical relation to each other for so long, then, the strategic error of the post-1976 regularization drive may have been to assume that the system could be made to exist on that basis alone, freed at last from the antiestablishment undertow.

By 1980–81, in any event, tensions were already such that they could no longer be ignored or dismissed as interventions of recalcitrant Maoist troublemakers. Without actually admitting that fault perhaps lay within the newly restored system itself, education authorities nevertheless began acknowledging the critical "opinions in society" it was arousing. Consequently, a steady stream of supplementary adjustments and reforms within reforms continued throughout the decade. These changes were clearly designed to accommodate various "opinions" and "interests" while avoiding any direct mention of the antithetical concerns underlying them. In 1985, the Education Ministry was upgraded into the more powerful State Education Commission, as a mark of official recognition that the wide-ranging problems within the education sector needed a stronger hand to resolve them.

Two years later, in September 1987, the *People's Daily* published an unusually forthright commentary on the conflicts being created by the post-Mao reforms generally. It described the contradictions that had developed as the reformers of the 1980s found themselves increasingly blocked by the realities of a China that pre-1949 critics would have understood very well. The author of the article was the then Minister of Culture, Wang Meng, and his topic was how literature might best contribute to the intensifying reform debates. As Minister of Culture, Wang Meng's job was to prescribe the proper orientation for China's writers and artists, so his perspective was not that of a laissez-faire Western liberal. Nevertheless, he stressed the importance of openness, choice, and enthusiasm in portraying the reforms. But his main point was the need for an accommodation with "conservative ideas"—reflecting their growing strength within the Party as the reformers were being forced on the defensive by problems for which they seemed to be running out of solutions. Wang Meng was essentially challenging the reformers to acknowledge the legitimacy of their opposition on three counts.

The first was an overly simple "shallow and childish" concept of reform, as though it was just a literary debate that once won would produce instant success. Another unfortunate trend was polarization. The reform process was being portrayed as a struggle between its adherents and the conservatives, wherein the former would prevail once the latter were vanquished. This trend showed the continuing influence of "the line struggle as the key link." Finally, reformers also had too great a tendency to look to the West for solutions. They mouthed high-sounding borrowed phrases, going on and on with their big talk and ambitious plans, as if reform could be achieved with the flick of the wrist, and then China would be saved. "In fact, during the past century of China's history, there were often people of the so-called modern school and the false foreign devils who learned a few superficial things from the West. But they ended up isolated and pitiful with not a single thing achieved."[5]

Wang Meng challenged the reformers to overcome their misconception on all three counts. "Any seemingly conservative concept," he claimed, "is related to various actual interests, to the actual level of productive development." Overcoming the commitment to egalitarianism and eating from the same big pot would be difficult until real alternatives were devised. And such solutions depended "not just on struggle but on construction and development." Conservatives, for their part, fretted over the degeneration of society and mourned the passing of their austere revolutionary traditions. They should realize that they could not return to the wartime communism and camaraderie of the 1940s. But neither would it be possible to achieve true modernization if the contemporary one-sided obsession with wealth continued. In the countryside, for instance, the agricultural reforms had begun to bring "wealth without civilization." In other words, the debate over reform remained "very active and heated," while an effective grasp of the complexities and difficulties had yet to be achieved.[6]

The implications of Wang Meng's commentary obviously extended beyond the literary realm to the crisis developing around the reforms as a whole. Had such an advisory been issued and heeded a decade earlier, the history of Deng Xiaoping's reform administration might have been very different. In the late 1970s when all its key decisions were being made, however, the grand coalition of Cul-

---

[5] *Renmin ribao*, Beijing, Sept. 8, 1987. All references to *Renmin ribao* below cite the national domestic edition.

[6] Ibid. See chap. 7, n. 2, for a postscript on Wang Meng's political status in the wake of the June 1989 crackdown against the student democracy movement.

tural Revolution victims seemed more than willing to sacrifice both their political hindsight and foresight to the uncompromising logic of the two-line struggle. In the process, of course, they also slipped easily into China's twentieth-century modernization mode as they abandoned one line and took up another, rushing forward yet again with a new formula and little concern for the dislocations that would inevitably follow. The resulting debates and complications that developed within the education sector during the 1980s are discussed in the following chapters.

CHAPTER FIVE

Elementary Schooling and the 1986 Compulsory Education Law

The weak link at the elementary level remains the countryside. All Chinese governments since the 1920s have proclaimed their commitment to universal elementary education, but all sources agree that it is only in the post-1949 era that the commitment has been "basically" realized (see table 2 for enrollments since 1949). The achievement is especially noteworthy, in international development terms, because of China's large rural population. The particular difficulties of developing a reliable system of mass education for the rural sector are not unique to China. They concern both supply and demand. On the supply side, the immediate obstacles are locational and financial. Rural populations are scattered over the landscape and elementary schools for young children must be scattered accordingly. The general principle, which educators everywhere (including those in Yan'an) have known for decades, is that the more distant the school, the smaller the proportion of children it will be able to serve. Terrain and lack of mechanized transport make it impossible for youngsters to travel long distances each day. And most rural families cannot afford the added expense of boarding school. In order to universalize elementary education in the rural areas, then, large numbers of small (and therefore inefficient) schools must be located throughout the countryside. This means that someone must pay to build and maintain them and find teachers to staff them as well.

These difficulties are compounded by others on the demand side. In relatively stable communities where the ways of life have remained largely unchanged, people who work the land and have never been educated tend not to grasp the advantages of sending their children to school. Many parents will not begin to do so voluntarily unless the benefits can be seen in clear and simple terms to outweigh the costs, which invariably include some fees, income foregone, and loss of parental control. Such "passive resistance" on the demand side naturally inhibits supply, since the kind of local village schools necessary cannot possibly survive without the support of the communities they serve. Such resistance can also be used to rationalize passive responses from local elites and others who have been heard to argue that "the peasants do not want to send their children to school" or that their children do not need schooling because "people who till the land can learn all they need to know from their fathers."

The circle of mass illiteracy and educational underdevelopment is thus difficult to break. Some countries, such as India and Pakistan, are inclined to let nature take its course. Local elites look after their own as they always have; the forces of economic development and mobility work to the advantage of some; and the majority of rural children grow up largely unschooled as their parents did before them. Since 1949, China has generally maintained a more interventionist approach, working with elaborations of the 1944 Yan'an formula. The essentials of that formula developed into an activist central government that kept up the pressure and became increasingly effective in enforcing its will via the collective structures at the grassroots level. The central government set general policy, provided financial assistance in the form of regular budgetary allocations, fixed curricula or issued guidelines, and did the same for books and materials.

The all-important budgetary allocation came down the bureaucratic chain through the provinces and counties, which apportioned funds for their commune elementary schools. Only city schools were fully state-funded, however. In the countryside, throughout the 1960s and 1970s, the crucial intervening variable was the commune or more specifically its constituent parts, the village-level production brigades. These were roughly the equivalent of the agricultural producers cooperatives set up in the 1950s. Allocations were made in such a way that the communes and brigades had to rely on their own local resources to make up the difference between their small share of state funds and the total cost of maintaining their village elementary schools. The state money typically covered a school's construction costs, operating expenses, salaries for a few of its teachers, and by the mid-1970s a small subsidy for the remainder of a school's teaching staff, most of whom were hired locally (called *minban* teachers for that reason). Other costs were met locally by a combination of collectively produced grain for the local teachers (who were paid in work points the same as the peasants, except for the small monthly state subsidy), collective labor power for maintenance and repairs, some student fees, and sometimes small-scale school-run farms and enterprises.

This formula, according to official statistics, succeeded in bringing 85 percent of the relevant age group into elementary schools by 1965 and upwards of 95 percent a decade later. However exaggerated the official figures might be, former rural schoolteachers and rural residents interviewed by myself and others in Hong Kong in the 1970s and early 1980s corroborated the high enrollment claims. These informants, despite a basically dissident orientation that had led to their common decision to leave China, nevertheless included the rural elementary school enrollment figures in their assessment of the Communist government's achievements.[1]

For the former schoolteachers, it was their achievement as well, since it had often been the teachers' responsibility to mobilize reluctant parents primarily through home visits and persuasive arguments. Interestingly, they all regarded "compulsory" (*qiangpo*) education as an alien Western concept that would have aroused undue resentment. Reports of actual penalties for noncompliance were very rare. Speaking primarily with reference to the 1970s, they recalled that such enforcement really was not necessary. Except for the few who had been teaching in national minority areas of Yunnan and Xinjiang, their mobilization efforts were directed mainly at bringing dropouts (more often girls than boys) back to the fold. Given the network of collective pressures and inducements that had grown up around them, rural people had by that time accepted the importance of learning to read and write and do simple calculations. A few of the teachers with longer memories could recall this as a mark of the difference between the 1970s and the 1950s, when mass mobilization efforts were just getting underway and the peasants still needed to be convinced. The circle had been broken, but the achievement was hard-won and based on a fragile balance. Regression was the price of failure to maintain the formula based on activism from the center, collectively supported enforcement, and local mobilization efforts.

---

[1] My own interviewees include some sixty former teachers from China. More than forty were former rural schoolteachers from all parts of the country. The interviews concentrated on the 1970s and were conducted between mid-1980 and mid-1983. (Write-up is currently in progress.) For rural Guangdong only, see William L. Parish and Martin King Whyte, *Village and Family in Contemporary China* (Chicago: University of Chicago Press, 1978), pp. 78–85.

The drag or pull exerted by the past was marked in turn by the dropout rates and by the 1982 census figures showing 235,825,000 (or 31.9 percent of the population) to be "illiterate or semi-literate" (that is, 12 years of age or over and knowing fewer than 1,500 characters.)[2] Questions might be raised about why illiterate and semiliterates were lumped together (note Evelyn Rawski's efforts to differentiate the two)[3] and how the census takers were able to ascertain that each person did or did not know 1,500 characters. Nevertheless, that number, which was used to define the category, is approximately what a person would retain from three or four years of elementary schooling, which is the sum total received by many village youth and thus the most basic qualification for the universal enrollment claim.

Beginning in 1978, the formula that had made all this possible began to unravel. The forces working against it came from two directions: (1) the regularization trend within the education sector itself and (2) the decollectivization of agriculture. Deriving from the former, the center's activist pressures that had accelerated during the early 1970s eased almost immediately after 1976. Local governments and education authorities similarly ceased their active promotion of rural schooling, as all attention focused on rebuilding the regular urban-based, quality-oriented system. Responding to the regularization trend within the system as a whole, local authorities began demanding that all rural schools be regularized as well. By this they meant that the state should assume full responsiblity for the cost of running the schools and that all *minban* teachers should be transferred onto the state payroll. In deference to quality and the sudden disfavor into which labor and practical learning had fallen, many schools also stopped running the various farms, workshops, and projects that had contributed to school budgets. Further in the interests of quality, local teachers began to be tested. Some areas required refresher courses for those who failed; others simply sent them back to the "front line of production." Millions of "sent-down" city youth also returned to their urban homes in 1978–79. Many had served as village schoolteachers and left

---

[2] *Zhongguo 1982 nian renkou pucha 10% chouyang ziliao* (Ten Percent Sampling Tabulation on the 1982 Population Census of the People's Republic of China) (Beijing: Zhongguo tongji chubanshe, 1983), pp. 316–17; *Beijing Review,* April 2, 1984, pp. 22–23.

[3] Evelyn Sakakida Rawski, *Education and Popular Literacy in Ch'ing China* (Ann Arbor: University of Michigan Press, 1979), passim.

without knowing who their replacements might be.

The first steps toward agricultural decollectivization also began in 1978, with the campaign to "reduce the peasants' collective burdens." This meant, among other things, that peasants had to be remunerated for any labor they performed for the collective. The costs of rural schooling began to climb as the advantages of nonattendance rose under the new household responsibility system. On the one hand, families were given more incentives and more opportunities to make money, while, on the other, their economic well-being suddenly depended solely on their own resources.

The results of these combined pressures were registered very quickly in terms of closing or "merging" schools, declining enrollments, rising dropout rates, and the unmet payrolls of locally hired teachers. According to official statistics, the number of students enrolled in elementary schools declined from a high of 150 million in 1975–76 to 140 million in 1982 and on down to 128 million in 1987. The number of elementary schools declined from just over one million in 1976 to 894,000 in 1981 (see table 2). Between 1979 and 1981, the number of students enrolled in the first grade declined from 37.79 million to 27.49 million.[4]

After the single-child-family campaign was launched in 1979–80, with all the attendant publicity, shrinking age cohorts became a standard rhetorical defense. In early 1984, an authoritative presentation of education statistics acknowledged that the number of elementary schools in 1983 was 18,000 fewer than the year before, and the number of students in school had fallen by 3.9 million during the same year. But the decline was dismissed as being due "mainly to the falling birth rate in recent years."[5]

Nevertheless, official statistics have acknowledged the decline not just in absolute numbers but also in the percentage of the age group entering school. The latter fell from 96 percent in 1976 to 93 percent between 1979 and 1982 (see table 3). These figures need clarification particularly as regards the considerable discrepancy

---

[4] The 1979 figure for the first grade enrollments is from *China: Socialist Economic Development* (Washington, D.C.: The World Bank, 1983), 3:205; the 1981 figure is from *Zhongguo baike nianjian, 1982* (China Encyclopedic Yearbook, 1982) (Beijing and Shanghai: Zhongguo dabaike quanshu chubanshe, 1982), p. 568.

[5] Guojia tongji ju, shehui tongji si (State Statistical Bureau, Division of Social Statistics), "Woguo jiaoyu shiye zai tiaozhengzhong fazhan" (The Development of Our Country's Educational Enterprise During Consolidation), *Tongji* (Statistics) (Beijing), June 17, 1984, p. 16.

Table 2

Elementary Schools and Enrollments

Year	Number of Schools	Number of Students in School (millions)
1949	346,800	24
1965	1,681,900	116
1966		103
1971		112
1972		125
1973		136
1974		145
1975		151
1976	1,044,300	150
1977		146
1978		146
1979	923,500	147
1980		146
1981	894,074	143
1982	880,516	140
1983	862,165	136
1984	853,740	136
1985	832,309	134
1986	820,846	132
1987	807,406	128
Six-year schools	458,671	75
Five-year schools	348,735	53
1988		125

SOURCES: Number of schools for 1949 to 1979 from *Zhongguo baike nianjian, 1980* (China Encyclopedic Yearbook, 1980) (Beijing and Shanghai: Zhongguo dabaike quanshu chubanshe, 1980), p. 535. Number of students for 1949 and 1965 from *Peking Review,* Feb. 3, 1978, pp. 16–17. Number of students for 1966 to 1980 from *Zhongguo tongji niangian, 1981* (China Statistical Yearbook, 1981), State Statistical Bureau, ed. (Beijing: Zhongguo tongji chubanshe, 1981), p. 441. Schools and students for 1981 to 1987 from *Zhongguo tongji nianjian, 1988* (China Statistical Yearbook, 1988), State Statistical Bureau, ed. (Beijing: Zhongguo tongji chubanshe, 1988), pp. 873, 876. Breakdown for 1987 between six-year and five-year schools from *Zhongguo jiaoyu tongji nianjian, 1987* (China Education Statistical Yearbook, 1987), State Education Commission, Planning and Financial Affairs Bureau, ed. (Beijing: Gongye daxue chubanshe, 1988), pp. 78–79. Schools and students for 1988 from State Statistical Bureau communiqué for 1988, *Renmin ribao,* March 1, 1989).

NOTE: Official statistics issued in the 1980s for the Cultural Revolution decade are roughly similar to those given earlier in other sources. One source of confusion in the later official compilations is the failure to distinguish between the academic and calendar years. One major unexplained discrepancy appears in the figures for 1965. The World Bank figures (*China: Socialist Economic Development* 3:134) show 682,000 primary schools instead of 1,681,900 as shown above, and 70 percent of the age group enrolled instead of 84.7 percent, as shown in table 3. The number of students in school is, however, the same in all sources that cite such a figure.

between the "number of school age children who have entered school" (shown in table 3) and the much larger widely cited figure for "number of students in school" (shown in table 2). In addition, the "percentage of the age group" figures are now compromised by the recent admission of probable substantial errors in the official birth rate statistics themselves, to exaggerate the success of the birth control campaign. This raises questions about the accuracy of the figures in table 3, showing the size of the national elementary school age cohorts.[6]

Whatever the accuracy of the figures, however, the officially acknowledged decline in the percentage of the age group entering school reflected the reality of a weakened elementary school delivery system in the countryside, which placed central policy makers on the defensive. Initial reports—and especially those not originating from central government sources—did not, in any case, cite the declining birth rate but rather blamed the new education and agricultural policies directly. "Quantity and quality are two

---

[6] For some probable reasons to explain the discrepancy between the "number of school-age children who have entered school" and the "number of students in school," see table 3, note. On the problems with the official birth rate figures, a national sample family-planning survey revealed that the gap between the reported figures and the actual figures for 1987 birth rates was: (1) less than 10 percent in only four provinces/municipalities/regions; (2) 10–20 percent in three such units; (3) 20–30 percent in six such units; (4) 30–40 percent in ten; and (5) over 40 percent in six. The errors were attributed primarily to fraudulent reporting by local cadres anxious to appear to have met their family planning targets in the face of local recalcitrance and to statistical recording procedures that lack adequate supervision or verification mechanisms (*Renmin ribao,* Oct. 24, 1988; also on the 1988 sample survey, see *Zhongguo renkou bao* [China Population] [Beijing], July 1, 22, 1988; Aug. 19, 1988; and Oct. 31, 1988).

China has 22 provinces, 3 municipalities, and 5 autonomous regions. Hence, 29 of its 30 provincial-level administrative divisions underreported their birth statistics. Although not identified in the report cited, the one nonoffender is probably Shanghai, which has consistently maintained the strictest birth-control program and the lowest birth rates in the country, dating back to the early 1970s.

Table 3

School-Age Children Enrolled at the Elementary Level

Year	National Elementary-School-Age Cohorts (millions)	School-Age Children Who Have Entered Elementary School (millions)	School-Age Children Entering Elementary School (percent)
1949			25.0
1965	116.03	98.29	84.7
1976	121.94	118.39	96.0
1977	121.01	116.79	95.5
1978	121.31	115.85	94.0
1979	123.23	115.80	93.0
1980	122.20	114.78	93.0
1981	120.18	111.75	93.0
1982	117.63	109.58	93.2
1983	112.51	105.78	94.0
1984	106.69	101.70	95.3
1985	103.62	99.43	95.9
1986	100.67	97.02	96.4
1987	97.51	94.77	97.2

SOURCES: Translated from *Zhongguo tongji nianjian, 1988* (China Statistical Yearbook, 1988), State Statistical Bureau, ed. (Beijing: Zhongguo tongji chubanshe, 1988), p. 889. The 1949 figure only is from *China: Socialist Economic Development* (Washington, D.C.: The World Bank, 1983), 3:134.

NOTE: The original table did not contain an explanation of how the age cohort was defined. Nor did the table carry an explanation for the significant difference between the number of school-age children who have entered elementary school and the much larger number of students in school shown in table 2. Both sets of figures are from the State Statistical Bureau. Presumably, the gap might be due to one or a combination of the following: (1) Under- and over-aged children actually in school. (2) A definition of "school-age children" based on the five-year elementary school course, perhaps in deference to the informal five-year/six-year difference between urban and rural schools. Thus, the conventional school age is 7 to 12 years for elementary students. But Jiangsu Province, for example, uses 7 to 11 years in calculating the "percentage of the age group entering school" ("Zhong xiao xue zonghe baobiao tianbiao shuoming" [Instructions for Filling Out the Comprehensive Statistical Report Forms for Secondary and Elementary Schools], Statistics and Finance Office of the Jiangsu Provincial Education Committee, June 1987). (3) The practice of repeating the final year of elementary school by those who have failed to gain admission to the junior secondary level on the first try. (4) Rural students tend to drift in and out, thus prolonging their stay "in school." Operating expenses allocated per student are the incentive for keeping them on the rolls for an extended period during which they are not necessarily physically present (according to former rural schoolteachers interviewed in Hong Kong in the early 1980s). (5) The larger "number of students in school" figure may also reflect a greater absolute number of youngsters in the age group than the official statistics acknowledge because of deliberate under-reporting of birth rates.

opposites in unity," admonished one writer in 1980. "It is onesided for attention to be paid only to quality but not quantity. We have to think about this point and to correct it right now, rather than wait until future generations sum up lessons when they write history." The comment was with reference, among other things, to the estimated 20 million new illiterates that would grow up during the coming decade given the elementary school enrollment ratios and the size of the relevant age cohorts.[7]

In the same vein, a report from Hebei Province complained that the number of primary and secondary school students in the province had declined by 700,000 during 1982 alone. "We should seriously investigate this question and take steps," noted the report. "We cannot eliminate illiteracy on the one hand and produce new illiterates on the other."[8] A complaint from Yunnan asserted that the rate of attendance at the elementary school level dropped for three consecutive years between 1979 and 1981.[9] Yunnan placed the blame on the household responsibility system in the countryside. As a result, teachers were leaving their jobs, students were dropping out, attendance rates had declined, and some rural schools had been closed.[10] Out in Qinghai Province, where school attendance rates were among the lowest in the country anyway, over 1,000 rural schools closed down in 1980. Also, because of the new agricultural policies, locally hired teachers were not being issued their grain ration and work points (collective payment under the old system).[11] In Ningxia, the number of children enrolled in elementary school also dropped (from 628,867 in 1977 to 553,900 in 1982), and there were "many more new illiterates."[12]

---

[7] Song Jian, "Population and Education," *Ziran bianzhengfa tongxun* (Journal of the Dialectics of Nature) (Beijing), no. 3 (June 1980), translated in Joint Publications Research Service of the Foreign Broadcast Information Service (Washington, D.C.), *China Report: Political, Sociological and Military* (hereafter, JPRS, *CR:PSM*), no. 178 (April 3, 1981), pp. 44, 47.

[8] Xinhua in Chinese for *Hebei ribao,* June 12, 1983, translated in ibid., no. 437 (July 11, 1983), pp. 109–10.

[9] Kunming, Yunnan service, Feb. 17, 1983, translated in ibid., no. 403 (March 21, 1983), p. 92.

[10] *Guangming ribao,* Oct. 8, 1980.

[11] Xining, Qinghai service, Jan. 8, 1981, translated in JPRS, *CR:PSM,* no. 159 (Jan. 26, 1981), p. 101.

[12] Chen Li, "My Humble Opinion about Investment in Intellectual Resources in Ningxia," *Ningxia shehui kexue* (Social Science in Ningxia) (Yinchuan), no. 3 (August 1984), translated in ibid., no. 089 (Dec. 19, 1984), p. 80.

The Shaanxi provincial Party committee and government issued a "proposal" regarding the locally hired teachers in late 1983. Among other things, it noted that "all counties must implement the related decisions of the State Council and grant subsidies in full to the teachers themselves, as stipulated, on a monthly basis. All communes and brigades must not delay in paying teachers."[13]

A survey of 7,000 production brigades conducted a few years earlier in Anhui Province suggested why the communes and brigades were finding it so difficult to pay their teachers. Essentially, they lacked the means to do so. The problem was to find a reliable source of school funding when the local collective unit was losing control over local income. About one-third of the brigades still retained some collective control with an assessment, for brigade expenses including the *minban* teachers' salaries, levied against every household contract. The amount was then withheld when the crops were sold to the state. This was the preferred method at the time, but it could only be used where local farm incomes were derived from growing government contract crops. Some 20 percent of the brigades were supporting their schools mainly by levying a tax on brigade-run enterprises, but not all were run well enough to encourage the widespread use of this method. Nevertheless, these were the two most reliable sources of funding. The other half of the brigades surveyed were using one of two other unsatisfactory methods. One was to divide education costs among all households in the brigade, whether they had children or not, and send the teachers out door-to-door to collect—which they did not like. The other way was to divide up costs only among those households with school-age children, which increased the dropout rates because many families could not afford the higher fees.[14]

The same decollectivization process that precipitated these trends has also inhibited the search for funding alternatives. Toward that end, the central government has issued a steady stream of directives reiterating its commitment to universal elementary schooling and, given its other competing goals, has probably done as much as it can to promote solutions. Their systematic enforcement remains dependent on the institutionalization of a viable sys-

[13] Xian, Shaanxi service, Nov. 5, 1983, translated in ibid., no. 475 (Nov. 30, 1983), p. 75.

[14] Ming Kecheng, "Renqing nongcun jingji xingshi; banhao nongcun jiaoyu" (Have a Clear Understanding of the Rural Economic Situation; Manage Village Education Well), *Jiaoyu yanjiu* (Education Research) (Beijing), no. 6 (1981), pp. 18–19.

tem of local township government and especially township financial administration to replace the now defunct collective. Official recognition and responses to the crisis began in 1979 and culminated in the 1986 compulsory (*yiwu,* more accurately translated as "obligatory") education law.

First, an official clarification was issued in 1979, in response to the local demands for more state funds that began to grow with the onset of regularization and decollectivization. The local authorities were advised that they must continue to run rural schools because the state would not be able to take over any more of that responsibility for the time being. In 1980, the Party Central Committee and the State Council issued a "Resolution Regarding Certain Questions in Popularizing Elementary Education," which called for the realization of universal elementary education by the end of the decade, albeit without specifying how the growing obstacles were to be overcome.[15] Local officials responsible for implementation were caught in the middle. They were supposed to continue to keep their schools open, but they had also been ordered not to mobilize peasants for unremunerated labor or otherwise increase their burdens for collective undertakings. No one seemed to know who should be responsible or where to start. Official support was reiterated for school-run workshops and farms, primarily for income-earning purposes rather than for labor education and practice as before. Newly rich peasants and others were encouraged to make voluntary private contributions. Soliciting contributions from Overseas Chinese compatriots resumed, also with official blessing. This custom had sustained many rural schools in Fujian and Guangdong prior to 1966. But these were all ad hoc expedients, incapable of maintaining universal elementary education on a nationwide basis.

A 1982 article in *People's Education,* published by the Ministry of Education, pleaded for a solution to the dilemma: "Of course, in solving these problems we cannot rely completely on the state. So long as we are reasonable, the peasants will be happy to take on the burden. Moreover, for many years they have already been bearing the expenses of making needed repairs and maintaining the desks

---

[15] *Renmin ribao,* Aug. 12, 1979; *Guangming ribao,* July 24, 1979; Zhongyang jiaoyu kexue yanjiusuo (Central Education Research Institute), ed., *Zhonghua renmin gongheguo jiaoyu dashiji, 1949–1982* (Chronicle of Events in Education in the People's Republic of China, 1949–1982) (Beijing: Jiaoyu kexue chubanshe, 1983), pp. 598–99.

and chairs. In this matter, it would be best to have some stipulated guiding principles, the better to be followed uniformly in the various areas."[16] Provincial leaders in Henan reached the same conclusion at a 1983 education work conference. The sense of the meeting was that "we cannot regard taking money from the peasants to run education as an increase of the burden on them."[17]

In Hunan, provincial Party and government leaders held an "urgent" telephone conference in July 1982 on pressing matters in education work. Local leaders reportedly moved at once to implement the "spirit of the meeting." By September, 8,000 *minban* teachers had received their back pay. Steps were also taken to stem the rash of peasant attacks against schools (over 300 cases of physical assaults against teachers and school property). Regarding the problem of school maintenance, Hunan's leaders simply broke the new rules. Commune and brigade cadres reportedly, "launched the masses to contribute labor and material to repair the buildings and make some teaching equipment."[18]

In Sichuan, by contrast, local leaders blamed those at the provincial level: "Education reform in our province started late and failed to make good progress. No noticeable successes have been achieved. There are many problems.... Up to now, the provincial department of education has not yet been able to put forward any concrete reform plan and there has been no experience of experimentation gained at any selected point from which we can learn. Even if the lower levels want to carry out reform, they do not know how to start it."[19]

In Shaanxi, the head of the provincial education bureau seemed totally at a loss. "In many localities," wrote Director Zhang, "the desolate situation exists where they rely on a small number of people in the education departments to run the schools. General education is an enterprise for local management, for our schools are found in nearly every inhabited locale.... How to arouse the enthusiasm toward running schools at the county and township lev-

---

[16] Zhang Zhiyuan, "Putong jiaoyu gongzuozhong de liangge tuqu wenti" (Two Pressing Questions in General Education Work), *Renmin jiaoyu* (People's Education) (Beijing), no. 10 (1982), p. 10.

[17] Zhengzhou, Henan service, Aug. 8, 1983, translated in JPRS, *CR:PSM*, no. 457 (Sept. 15, 1983), p. 29.

[18] Changsha, Hunan service, Sept. 4, 1982, translated in ibid., no. 340 (Sept. 24, 1982), p. 87.

[19] *Sichuan ribao* (Chengdu), June 27, 1984, translated in ibid., no. 071 (Oct. 22, 1984), p. 38.

els, particularly under the conditions of the current transformation of the rural economic structure, and how to reform the management system of rural education are the new problems facing education departments at every level, which should issue many articles on reform."[20]

The cause of Director Zhang's apparent consternation was undoubtedly the increasing pressure on the localities to bear even more responsibility for funding rural schools. The pressure from the center increased during 1984, with the national publicity given to the Hebei experiment. By April, 51 Hebei counties participating in this experiment had reportedly converted to the new system with good results. It apparently entailed the withdrawal of all state funds from all rural schools, both elementary and junior secondary, and including the state subsidy for the *minban* teachers. The state money thus saved within any given county was to be concentrated in its "elite" state-supported sector, that is, in its keypoint schools, senior secondary and technical education, and used to increase the salaries of the teachers therein. Limited and temporary state subsidies were promised to help out very poor districts. The official rationale was that state appropriations were scarcely adequate to maintain existing levels of education. Meanwhile, the peasants were growing wealthy due to the new agricultural policies and should be able to fund all their own schools locally from their own resources.[21]

It is impossible to ascertain, from a distance, whether this Hebei experiment was mainly just a publicity effort aimed at giving local authorities the guiding examples they were demanding; or whether the experiment really aimed to test the feasibility of withdrawing all

---

[20] *Shaanxi ribao* (Xian), Sept. 22, 1984.

[21] Ten-part series by Zhang Tianlai and Mei Zhanyi, *Guangming ribao,* Feb. 22–28, 1984; Gao Baoli, "Guanyu Hebeisheng nongcun jiaoyu gaige de lilun tantao" (A Theoretical Inquiry into Hebei's Rural Education Reform), and Zhao Qin, "Hebeisheng nongcun jizi banjiaoyu de kexingxing yanjiu" (Research on the Feasibility of Raising Funds for Rural Education in Hebei Province), *Jiaoyu yanjiu,* no. 9 (1984), pp. 39–43 and 44–46, respectively; Zhongguo jiaoyu ninjian (China Education Yearbook), ed., *Zhongguo jiaoyu nianjian (difang jiaoyu), 1949–1984* (China Education Yearbook, Local Education, 1949–1984) (Changsha: Hunan jiaoyu chubanshe, 1986), pp. 129–30; Xin Xiangrong, "Peasants Run Their Own Schools," *Beijing Review,* April 9, 1984, pp. 4–5; Hubert O. Brown, "Teachers and the Rural Responsibility System in the People's Republic of China,"*Asian Journal of Public Administration* (Hong Kong University) 7:1 (June 1985):2–17; and idem, "Primary Schooling and the Rural Responsibility System in the People's Republic of China," *Comparative Education Review,* August 1986, pp. 373–87.

state funds from all rural schools, as published descriptions indicated. If the latter, the results should have been anticipated, namely that such a plan, implemented generally, would have dealt an even greater blow to rural education than that already experienced. In any event, the State Council issued a clarification in late 1984, promising that "educational operating expenses allocated by the state will continue to be issued on the original basis, and be sent down from the county to the township; they cannot be reduced or held back." But, "henceforth any increase in educational appropriations issued by the state and local governments will be used primarily to develop teacher training education and subsidize poor districts. Rich districts must rely on themselves for any increase in township education operating expenses." To facilitate the latter endeavor the same circular also, finally, authorized the township governments to collect an educational surtax to be levied against agricultural and township enterprises. The circular did not suggest alternatives for localities without profit-making enterprises, but the unpopular head-tax and land-tax methods were forbidden.[22]

The current state of the Hebei experiment has not been publicized. But despite the State Council's claims and subsequent clarification, one recent report noted that eighteen city and county governments in Hebei Province reduced educational funds by up to 10 percent in 1987. As a result, some schools were unable to pay their teachers' salaries, which remains a common problem.[23] For example, according to reports from Liaoning Province in the Northeast, several million dollars (*renminbi*) in back pay was owed to teachers in locally run schools throughout the province as of early 1989. Because of limited budgets in many rural areas there, some schoolteachers had received no cash payment for as long as two years.[24]

Given such unsteady foundations, the plans for a compulsory education law announced in mid–1985 appeared somewhat prema-

---

22 "Guowuyuan guanyu choucuo nongcun xuexiao banxue jingfei de tongzhi" (State Council Circular on Raising Funds for Rural School Operating Expenses), Dec. 13, 1984, *Zhonghua renmin gongheguo guowuyuan gongbao* (Bulletin of the State Council of the People's Republic of China) (Beijing), no. 31 (Dec. 30, 1984), p. 1046.

23 *China Daily,* Jan. 27, 1989.

24 Xinhua (New China News Agency), English, Jan. 26, 1989, in *Summary of World Broadcasts* (hereafter, *SWB*), British Broadcasting Corporation, Reading, England, FE/0375 B2/6, Feb. 3, 1989; Shenyang, Liaoning provincial radio, Feb. 1, 1989, in *SWB*, FE/0381 B2/4, Feb. 10, 1989; *China Daily,* March 18, 1989.

ture. The law itself was promulgated a year later and now stands at least as an official declaration of intent. As such it also plays an important political role in countering the initial charge that the new policies are onesided in their pursuit of quality to the detriment of mass education. Publicity surrounding the law claimed it placed China among the many advanced nations that have ten to twelve years of compulsory education. The law formally institutes a nine-year compulsory education system, including both elementary and junior secondary schooling. According to the law, compulsory education is to be tuition free. Organizations and individuals are forbidden to employ school-age children, that is, aged 16 or younger. Local governments are authorized to take action against parents who do not send their children to school and employers who might hire them.[25]

Official explanations of the new law, however, place it more clearly within the context of Chinese realities. Commenting on the various provisions, He Dongchang (formerly minister of education; now a vice-minister of the Education Commission) acknowledged that "in many rural areas, elementary education is still not universal, and new generations of illiterates continue to emerge." He also acknowledged further that unlike the cities, most rural elementary schools had not reverted to the (pre–Cultural Revolution) six-year format.[26] Hence, elementary and junior middle school combined were only eight years at most in the countryside and should remain so for the time being. Indeed, the overall time table for implementing the law remains very open-ended. Cities and certain developed areas of the hinterland should strive to fulfill its provisions by 1990, less-developed cities, towns, and rural areas by 1995, and "areas with poor economic and cultural background" as conditions permit. A similarly flexible interpretation was authorized for the "tuition-free" regulation as well. Given their financial difficulties, schools can (and do) continue to collect "miscellaneous fees."[27]

---

[25] *Renmin ribao,* April 18, 1986.

[26] See table 2 for the year 1987, which shows the breakdown between five- and six-year elementary schools.

[27] He Dongchang's explanation was widely reprinted prior to the law's promulgation, for example, in *Zhongguo jiaoyu bao* (China Education News) (Beijing), Jan. 18, 1986. The same points were reiterated by Li Peng, then vice-premier and chairman of the newly created State Education Commission, in his formal explanation of the compulsory education law (*Renmin ribao,* April 18, 1986).

Clearly, the administration has taken the initiative in its effort to counteract the initial damaging effects of its policies on rural mass education. But He Dongchang's claim at a press conference in March 1989 remains to be substantiated. He said that during the previous year, 97 percent of all school-age children were attending elementary school and that 97 percent of all such students completed their education. He did not clarify whether they completed five or six years of schooling. Nor did he explain how this figure could have been achieved given his subsequent admission that only 1,326 of China's 2,017 county-level administrative divisions have achieved universal elementary education.[28] Nor did he explain how enrollments have continued to grow even as the number of schools continue to decline. In the countryside, as noted, fewer schools conventionally mean lower attendance rates because of distances and transportation difficulties.

Also not explained were the contradictions between the official claim of 97 percent of the age group in school (see also table 3) and the results of various surveys conducted in 1987 and 1988. One such survey in Anhui Province, for example, found that about 19 percent of the elementary-school-age group (children aged 7 to 12 years) in the province were unable to attend school.[29] Another survey conducted by the Rural Investigation Team of the State Statistical Bureau found that the number of rural schools in Hubei Province was 10 percent less in 1986 than in 1980, while close to 1.5 million students had dropped out in 1987. Similarly, in Shaanxi Province, 2,890 elementary schools had closed between 1982 and 1986, while over half-million children between the ages of 6 and 11 years had recently dropped out. Rising tuition costs were cited as a major cause of the dropouts.[30] In the State Statistical Bureau's

---

28 The press briefing was carried live on Beijing television, March 24, 1989, translated in *SWB*, FE/0420 C1/1–5, March 29, 1989. Only a portion of the briefing was printed in *Renmin ribao*, March 25, 1989. The same county-level figure was also given in the State Statistical Bureau's communique for 1988 (*Renmin ribao*, March 1, 1989). The announced standards for "universalizing" elementary education would seem to make the figures irreconcilable. See, for example, the discussion of the Ministry of Education's Aug. 16, 1983, "Provisional Decision on the Basic Demands for Universalizing Elementary Education," in Zhongguo jiaoyu nianjian, ed., "Xiaoxue jiaoyu" (Elementary School Education), *Zhongguo jiaoyu nianjian, 1982–84* (China Education Yearbook, 1982–1984) (Changsha: Hunan jiaoyu chubanshe, 1986), pp. 76–78. Official statistics on the rising percentage of the age group in school during the mid-1980s are shown in table 3.

29 *China Daily*, Feb. 20, 1989.

30 Ibid., June 4, 1988.

1987 sample survey of 9 provinces (Inner Mongolia, Heilongjiang, Zhejiang, Shandong, Hubei, Guangdong, Sichuan, Yunnan, and Liaoning), 15 percent of the 6 to 14 year olds were not in school in the cities and 25 percent in the countryside (or 17.9 percent and 26.4 percent respectively for 6 to 12 year olds). This survey found that location was the major cause of children not in school. Schools located too far from home was the reason given for just over 63 percent of all those not in attendance while poverty and helping with family work accounted for only 7.8 percent. The comparable figures for cities and countryside respectively were 43 percent and 66 percent for the distance factor, while economics accounted for 2.3 percent in the cities and 8.6 percent in the countryside.[31]

In fact, such clarifications must more realistically await further progress in the collection and use of the education surtax as well as the developing township financial structure. These will have to guarantee stable funding in good years and bad, even when local enterprises are in a state of decline, and not just in the rich coastal provinces. These are the new prerequisites for popularizing rural educaiton and overcoming the recent losses. In particular, it must be shown that the new township and village authorities, which replace local collective leadership at the commune and production brigade levels, have the will and the wherewithall to make up the difference between the small share of the state education budget that reaches a village school and the sum total of its expenses.

Education officials remained understandably vague on these points because the basic problems were rooted in the policy of agricultural decollectivization which, at least until mid-1989, could not be directly challenged. Throughout the 1980s, however, solutions were dependent not just on the state education bureaucracy but on a rural political economy not yet sufficiently reconstructed to define, much less enforce, the new more limited scope of its public authority.[32]

---

[31] Zhongguo ertong qingkuang chouyang diaocha bangongshi, guojia tongjiju shehui tongji si (The Circumstances of Children in China Sample Survey Office, State Statistical Bureau, Division of Social Statistics), ed., *Zhongguo 1987 nian ertong qingkuang chouyang diaocha ziliao: zongce* (Materials on the 1987 Sample Survey of the Circumstances of Children in China: Summary Volume) (Beijing: Zhongguo tongji chubanshe, 1989), pp. 95–96, 165–67.

[32] The above discussion is based on conditions prior to June 4, 1989. Even before that date, however, the official press seemed to be in the early stages of "preparing public opinion" for a more favorable assesssment of collectivized agriculture. Under the new post–June 4th administration, this trend has intensified. As of Oc-

Minister of the State Education Commission Li Tieying could therefore say only that current thinking is still focused on the education surtax, when reporters asked about current plans for solving rural education problems at the March 1989 press conference. The aim, he said, was to "gradually set up a mechanism through which we have state appropriations and education tax in the main to be aided by the funds raised through various channels." On the contradiction between the provisions of the existing compulsory education law and the universally acknowledged realities of rising dropout rates, child labor, poor facilities, arbitrary school fees, and underpaid teachers, he replied similarly that "we should gradually introduce a legal regime so that laws can be used for developing education." Added He Dongchang, "The law governing compulsory education in China still has to be supported by other relevant laws, and our work in this regard is quite inadequate."[33]

---

tober, well-sourced rumors in Hong Kong indicated that recollectivization was imminent. The most authoritative source was Roger Sullivan, president of the U.S.-China Business Council, who was told in October by national Chinese leaders in Beijing that the plan was to recollectivize agriculture uniformly in the North and on a more flexible or voluntary basis in the South (according to a subsequent talk given by Mr. Sullivan to the American Chamber of Commerce in Hong Kong and an article he contributed to the *Asian Wall Street Journal,* Hong Kong, Nov. 3–Nov. 4, 1989).

[33] *SWB,* FE/0420 C1/1–5, March 29, 1989.

CHAPTER SIX

Secondary Schooling

Even an unqualified success in solving the rural elementary school problem would, however, only go part way toward counteracting the charge that education policies in the 1980s were elitist and detrimental to the aim of mass education. The biggest case to answer on that score concerns their impact at the secondary level, where the regularization patterns inherited from the past have been most faithfully reproduced. And it is at this level that policy makers have been placed most clearly on the defensive by the critical "opinions in society" aroused in the process.

The patterns from the past resurfaced with the attempt to reimpose quality and order on the Cultural Revolution system, which had contradicted the assumptions of professional educators about how schools should be run. In Yan'an, newly arrived intellectuals sought to impose order on the hastily built young system; hence the impact of their 1938–42 regularization drive was greatest at the elementary level. By 1976, the commitment to mass elementary education had developed sufficiently to withstand the anti–Cultural Revolution backlash, albeit with shaken foundations as we have seen. Instead, the full force of regularization was directed at the secondary level, where it was nevertheless imposed via the same pattern of school closures, reduced enrollments, and reconcentrated resources that educators had applied to Yan'an primary schools between 1938 and 1942. That this pattern represents some very deep cultural assumptions and not just the economics of scarcity, as sometimes suggested, was reflected in the reaction of a Shanghai middle school principal and a representative from the Shanghai Bureau of Higher Education during an interview in 1980. Both were incredulous that American high schools, also worried about quality, were not considering the general use of unified entrance exams to weed out the undeserving and concentrate the best students in a few good institutions.

The problem with a national school system based on these assumptions, of course, is the same today as it was fifty years ago,
namely, what it does to everyone who is left out. But fifty years
ago the system rested on a largely illiterate mass base. In the interim, with the twentieth-century commitment to universal education
having taken root and developed accordingly, the social consequences of such a system are more difficult to contain. And it is at
this point that Wang Meng's above-cited cautionary is especially
relevant. The "seemingly conservative viewpoints" in favor of egalitarianism belong to people whose interests are not being served by
the present reforms. In this case, furthermore, these people
represent a complex mix of interests, potentially exploitable by
some radical ideologue to be sure, but in essence still tied to those
endemic divisions and concerns within Chinese society that gave
rise to the radical critique of the established education system in
the first place. The pressure points today at the secondary level are
threefold: (1) the reduced numbers of secondary school students, (2)
vocational training for the majority, and (3) the restored quality or
keypoint stream for the privileged few.

To recapitulate, the basic tasks that should be performed at the
secondary level are to provide education that will be terminal for
most and college preparatory for some, in ways the economy can
afford and society can accept as fair. An added challenge is to provide kinds of education that will realistically prepare young people
for the lives they must lead after leaving school. During the early
1960s, the formula for achieving these tasks that emerged in the
wake of the Great Leap Forward experiments was an increasingly
stratified one with the urban-based, quality-oriented keypoint
schools emerging clearly as the college-preparatory stream. Other
less regular work-study and vocational options were used to meet
the inevitable demands for some kind of mass secondary schooling
that grew out of the rapidly developing elementary school system.
Liu Shaoqi is now credited with (as he was blamed during the Cultural Revolution for) the transformation of Mao's "walking on two
legs" slogan into the formula for "two kinds of education."[1] Liu
did not dwell on conditions within the quality stream that perpetuated all the old regular education traditions with one new addition, namely, the political and class background considerations that

---

[1] "Bangong bandu, yigong yinong" (Half-Work Half-Study, in Both Industry and
Agriculture), Aug. 1, 1964, in *Liu Shaoqi xuanji* (Selected Works of Liu Shaoqi)
(Beijing: Renmin chubanshe, 1985), 2:465–69.

became increasingly important admissions criteria in the 1960s. These considerations, when added to the regular academic criteria, meant that the children of the new political and old intellectual elites were congregating together as the chief beneficiaries within the college-preparatory stream.

The "Maoist" solution as it finally crystallized during the 1966–76 decade, after the Red Guard phase had run its course, was to break up the whole bifurcated system. Despite all the rhetoric, the net effect was not just to politicize education but also to popularize and vocationalize it, much as the 1944 Yan'an reforms had broken the 1938–42 regularization trend. The aim, after schooling resumed in the late 1960s, was to popularize secondary education as quickly as possible based on the shortened ten-year system (five years each of primary and secondary schooling, down from six years at each level). For the countryside, the immediate goal— which interviewees indicate was widely achieved—was to attach junior middle classes to production brigade elementary schools and establish one complete junior/senior middle school in every commune. By the end of the Cultural Revolution decade, the goal was to achieve universal senior secondary schooling in all cities and universal junior secondary education in the countryside by 1985.[2] According to more recently released official statistics, the "pass rate" for primary school graduates promoted to the junior secondary level was 90.6 percent in 1975 and the rate for junior secondary graduates moving on to the senior secondary level, 60.4 percent (see table 4).

The keypoint function of concentrating the "best" students was abolished. Instead, the keypoint schools enrolled those living in closest proximity following the neighborhood school principle. Physics, chemistry, and biology courses were revised uniformly to become classes in industrial or agricultural technology. Two years of work experience after middle school became the new prerequisite for admission to college along with the political and class background criteria. These latter were strengthened in importance by comparison with pre-1966, while academic qualifications became at best a secondary consideration.

In retrospect, teachers found it difficult to distinguish between the basic structural/academic changes and the overt political inter-

---

[2] Hua Kuo-feng, "Report on the Work of the Government," Feb. 26, 1978, *Peking Review*, Mar. 10, 1978, p. 28.

Table 4

Promotion Rates

Year	Elementary Graduates Entering Junior Middle School (percent)	Junior Middle Graduates Entering Senior Middle School (percent)	Senior Middle Graduates Entering College (percent)
1975	90.6	60.4	4.27
1980	75.9	43.1	4.56
1981	68.3	31.5	
1982	66.2	32.3	
1983	67.3	35.5	
1984	66.2	38.4	
1985	68.4	39.4	31.50
1986	69.5	37.8	
1987	69.1	35.7	24.99

SOURCE: Columns one and two from *Zhongguo tongji nianjian, 1988* (China Statistical Yearbook, 1988), State Statistical Bureau, ed. (Beijing: Zhongguo tongji chubanshe, 1988), p. 889; column three calculated from ibid., pp. 878, 881.

ventions including a variety of "extracurricular" political activities that constantly disrupted teaching schedules. As a whole, this new politicized "irregular" system generally appalled professional educators. It also worked against the interests of all those in the keypoint stream whose route to college was disrupted. After having spent two years in the countryside or in a factory, however, one could be recategorized as a peasant or worker for purposes of college admission. Thus, many (although not all) of those who began making their way back to college in the early 1970s were young people who would have been there anyway. Some interviewees nevertheless recalled that their communes were able to send local youth to college for the first time ever from their new middle schools. In at least two cases, youths from those schools even passed the national college entrance exams when they were restored in 1977. But by and large, the quality stream was destroyed; the lives of everyone within it were disrupted; and traditional views about regularity in education were turned upside down.

Perhaps not coincidentally, the same coalition of new political and old intellectual interests that united to overthrow the Maoist political legacy became the chief beneficiaries of the education system they also immediately restored. According to the official argument, the Cultural Revolution policies not only tried to universalize (*puji*) secondary schooling prematurely, but also sought to unify (*danyihua*) education in a manner inappropriate to China's level of economic development. The new policies therefore set about reversing the consequent equalization of quantity and quality that took place between 1966 and 1976. As a result, the education system at the secondary level has been drastically reduced in size. It has also been retracked and streamed in a manner deliberately designed to exploit and reinforce the existing social divisions of labor.

Quantitative Declines

The reduced enrollments were enforced uniformly in city and countryside between 1978 and 1983. No direct or immediate effort was made to coordinate the declines with demographic trends or the expansion of vocational education (as indicated in tables 5 and 6). Quotas were never made public, but they were imposed even on the largest cities, including Beijing, Shanghai, Hangzhou, and Guangzhou, which had achieved universal or near universal ten-year schooling. In the countryside, a plan to close down the senior sections of the commune middle schools, leaving only one or a few complete secondary schools in each county, was announced in the late 1970s. Also to be abolished were the junior middle classes attached to production brigade primary schools. At most, only one junior middle school was to be retained in each commune.

The secondary system had grown overall from 14 million students enrolled in 1965 to about 68 million during the 1977–78 academic year, when the new line began to be implemented. When the decline finally stopped in 1983, enrollments stood at 43.9 million. During 1980 alone, more than 20,000 secondary schools were closed. The cutbacks have been more severe at the senior secondary level where, according to one claim, enrollments for 1981–82 were down by approximately two-thirds from 1978.[3] The argument used to justify the reductions at the senior level is that since such a small proportion of students are able to enter college, large senior secondary enrollments are unnecessary. Following this logic, the ratios have now been appropriately adjusted. The number of senior middle graduates has declined from an all-time high of 7.2 million

[3] *Guangming ribao*, Oct. 12, 1981.

in 1979 to 1.96 million in 1985. The annual intake at the tertiary level is now about 600,000.[4]

Of the 75,000 junior middle graduates in all of Shanghai Municipality in 1981, only a little over 20,000, or at most 30 percent, were allowed to pass the entrance exams and continue on to the senior secondary level. About 200 of Shanghai's 1,000 middle schools were closed at this time, and many of the remaining 800 were changed from complete secondary schools into junior secondaries only. About 100 were reorganized into vocational schools.[5] Similarly, only 54,000 or 39 percent of Beijing's total 139,000 junior secondary graduates were admitted to the senior middle level for the fall 1981 semester.[6] Assuming these figures are accurate, the smaller size of Shanghai's secondary school population overall reflects the earlier and more rigorous attention paid to family planning in that city, where it was already being strictly enforced by the mid-1970s.

Reports from Liaoning Province claimed that the province's junior and senior middle schools had been reduced to about 600 in 1980 from more than 3,000 in 1978.[7] In addition, 6,000 schools that had been designated as junior secondaries were said in fact to be only elementary schools. Almost 2,000 of these were closed and the remainder appropriately redesignated.[8] As a result of cutbacks nationwide, the promotion rate of elementary school graduates on to the junior secondary level fell from 90.6 percent in 1975 to 66.2 percent in 1984. For junior middle graduates moving on to the senior level the rate fell from 60.4 percent in 1975 to 31.5 percent in 1981 (see table 4).

---

[4] *Zhongguo baike nianjian, 1980* (China Encyclopedic Yearbook, 1980) (Beijing and Shanghai: Zhongguo dabaike quanshu chubanshe, 1980), p. 538; *Zhongguo baike nianjian, 1986* (China Encyclopedic Yearbook, 1986) (Beijing and Shanghai: Zhongguo dabaike quanshu chubanshe, 1986), p. 433.

[5] *Wenhuibao* (Shanghai), Oct. 21, 1981, p. 4. On the small size of Shanghai's secondary school age group, see ibid., Feb. 25, 1982; *Guangming ribao*, Nov. 10, 1987.

[6] *Renmin ribao*, Nov. 12, 1981.

[7] Shenyang, Liaoning service, Sept. 27, 1980, translated in Joint Publication Research Service of the Foreign Broadcast Information Service (Washington D.C.), *China Report: Political, Sociological and Military* (hereafter, JPRS, *CR: PSM*), no. 128 (Oct. 15, 1980), p. 72.

[8] Shenyang, Liaoning service, Jan. 2, 1981, translated in ibid., no. 161 (Feb. 3, 1981), p. 80.

The press, both national and provincial, has been extremely cautious in publicizing the cutbacks and, especially, any public response to them. The most forthright published criticism, from the *Journal of the Dialectics of Nature*, argued that quality and quantity were two sides of the same question. The author's calculations for the 322 million young people aged 6 to 18 years indicated that, given the existing level of education in 1980, 20 million would grow up illiterate, at least 133 million would have no more than a primary school education, and only 10 million would receive any kind of professional or tertiary schooling. "It is unthinkable," admonished the writer, "to rely on such a composition of the population to build a modern nation."[9]

The authorities have yet to devise an answer to this challenge. Nevertheless, the increase in general secondary school enrollments since 1984 seems to indicate a recognition that reductions had gone too far, given the mass pressures building up form below. In 1984, localities were instructed not to continue reducing secondary enrollments. In some places where reduction had "gone too far," increases could be permitted "in order to satisfy the demand of the broad masses of youth to continue their studies."[10] In 1983, nationwide, 67.3 percent of primary school graduates continued on to junior middle school, and only 35.5 percent of the junior middle school graduates were able to continue on to the next level (see table 4). Pressures must have been intense if Beijing's experience is any indication. Three years later, in 1987, when the class that entered secondary school in 1984 was about to graduate, authorities in the capital had to cope with a junior middle graduating class of 150,000—up from only 80,000 the year before.[11]

---

[9] Song Jian, "Population and Education," *Ziran bianzhengfa tongxun* (Journal of the Dialectics of Nature) (Beijing), no. 3 (June 1980), translated in ibid., no. 178 (April 3, 1981), pp. 44, 47.

[10] Guojia tongji ju, shehui tongji si (State Statistical Bureau, Division of Social Statistics), "Woguo jiaoyu shiye zai tiaozhengzhong fazhan" (The Development of Our Country's Educational Enterprise during Consolidation), *Tongji* (Statistics) (Beijing), June 17, 1984, p. 17; also, *Zhongguo jiaoyu bao* (China Education News) (Beijing), Oct. 16, 1984. According to the figures presented in the above *Tongji* article, there were 66,000 fewer ordinary middle schools in 1983 than in 1978, or a reduction of 40.7 percent, and 21.5 million fewer students, or a reduction of 32.8 percent. In 1983, only 31 percent of the 12 to 16 year olds were attending secondary school (p. 17).

[11] "Beijingshi dui 1987 nian chuzhong biyesheng ruhe anpai" (How to Take Care of Beijing's 1987 Junior Middle Graduates), *Liaowang* (Outlook) (Beijing), domestic ed., Feb. 16, 1987, p. 48.

Initially, when the reductions began to go into effect, schools everywhere allowed students at all levels—primary, junior secondary, and senior secondary—to remain behind for a year of restudy when they failed to gain admission to the next level. This practice, aimed at giving those students who seemed to deserve it a second chance to pass entrance exams, was officially discouraged in the early 1980s. But no one could figure out what to do about the rising juvenile delinquency rates among school dropouts or how to keep 16-year-old "senior middle school rejects" otherwise occupied.

Within schools themselves, the curtailed opportunities led essentially to one of two results: demoralization for some and intense pressure to succeed for others. Those who anticipated failure often gave up and dropped out before confronting it. In rural schools, even the elementary level was affected. The sudden lost opportunity to continue their studies in middle school was said to be one of the reasons, along with the new household responsibility system, for the rising dropout rates from rural elementary schools in Shanxi.[12] In the cities, demoralization was more likely to set in at the junior secondary level. One commentary from Shenyang blamed the schools themselves, some of which had simply abandoned students to their own devices, even to the point of urging them to leave before graduation and refusing to assign enough instructors to teach them.[13] More recently, an official in Beijing acknowledged that junior middle schools such as his, which received the academically poorer students, were referred to as "Third World schools." Morale was so low that about 20 percent of the students gave up before graduation.[14]

By contrast, students who have a chance are pushed to the opposite extreme in order to pass the entrance exams for the next level. Homilies appear in the educational press each year as examination time approaches blaming parents and teachers for the pressures placed on students. Perhaps it is just coincidental that in 1987, as "conservative" winds were rising in Beijing, publicity on the issue shifted direction to focus instead on the more basic nature of the problem. The "new" concern was the contradiction between the mass pressures from below for more schooling and the curtailed op-

12 *Shanxi ribao* (Taiyuan), Oct. 26, 1982, translated in JPRS, *CR: PSM*, no. 371 (Dec. 10, 1982), p. 123.
13 *Liaoning ribao* (Shenyang), Jan. 5, 1981, translated in JPRS, *CR: PSM*, no. 183 (April 17, 1981), pp. 40–41.
14 *China Daily*, April 8, 1987.

portunities at the senior middle level. In 1986, the junior middle graduating class was 80,000 in Beijing, and 60,000 went on to the senior level. In 1987, room at the senior level was made for 90,000. But with 150,000 junior middle graduates, reflecting the expanded enrollments permitted in 1984, 4 out of 10 would still be unable to continue their studies. About 40 percent of the graduating class was under 16. When these figures were publicized as examination time approached, to prepare everyone for the ordeal ahead, many worried parents wrote letters of complaint challenging the city authorities to find ways of keeping their children off the streets.[15]

Without actually acknowledging in so many words that a policy change has occurred, the new oficial trend is nevertheless to respond to the politically controversial mass pressures for more schooling. The city of Fuzhou was another that shifted its emphasis in 1987 from concentrating on the college preparatory stream to "energetically raising the quality of the laboring people." The pass rate from elementary school on to the junior secondary level had been maintained "for a long time" at under 60 percent in the greater Fuzhou area. This meant that some 30,000 elementary school graduates each year were unable to continue on to middle school in Fuzhou's eight suburban counties. In 1987, however, the city increased educational expenditure and expanded enrollments so that 16,180 of the 17,040 primary school graduates in the city proper were able to continue on to middle school along with 76.7 percent of their counterparts in the surrounding counties. This latter proportion was up by 35 percent over the year preceding. Youngsters who failed to pass were allowed to repeat the final year of primary school if they were under 14 years of age. Those over 14 could be channeled into vocational training classes.[16]

As the Fuzhou report indicates, the practice of allowing youngsters to repeat the final year at school in order to prepare for a second chance at continuing their studies is apparently being permitted again as a solution at the mass level. Also legitimate once more is the practice of attaching junior secondary classes to estab-

---

[15] "Beijingshi dui 1987 nian chuzhong biyesheng ruhe anpai," p. 48; *Zhongguo jiaoyu bao*, Feb. 24, 1987; *Beijing ribao*, July 5, 1987; *China Daily*, April 8 and 23, 1987.

[16] *Zhongguo jiaoyu bao*, Oct. 10, 1987; *Guangming ribao*, Oct. 10, 1987. The new emphasis is evident in Guangzhou as well. *Nanfang ribao* (Southern Daily) (Guangzhou), June 21, 1987; Jan. 14, 1988; July 12, 1988.

lished elementary schools. According to official statistics for 1987, of the total 41.7 million students nationwide at the junior secondary level, some 3.5 million were studying in such attached classes.[17]

Vocational Education

Another major plank in the reform platform at the secondary level is to create separate academic and vocational streams, claiming authority from Liu Shaoqi's "two kinds of education and labor systems" formulation. The intention was never to replace all of the closing general middle schools with vocational equivalents, although public announcements were often deliberately phrased so as to give that impression. Rather, the proclaimed objective was to build upon and restructure the reduced base so that by 1990 there would be at the senior secondary level one student receiving some kind of technical or vocational education for every one in the general academic stream.[18]

In 1978–79, it was claimed that Cultural Revolution policies had deliberately destroyed technical and vocational education. More recently published statistics (see tables 5 and 6) indicate that such education was never very extensive. What Cultural Revolution policies had opposed was the "two kinds of education" format, which was criticized as a device for perpetuating existing social inequalities. The Cultural Revolution solution was a uniform kind of schooling that offered some variation on the practical work-study theme for everyone within the structure of the existing general middle school.

The basic problem with the revived two-track approach, however, has been its apparent lack of appeal to everyone except central decision makers and those whose interests are tied so firmly to one of the tracks that they have neither the opportunity nor the need to choose between them. Otherwise, if there is a choice between vocational and academic tracks, whether in town or countryside, people seem to entertain the same basic preference as does the professional

17 Guojia jiaoyu weiyuanhui jihua caiwu ju (State Education Commission, Planning and Financial Affairs Bureau), ed., *Zhongguo jiaoyu tongji nianjian, 1987* (China Education Statistical Yearbook, 1987) (Beijing: Gongye daxue chubanshe, 1988), p. 58.

18 For a survey of vocational education, 1976–83, see Jurgen Henze, "Developments in Vocational Education Since 1976," *Comparative Education* 20:1 (1984):117–40.

educator for "regular" education. Thus everyone's inherited instincts tell them that a general academic education is more valuable than any other. The traditional bias is enhanced by the better access to life's benefits that an academic education is presumed to make possible. This assumption was reinforced in 1977–78, when academic secondary schooling was restored as the one prerequisite for a college education. The benefits of the latter in terms of status, security, and career opportunities, including study abroad, were also greater in the post-Mao decade than at any time since 1949. That comparative advantage only began to be eroded in the late 1980s under the impact of the concurrent market-oriented economic reforms (discussed below).

The official argument for the vocational alternative is that since most youth cannot aspire to a college education, they should be satisfied with practical and relevant alternatives. The logic of the argument cannot be faulted. School and job placement systems based the two-track approach would undoubtedly be the most efficient of all possible solutions. Nevertheless, many perceive it as unfair, and many others consider vocational training as a waste of time. Dropping out (especially if remunerative work is available) is often elected as a more useful personal strategy than vocational training.

The full implications of the plan to resegregate vocational and academic training were not immediately apparent in 1978–79, when the plan was first announced, perhaps because no one seemed to take it seriously. Interviewees both in Hong Kong and China were amused by the proposal and assumed it was merely part of the immediate post-Mao rhetoric, which would be modified to accommodate the general dislike of vocational schooling. One typical report from 1980, noting that three meetings of the entire leadership of Dehua county (Fujian) had been necessary before agreement could be reached on collapsing the county's eleven middle schools into only five, continued: "If so much difficulty is encountered in modifying middle schools, even greater difficulty will be encountered in developing vocational and technical education."[19] The initial unenthusiastic response was nevertheless countered with more determined directives from the center.

---

[19] *Fujian ribao* (Fuzhou), Nov. 8, 1980, translated in JPRS, *CR: PSM*, no. 174 (March 25, 1981), p. 82.

Table 5

Secondary Schools and Students

(general secondary, including keypoints)

Year	Schools	Students (millions)
1949	4,045	1.04
1965	18,102	9.34
1966		12.50
1968		13.92
1970		26.42
1972		35.82
1974		36.50
1975		44.66
1976	192,152	58.36
Junior		43.53
Senior		14.84
1977		67.80
1978		65.48
1979	144,233	59.05
Junior		46.13
Senior		12.92
Keypoint	5,200	5.20
1980		55.08
1981	106,718	48.60
Junior		41.45
Senior		7.15
1982	101,649	45.28
Junior		38.88
Senior		6.40
1983	96,474	43.98
1984	93,714	45.54
1985	93,221	47.06
1986	92,967	48.90
1987	92,857	49.48
Junior		41.74
Senior		7.74
Keypoint	2,243	3.08

SOURCES: Schools from *Zhongguo baike nianjian, 1980* (China Encyclopedic Year-book, 1980) (Beijing and Shanghai: Zhongguo dabaike quanshu chubanshe, 1980), p. 535; *Zhongguo baike nianjian, 1982* (China Encyclopedic Yearbook, 1982) (Beijing and Shanghai: Zhongguo dabaike quanshu chubanshe, 1982), p. 568; and *Zhongguo tongji nianjian, 1988,* State Statistical Bureau, ed., p. 873. The pre-1980 figures do not agree with those given in other sources, for example, *Zhongguo jingji nianjian, 1981* (China Economic Yearbook, 1981) (Beijing: Jingji guanli zazhi she, 1981), pp. IV-205, IV-206; and *China: Socialist Economic Development* (Washington, D.C.: The World Bank, 1983), 3:134.

Students from *Zhongguo baike nianjian, 1980,* p. 536; *Zhongguo baike nianjian, 1982,* p. 568; *Zhongguo tongji nianjian, 1988,* p. 876.

Keypoint schools and students figures for 1979 and 1987 only, from *Zhongguo baike nianjian, 1980,* p. 541; and *Zhongguo jiaoyu tongji nianjian, 1987* (China Education Statistical Yearbook, 1987), State Education Commission, Planning and Financial Affairs Bureau, ed. (Beijing: Gongye daxue chubanshe, 1988), pp. 58–59, 65, respectively.

NOTE: Keypoint schools are included in the category of general or ordinary (*putong*) schools, which are academic rather than technical or vocational in orientation. Separate figures for key schools are shown for the years 1979 and 1987 only.

A second problem with the revived two-track idea that all sides readily recognized was the added expense of converting ordinary into specialized schools. One alternative was to introduce vocational subjects and "labor education" into the curriculum of ordinary non-key schools at the senior secondary level. This practice was approved by the State Council in 1980, and remains the official solution.[20] To the extent that a general secondary school takes this assignment seriously, its students will not be able to compete successfully for admission to college—which is, of course, the official intention, despite the carefully preserved legal fiction that every qualified person has the right to compete on the entrance examinations. For their part, however, general middle schools have been slow in setting up such courses. When they do, they tend to keep

---

[20] "Guowuyuan pizhuan jiaoyubu, guojia laodong zongju guanyu zhongdeng jiaoyu jiegou gaige de baogao" (Report of the Education Ministry and the National Labor Bureau on Restructuring Secondary Education, as Approved and Circulated by the State Council), Oct. 7, 1980, *Zhonghua renmin gongheguo guowuyuan gongbao* (Bulletin of the State Council of the People's Republic of China) (Beijing), no. 16 (Dec. 1, 1980), pp. 492–93; "Jiaoyubu, laodong renshibu, caizhengbu, guojia jihua weiyuanhui guanyu gaige chengshi zhongdeng jiaoyu jiegou, fazhan zhiye jishu jiaoyu de yijian" (Opinion of the Education Ministry, the Labor and Personnel Ministry, the Finance Ministry, and the State Planning Commission on the Reform of the Structure of Urban Middle Schools and the Development of Vocational and Technical Education), May 9, 1983, ibid., no 12 (July 10, 1983), pp. 552–56; "Jiaoyubu guanyu jinyibu tigao putong zhongxue jiaoyu zhiliang de jidian yijian" (A Few Opinions from the Education Ministry Concerning the Progressive Raising of the Quality of Education in Ordinary Middle Schools), Aug. 10, 1983, ibid., no. 18 (Sept. 20, 1983), pp. 839–44.

Table 6

Secondary Schools and Students: Specialized and Vocational

Year	Professional (*zhuanye*): Technical (*jishu*) and Teacher Training (*shifan*)		Vocational (*zhiye*) and Agricultural (*nongye*)	
	Schools	Students	Schools	Students
1949	1,171	229,000		
1957	1,320	778,000		
1965	1,265	547,000	61,626	4,433,000
1976	2,443	690,000		
1979	3,033	1,199,000		
1980	3,069	1,243,000	3,314	453,600
Vocational			390	133,600
Agricultural			2,924	320,000
1981	3,132	1,069,000	2,655	480,900
Vocational			561	213,100
Agricultural			2,094	267,800
1982	3,076	1,039,000	3,104	704,000
1983	3,090	1,143,000	5,481	
1984	3,301	1,322,000	7,002	
1985	3,557	1,571,000	8,070	2,295,000
1986	3,782	1,757,000	8,187	
1987	3,913	1,874,000	8,381	2,676,000

SOURCES: 1949–1979 from *Zhongguo baike nianjian, 1980,* pp. 535–36; 1980 from *Zhong-guo jingji nianjian, 1981,* pp. IV-205, IV-206; 1981 from *Zhongguo baike nianjian, 1982,* p. 568; 1982–1987 from *Zhongguo tongji nianjian, 1988,* pp. 873, 876.

the vocational students separate from the academic stream within the school. The senior secondary sections of non-keypoint schools, although now greatly reduced in number, nevertheless know that their students cannot compete as successfully as those in the keypoint stream. Still, everyone wants to try, because entrance into college continues to be regarded by all—teachers, parents, and students—as the most "glorious" culmination of a secondary school career. Hence, the determination to maintain a separate academic stream within the general non-key schools remains strong.

Yet another major problem with vocational education is that it does not necessarily provide training that is vocationally relevant. The Chinese immediately encountered the same problem experienced by others who have tried to introduce such training into schools (by contrast with specific apprenticeship or job training programs). The difficulty always is to match teachers and training programs with the jobs available to the students upon gradation. For example, one of the first vocational courses introduced into a

Fujian middle school was production-line garment making. But there were no such factories in the area, and the students were not being taught to make the whole garment, which would at least have allowed them to go into business as private tailors. The course was therefore regarded as a failure, according to a former teacher from the locality interviewed in Hong Kong in the early 1980s.

This experience has now been reproduced many times over as local schools try to implement the central directives. The first graduates of Hangzhou's vocational courses also had trouble finding employment, because the specialties they had studied were not those needed that year by work units with job openings.[21] Local education departments were advised to learn not only which subjects were needed but also which kinds of jobs were likely to become available, and to synchronize this information with their course offerings. "The labor force that may be scarce today in a given occupational category may tomorrow be in large supply. Without a basic estimate and forecast of the need for a given labor force, vocational education will develop blindly and create passivity."[22] Essentially, this long-recognized problem concerns the extent to which schools can and should be expected to provide what is essentially job-specific apprenticeship training.[23]

For rural schools, the problem is further compounded by changes that are occurring due to the agricultural reforms. Thus, the challenge for urban education officials is to "correctly predict the kind of talent needed in various sectors with the same foresight that formed the open-door policy and made the economy more responsive." In the countryside, the difficulties entail predicting job opportunities and providing relevant courses for young people likely to "drift out of agriculture but not from the rural area."[24]

---

[21] *Renmin ribao*, Sept. 17, 1981.

[22] Zhang Zhiyuan, "Putong jiaoyu gongzuozhong de liangge tuchu wenti" (Two Pressing Problems in Ordinary Education Work), *Renmin jiaoyu* (People's Education) (Beijing), no. 10 (Oct. 1982), p. 11.

[23] The classic account of this dilemma in the educational development literature is Philip J. Foster, "The Vocational School Fallacy in Development Planning," reprinted in C. Arnold Anderson and Mary Jean Bowman, eds., *Education and Economic Development* (Chicago: Aldine Publishing Company, 1965), pp. 142–66.

[24] *Zhongguo jiaoyu bao*, Aug. 25, 1984; Zhang Enhua, "Nongcun zhiye jishu jiaoyu bixu wei zhenxing nongcun jingji fuwu" (Rural Vocational and Technical Education Must Serve the Development of the Rural Economy), *Jiaoyu yu zhiye* (Education and Occupation) (Shanghai), no. 6 (1986), pp. 9–10.

In the countryside, moreover, the vocational school becomes the
current equivalent of the old agricultural middle school, especially
since the work-study idea has been promoted along with it to help
finance costs. But agricultural middle schools have already failed in
at least two pre-1966 attempts. Some university intellectuals still
profess genuine surprise at the unanimity of the rural dislike of
these schools, which local officials and rural school teachers all
confirm. Rural people generally do not like to send their children
to such schools for the same reasons as in the early 1960s. If a
child could not attend a regular school in the county town, then a
similar school in the commune seat was acceptable. But to attend
school to learn about agriculture, on a work-study basis, was regarded as a waste of time. Students could learn much the same from
their elders and begin contributing to the family income at the
same time. The few such schools initially set up in the late 1970s
were already declining in number by 1981 (see table 6).

Yet new directives have since reaffirmed the determination to
establish agricultural middle schools. Primary schools are to begin
the process of vocationalization, orienting their curriculum to agricultural production and rural life. Junior middle schools must re-
vise their curricula so that 30 percent of their courses are vocational. At the senior secondary level, there should be, by 1990, at least
as many students in agricultural vocational schools as in general
schools, and vocational courses must not make up less than 30 percent of the total taught in the former. However, the directives seem
to mean that even a general middle school, if located in a rural
area, should introduce vocational production-oriented subjects.
The directives also suggest that students graduating from rural
secondary schools should be given preference in admission to agricultural colleges. This last is in deference to current conventional
wisdom (impossible to verify for lack of data) that the county-town
middle school education available to rural youths places them at a
competitive disadvantage on the college entrance exams. Since
places in agricultural colleges are difficult to fill, such schools in
practice maintain lower admissions standards and can enroll lower-
scoring rural youth on a "preferential" basis.[25]

25 "Zhonggong zhongyang, guowuyuan guanyu jiaqiang he gaige nongcun xuexiao
jiaoyu ruogan wenti de tongzhi" (Notice by the Party Center and the State Council
on Some Questions Concerning the Strengthening and Reform of Rural Schools and
Education), May 6, 1983, *Zhonghua renmin gongheguo guowuyuan gongbao*, no. 12
(July 10, 1983), pp. 528–32. Note: The definition of a "rural" secondary school is
inevitably imprecise. Urban and suburban schools are situated in cities and subur-

Not surprisingly, then, the rejection of the vocational stream has been acknowledged as "quite universal" on the part of parents, education bureaus, and local officials alike.[26] At issue was not so much vocational training itself as vocational training in competition with the more powerful regular system—just as decades ago the new modern schools could not gain acceptance because they could not compete with the advantages of a traditional education that served as the sole prerequisite for the all-important civil service career option. The central authorities nevertheless remain undeterred in their enthusiasm for technical and vocational education. But just as they have been unwilling to address directly the basic issue of unequal advantage between the academic and vocational streams, so have they also been unable to find viable solutions that all the concerned parties will accept for rebuilding the system on the basis of two separate streams. Recommendations acknowledge the "interests" and "opinions" involved by tiptoeing around them, to an ongoing lament over the general failure to popularize vocational training.

Hence, the 1985 Central Committee decision on education reform, which preceded the promulgation of the compulsory education law, noted as it reaffirmed the commitment to a bifurcated academic-vocational system that "we have stressed the importance of vocational and technical education for years, yet no significant progress has been made." To counteract the "contempt" in which vocational training continued to be held, the decision advocated that employers be required to give first preference in hiring to technical and vocational school graduates. The decision also held out the promise of continuing opportunities at the tertiary level for technical or vocational school graduates, as did the earlier rural directive, to make the option appear less unequal and therefore more attractive.[27] If actually implemented, of course, this practice

---

ban counties. But in the 1980s after the senior sections of commune middle schools were closed, most "rural" senior secondary schools were actually situated in county towns. There they typically served students from that town itself as well as those from the surrounding countryside. Hence such a school would include students from both "urban" and "rural" households, according to the formal household registration system based on family occupation. The school itself, however, would be regarded by all and referred to as a "rural" middle school. It is from such schools that the "rural" students at the Guangdong teachers training college mentioned in the next chapter originate.

[26] *Renmin ribao*, Oct. 29, 1983.

[27] Ibid., May 29, 1985. See also, Li Peng's formal explanation of the compulsory education law, in *Renmin ribao*, April 18, 1986; speeches by Li Peng and others at

would defeat the whole purpose of the two-track system, which is to prepare the majority of students not for college but for work.

In 1986–87, yet another solution was introduced, which was also designed to cast vocational education in a more equitable light. This entailed the "five-four system," or five years of elementary and four years of junior secondary schooling (by contrast with the recently revived "six-three" standard system). The draft teaching plans that accompanied the compulsory education law acknowledged this alternative, but at the time it seemed destined primarily for the countryside, where five-year elementary schooling is most prevalent.[28] Subsequent publicity, however, suggested the five-four solution for urban schools as well, without specifying whether the vocational "experiment" was perhaps anticipating another overall reversion to a national five-year elementary system, the better to promote what is essentially a four-year combined academic/vocational junior secondary school.

As of 1987, about 100 schools were participating in the nationwide experiment that had been underway for six years. It was advertised as a way of unifying basic culture and scientific knowledge with productive labor education by making more time available to work the latter into the regular curriculum throughout the entire four-year junior secondary course. Experimental schools reported devoting between 15 and 25 percent of their course work to vocational training. The experiment was said to be successful in producing students who could both pass their senior secondary school entrance exams and master vocational skills (although the publicity did not clarify that all schools succeeded equally at both tasks).

---

the national vocational education conference held just after the promulgation of the law and Li Peng's subsequent report in *Zhongguo jiaoyu bao*, July 5, and 8, 1986, and Aug. 30, 1986; "Jiaoyu jiegou he laodong renshi zhidu tongbu gaige jinzhande ruhe?" (How Is the Concurrent Reform of the Education Structure and the Labor Personnel System Progressing?), *Jiaoyu yu zhiye*, no. 5 (1986), pp. 15–19.

[28] See, for example, Li Peng on the compulsory education law, *Renmin ribao*, April 18, 1986; "Yiwu jiaoyu quanrizhi xiaoxue chuji zhongxue jiaoxue jihua, chugao" (Teaching Plans for the Compulsory Education Full-Day-System Elementary and Junior Middle Schools, First Drafts), "Guanyu yiwu jiaoyu quanrizhi xiaoxue chuji zhongxue jiaoxue jihua, chugao, de shuoming" (Explanation of the Draft Teaching Plans for the Compulsory Education Full-Day-System Elementary and Junior Middle Schools), and Wang Wenzhan, "Guanyu 'yiwu jiaoyu quanrizhi xiaoxue chuji zhongxue jiaoxue jihua,' chugao, de jige wenti" (Some questions on the First Drafts of the "Teaching Plans for the Compulsory Education Full-Day-System Elementary and Junior Middle Schools"), all in *Renmin jiaoyu*, no. 12 (1986), pp. 12–13, 14–15, 16–18, respectively.

Both urban and rural schools participated, including Beijing's Jingshan School and the Number Two Middle School Attached to Beijing Teachers' Training University. But the experiment has received little publicity since early 1987, and its status remains uncertain—despite its advertised ability to produce two kinds of students without actually dividing them into two different kinds of school.[29]

The slow growth of vocational and technical education nationwide (as shown in table 6) testifies to the obstacles that continue to block its progress. Secondary education must be college preparatory for some and terminal for the majority, but Chinese society is obviously reluctant to accept a solution based on two separate and mutually exclusive streams. Current Chinese decision makers who remain committed, for whatever reason, to the "two kinds of education" formula have therefore found themselves caught between their own commitment and the popular resistance to the "inferior" half of the equation. Hence the ongoing effort to make the bifurcated system appear more equitable—by promising technical secondary school graduates a chance to go on to college and by publicizing the experimental attempt to combine vocational and academic training in rural schools as well as two of the country's most famous urban keypoints.

The Keypoint College-Preparatory Stream

The schools that constitute the keypoint stream are the best in the country. They are also the schools that everyone loves to hate. They represent the principal route of access to higher education, the value of which has been so greatly enhanced, even by comparison with the pre-1966 years, that the college-preparatory stream dom-

---

[29] Despite the lack of publicity, however, the "five-four" solution has not been abandoned. In mid-1989, the Shanghai Bureau of Education announced without fanfare a decision to introduce the system throughout the city beginning with the 1988–89 fifth grade class all of which would automatically be promoted to the the junior secondary level at the start of the fall semester 1989 (*Wenhuibao,* Shanghai, June 20, 1989). On this experiment generally, see *Guangming ribao,* Jan. 21, 1987; March 19, 1987; May 22, 1987. *Zhongguo jiaoyu bao,* June 3, 1986; Sept. 23, 1986; Feb. 10, 1987; and May 14, 1988. Li Qun, "Nongcun xiaoxue, chuzhong ying zhubu shixing 'wu, si' fenduan de xuezhi" (Rural Elementary and Junior Middle Schools Should Progressively Carry Out the "Five-Four" Division School System" *Renmin jiaoyu,* no. 10 (1987), pp. 6–7. Of the total 41.7 million junior secondary school students nationwide in 1987, only 88,307 were in four-year system schools. Guojia jiaoyu weiyuanhui, ed., *Zhongguo jiaoyu tongji nianjian, 1987,* p. 58.

inates the education system more absolutely than ever before. Thus, in the 1980s, a college education was (1) a prerequisite for study abroad; (2) a new prerequisite for leading cadre positions in the state bureaucracy, both civilian and military; (3) one of the few means of securing "iron rice bowl" state employment; and (4) a means of gaining access to high-paying non-state jobs, especially in the Guangzhou-Shenzhen-Hong Kong joint venture sector. The keypoint schools therefore stood at the apex of the secondary school hierarchy shown in tables 5 and 6.

Next in order of popularity after the keypoint stream were the non-key general or ordinary (*putong*) middle schools, to the extent that they could maintain respectable pass rates into college. Probably tied for second place, depending on a student's academic record, economic circumstances, and family connections, were the specialized technical secondary schools (*zhongdeng zhuanye xuexiao*). Their students could graduate into lower-ranking jobs on the state-salaried cadre pay scale. Vocational schools were in last place; their students graduate to become skilled workers at best.

In 1988, as will be noted below, this ranking was challenged suddenly from an unexpected direction, namely, the government's market-oriented economic reforms. The economic crises of 1988 were then followed by the political crisis of 1989, and at the time of writing it is still too early to discern what the long-term consequences of these events will be. Throughout the 1980s, however, the keypoint stream remained the dominant feature of the education system. Its "pagodas" of learning, which bore the brunt of the Cultural Revolution's antielitist wrath, were restored throughout the country at all levels from kindergarten through university. The specific task of the keypoint schools was to "concentrate strength," that is, the best teachers, administrators, students, facilities, and learning conditions, in a manner that would "guarantee quality." At the secondary level, there was usually one such key school per county located in the county seat, one or more in each city district, and additional super keypoints enrolling the very best students from a wider or all-city catchment area.[30]

---

[30] On the revival of this stream, see Stanley Rosen, "Restoring Key Secondary Schools in Post-Mao China: The Politics of Competition and Educational Quality," in David M. Lampton, ed., *Policy Implementation in Post-Mao China* (Berkeley and Los Angeles: University of California Press, 1987), pp. 321–53; also *Zhongguo jiaoyu nianjian, 1949–1981*, pp. 167–70.

Official policy now professes to be unconcerned with social consequences or what opportunities are offered to what kinds of students. Both the earlier 1950s practice of giving preference to qualified working-class youth when their academic standing was competitive and the later bias in favor of "good" class background candidates have been dropped. Everyone is now more-or-less "equal before marks." Unified city and county entrance exams were restored in the late 1970s, on the basis of which students were channeled into the hierarchy of schools both at the junior and senior secondary levels. Statistics on family background are not available, but the conventional wisdom among teachers and school administrators is that the children of cadres and intellectuals are most able to benefit from this system.

In the early 1980s, a majority of students entering key middle schools were said to have come from the key primary schools or key classes of ordinary schools. At the elementary level, children were supposed to enroll in their nearest neighborhood school without examination. But in the late 1970s, individual key schools began giving youngsters oral "entrance examinations" as part of their admissions procedure. Teachers indicated that parents' background was also considered by the key schools as part of the entrance procedure since it is a commonplace that the children of educated and economically secure parents perform better in school. Indeed, key schools are often located in the "better" neighborhoods with large concentrations of cadres and intellectuals.

Everyone also acknowledges the general criticism of the revived keypoint system that exists "in society." An outburst against them was aired briefly in the press in late 1981, the first time that any such statements concerning them had appeared in the press since 1976. The thrust of the commentary, which echoed the Cultural Revolution critique of such schools, was that the schools should be abolished because of the unfair advantages they gave to a small, privileged minority and the damage they were doing to the "enthusiasm for learning" among the majority. The best "backbone" teachers and students were just then being transferred from ordinary schools into the re-created keypoints. Secondary enrollments also fell to their lowest levels at this time. Tensions were such that at a National People's Congress meeting in December 1981 several delegates called for the abolition of the key schools at the elementary and junior secondary levels.[31] The debate was ter-

---

[31] Xinhua domestic service, Beijing, Dec. 11, 1981, translated in JPRS, *CR:*

minated abruptly at the end of the month with the announcement that, whatever their faults, key schools would be retained.[32]

The outburst against key schools in 1981 was actually part of a developing controversy then underway over many commonly acknowledged educational drawbacks of the newly rebuilt system. Probably given impetus by the cutbacks at the secondary level, the controversy nevertheless only skirted that issue, concentrating instead on a number of specific pedagogical concerns. Besides the keypoint stream itself, these were: the related practice of tracking or segregating students within schools and teaching them separately according to ability; the inflexible rigors reimposed on the system by the need to pass entrance exams at each level; and the ensuing competitive drive to achieve high pass rates. All sources agreed that the cramming and competition were if anything more intense in the late 1970s than ever before.

Teachers almost uniformly claim to prefer the "regularity" of the restored national unified curriculum with its clear standards, demands, and fixed progression of lessons, enforced by the full panoply of quizzes, tests, and examinations. Yet the logic of the pedagogical arguments against most of these features is also generally accepted. Streaming, for instance, was specifically not permitted in the original Soviet-style system of the 1950s. But because that prohibition contradicted the traditional Chinese assumption that "special talent" deserves special training, the issue was widely debated at that time. Such training was then allowed in the early 1960s but forbidden again during the 1966–76 decade. As a result, Chinese educators are very familiar with the pedagogical arguments for and against streaming. They generally agree, for example, that it benefits only the brightest students, leaving the others if not demoralized at least more intellectually passive. Hence, when such features of the system were allowed to develop unchecked in the late 1970s, there was a basis for criticism even among teachers otherwise instinctively committed to "regularity."

Yet correctives had to come from the central authorities responsible for fixing the centralized rules of the system, and, predictably,

---

PSM, no. 253 (Dec. 30, 1981), p. 66; *Guangming ribao*, Dec. 5, 1981.

[32] *Beijing ribao*, Dec. 25, 1981. On the press commentary that preceded this statement, see *Zhongguo qingnian bao* (China Youth News) (Beijing), Oct. 31, 1981; Nov. 21, 1981; Dec. 5, and 12, 1981; *Wenhuibao*, Oct. 21, 1981, and Dec. 12, 1981; *Guangming ribao*, Nov. 7, and 16, 1981, and Dec. 5, 1981; *Beijing ribao*, Dec. 12, 1981; *Renmin ribao*, Nov. 12, 15, and 17, 1981.

given the logic of the two-line struggle, the official decision came in the form of a rebuke for the previous system rather than its successor. Climaxing the 1981 controversy, then education minister Jiang Nanxiang conceded that the competition for college admission was being waged more intensely, with all the attendant evils, than at any time in the past. However, the problem was not the restored college entrance exams or the keypoint stream but the fact that too many senior middle school graduates were chasing too few seats in college. He recalled somewhat wistfully how much more manageable the secondary school system had been in the mid-1960s, when it had an enrollment of only 14 million. He seemed to be defending the reduction of enrollments then underway by suggesting that the tension within the system would be alleviated once it had fewer students to worry about.[33]

In fact, Jiang and his successors have discovered that turning back this particular clock is easier said than done. Tensions may be less at the college level, where only about 2 million senior secondary graduates are now competing annually for 600,000 college seats (by contrast with 7 million vying for half that number in 1979).[34] Equally important, the number of officially recognized keypoint secondary schools has also been halved (there were in 1987 only 2,243 such schools nationwide as shown in table 5), to produce about 600,000 graduates each year, or a number more or less exactly equal to the annual intake of college freshmen.[35] This probably has reduced tensions at the senior secondary level, where the keypoint schools regularly report pass rates into college of 90+ percent. But the competition, far from being eliminated, has only been forced down the line where sixth- and ninth-graders are

---

[33] *Beijing ribao*, Jan. 3, 1982.

[34] Guojia tongji ju, ed., *Zhongguo tongji nianjian, 1988*, pp. 878, 881.

[35] Guojia jiaoyu weiyuanhui, ed., *Zhongguo jiaoyu tongji nianjian, 1987*, pp. 58–59, 65. Unfortunately, this source does not provide an explanation for the number of key schools it provides. Other less official sources, for example, refer to 4,000 keypoint middle schools nationwide, a figure that includes the county keypoints (see Lin Shuangchuan, "Remen huati: zhongdian zhongxue deshi tan" [Hot Topic: A Discussion of the Advantages and Disadvantages of Keypoint Middle Schools], *Zhongguo funu* [Chinese Women] (Beijing), no. 7 (1988), p. 4; also, *Zhongguo qingnian bao* (Nov. 2, 1989). Apparently the State Education Commission now distinguishes between the "rural" keypoints and others, which university personnel also tend to do informally, but this distinction has not been officially acknowledged. There are some 2,000 counties in China. If the county keypoint middle schools are subtracted from the usually cited 4,000 figure, the result would be roughly the same as the 1987 State Education Commission compilation shown in table 5.

prepped and crammed in a valiant effort to push them into the keypoint stream.

The radical arguments with their antielitist implications can also be (and since 1981 have been) kept out of the newspapers. But it has not been possible to eliminate the "interests" that the Cultural Revolution policies created in the form of a mass education base with all the upward pressures arising from it. And whether the old radical arguments are used, or the currently acceptable professional ones, the keypoint stream loses out either way. Another upsurge of criticism, using the latter, occurred between 1984 and 1986, when calls were again raised to abolish such schools at the elementary and secondary levels. The main points in the mid-1980s critique were elaborated as follows:

- Non-key schools had lost all of the best teachers to their keypoint rivals.

- Key schools were ignoring their junior middle sections and putting all their efforts into the senior level in order to achieve high pass rates into college.

- As a result, key-school students were not only arrogant but had no interest in politics or social activities.

- Teachers in the non-key schools were demoralized because they knew their students were the rejects of the keypoint stream.

- Student morale in non-key schools was low because students knew that they had little chance of going on to college and that job opportunities for them were scarce.

- The keypoint system worked to the disadvantage of boys, whose intellectual development was slower than that of girls. Female students performed better on entrance exams, but "due to various social, historical, and psychological factors," their performance declined after the first year of senior middle school. Hence, "many promising male students are deprived of normal development because they have entered non-key schools that do not have...competent teachers, adequate teaching facilities, or enough funds."

- Finally, the keypoint stream worked to the detriment of intellectual development generally. Regardless of the resolutions issued each year, everyone judged key schools by their chief raison d'être, namely, the access they provided to the next level and especially to college. The key schools therefore had no choice but to base their teaching on the cram method in order to guarantee examination results and high pass rates.[36]

Such arguments were aired extensively in the national and provincial press between 1984 and 1986.[37] Delegates at the annual meetings of the National People's Congress and the concurrent Political Consultative Congress renewed their demand that the keypoint stream be abolished. Professor Qian Weichang, president of the Shanghai Polytechnic University, received much publicity as one of the most prominent critics among the delegates on this issue.[38] Unlike 1981, those who spoke out in the mid-1980s were careful to acknowledge the legitimacy of the keypoint concept "in principle" and its importance initially in counteracting the influence of the Gang of Four. Nevertheless, central policy makers on this matter, too, were ultimately caught between their "line" and the logic of the continuing arguments against it. Reflecting the dilemma, they have steadfastly refused to repudiate the keypoint concept or the system they recreated with such determination in the late 1970s. But they have responded with a series of gestures and measures that appear rather more substantive than those taken to defuse the vocational education controversy.

The gestures have included a steady stream of increasingly defensive publicity designed to cast the keypoint schools in a benign light by showing that they can correct their faults and work for the common good. Gone is the aggressive tone of the late 1970s, when the sole aim was to "concentrate resources" in order to "guarantee quality" for the tertiary level. Readers in Tianjin have been as-

---

[36] This summary of the mid-1980s arguments is from *Guangming ribao*, Sept. 6, 1984.

[37] For example, in 1984: *Wenhuibao*, Aug. 17, 25, and 31, 1984; Liu Huo, "Shi peiyang rencai haishi yayi rencai?" (Nurturing Talent or Suppressing Talent?), *Xin guancha* (New Observer) (Beijing), no. 18 (1984), pp. 14–15. In 1985: *Renmin ribao*, Sept. 22, 1985; Oct. 20, 1985; *Jiaoyu wenzhai* (Education Digest) (Beijing), Jan. 1, 1985; April 5, 1985; May 5, 1985; Nov. 5, 1985; *Wenhuibao*, July 26, 1985; Aug. 2, 9, and 23, 1985; Sept. 13 and 20, 1985. In 1986: *Wenhuibao*, May 7, 15, and 29, 1986; *Nanfang ribao* (Southern Daily) (Guangzhou), Nov. 8, and 29, 1986; *Renmin zhengxie bao* (People's Political Consultative News) (Beijing), April 18, 1986; June 3, 1986; Oct. 24, 1986; "Jiaoyu sixiang gaige zhuanti taolun jiyao" (Summary of a Special Discussion on the Reform of Educational Thinking), *Jiaoyu lilun yu shijian* (Theory and Practice of Education) (Taiyuan, Shanxi), no. 6 (1986), p. 17.

[38] See *Beijing ribao*, May 26, 1984; *Yangcheng wanbao* (Yangcheng Evening News) (Guangzhou), Aug. 1, 1984; *Guangming ribao*, April 7, 1985; *Tuanjiebao* (Unity News) (Beijing), April 6 and 13, 1985; *Renmin zhengxie bao*, April 5, 1985; *China Daily*, April 4, 1985; *Renmin ribao*, April 9, 1986.

sured, for example, that "keypoint schools and ordinary schools learn from one another, help one another, and improve together."[39] In Shenyang, readers learned that the city's key schools were opening their laboratories and libraries to teachers from ordinary schools and had set up "cooperative networks" to help them improve the quality of their teaching.[40] Authorities in Fuzhou later announced that they had begun establishing links between the city's thirty middle schools as early as 1979. All together nine key schools had been linked with nine ordinary junior middle schools. Teachers and administrators moved back and forth between them for observation, evaluation, and practice teaching.[41]

Beijing's Middle School No. 8, which boasted a 100 percent pass rate into college by the mid-1980s, announced in 1985 that it was no longer satisfied with its reputation as a prep school. Henceforth its aim would be to develop the all-around talents and abilities of its students.[42] To demonstrate that they were not obsessed with their pass rates to the exclusion of all else, keypoints were said to be taking the lead in education research, experimental teaching, demonstration teaching, developing extracurricular activities, introducing optional vocational courses, developing physical education, promoting student health, and bringing labor education back into the curriculum. Beijing's famous experimental Jingshan School even introduced housework into the labor class, requiring students to sweep floors and wash clothes as part of their homework.[43]

More substantive measures have focused on trying to reintroduce the neighborhood school principle for student enrollment at the elementary and junior secondary levels, while leaving the key schools themselves with all their other concentrated resources intact. This compromise was introduced for elementary schools when the first backlash against the keypoint stream escalated in late 1981, coming in the form of a proposal that key schools be changed into

---

39 Nankai zhongxue (Nankai Middle School), "Zhongdian xiao he yiban xiao yao huxiang xuexi, huxiang bangzhu, gongtong tigao" (Keypoint Schools and Ordinary Schools Learn from One Another, Help One Another, and Improve Together), *Tianjin jiaoyu* (Tianjin Education), no. 4 (1983), pp. 9–10.

40 *Zhongguo jiaoyu bao*, Nov. 27, 1984.

41 Ibid., Feb. 19, 1987.

42 *Renmin ribao*, Feb. 3, 1985; *Zhongguo jiaoyu bao*, June 11, 1985.

43 *Beijing ribao*, Nov. 17, 1987; *Guangming ribao*, May 11, 1987; July 20, 1987; Oct. 9, 1987; *Nanfang ribao*, May 21, 1986; *Renmin ribao*, March 9, 1986; Jan. 7, 1988; *Zhongguo jiaoyu bao*, Nov. 29, 1986; Aug. 18, 1987; Dec. 19, 1987; June 11, 1988.

"central" schools. The city of Shanghai took the lead in announcing this change.[44] The central school ideally does not seek only the best and brightest students, but rather enrolls everyone in the neighborhood. It does, however, concentrate the best staff and facilities and is supposed to serve as a leader or model demonstration center for other less well appointed schools in its vicinity. This version, already established before 1949 as we have seen in the Yan'an example, was the original one from which the keypoint system evolved and remains today a prominent feature of the education system in Taiwan.

A few months after Shanghai's announcement, the head of the Guangzhou Education Bureau visited Hong Kong and acknowledged in an informal interview that the central school idea was aimed at mollifying the "opinions in society" against keypoint schools. She said, however, that Guangzhou was not yet ready to change its newly restored key elementary schools and avowed that Shanghai had not really abolished them either except in name. She declared that Shanghai was running its central schools essentially like keypoints. There are two ways of doing this. One is for the school itself to continue to vet youngsters in some way preparatory to admission. The other is for the parents to use connections and relatives in order to establish an address for the child within the neighborhood of the school.

The central school compromise remains the favored arrangement and appears to have survived the promulgation of the compulsory education law. Thus key elementary schools have not really been abolished, but neither do they receive much publicity in deference to the "opinions" against them. In accordance with the compulsory education law, local regulations everywhere require elementary schools to enroll on the neighborhood principle without an entrance examination. Neighborhood enrollment is the established norm, but informal ways of "concentrating" students are allowed to continue. At the start of the 1986–87 academic year, for example, Beijing Municipality boasted over 4,000 elementary schools, of which 43 were district keypoints and 9 all-city keypoints. Parents were reported using all manner of stratagems to establish "residence" in the districts of the favored schools.[45] A year later, *China Education News* published a series of photographs showing

---

[44] *Guangming ribao*, Nov. 7, 1981.
[45] *Zhongguo qingnian bao*, Sept. 28, 1986.

anxious parents and youngsters gathered for the "entrance examinations" of "a certain" Beijing key primary school.[46] Such practices are not officially encouraged, but neither are they forbidden. Parents' hopes for a glorious future for their children (*wangzi chenglong*) by following the keypoint stream from primary school to college do the rest in maintaining the essence of the system intact even as it disappears officially in form.

The same compromise solution for the junior secondary level was introduced in the form of an "opinion" issued by the Education Ministry in 1983, which stated that "in principle," unified junior middle school entrance exams should be abolished in cities that had universalized schooling at that level.[47] The aim was to eliminate the elaborate procedure whereby elementary school graduates were channeled into the hierarchy of key and non-key schools within a city on the basis of unified entrance examinations scores. Key junior middle schools would then enroll only children from their own immediate neighborhoods, as was done during the 1968–76 period. The 1983 opinion was followed by a circular to the same effect in 1986, which continues to govern practice in this regard.[48]

At present, localities are in a "transitional stage," as they try to combine in practice the two contradictory concepts of neighborhood enrollment and keypoint schools. Because the latter remain otherwise unchanged, with the best teachers, facilities, and pass rates on to the keypoint senior middle level, parents outside the school district naturally continue to demand access. Thus when authorities in the northeastern city of Dalian abolished their unified entrance exams in 1986 for the neighborhood enrollment method, the results were uncertain. According to one source, the lack of success was due to "the most difficult problem" encountered, namely, the "uneven conditions of the junior middle schools including

---

46 *Zhongguo jiaoyu bao*, July 16, 1987.

47 "Jiaoyubu guanyu jinyibu tigao putong zhongxue jiaoyu zhiliang de jidian yijian," Aug. 10, 1983 (full citation in n. 20).

48 *Zhongguo jiaoyu bao*, March 8, 1986; May 30, 1987; also, "Jiaoyubu guanyu yinfa Changchun deng wushi chuzhong zhaosheng zhidu gaige cailiao de tongzhi" (Ministry of Education Circular on the Materials Issued Concerning the Reform of the Junior Middle School Enrollment System in Changchun and Four Other Cities), March 28, 1985, in Guojia jiaoyu weiyuanhui bangongting (Office of the State Education Commission), ed., *Jiaoyu gongzuo wenjian xuanbian, 1985* (A Selection of Education Work Documents for 1985) (n.p.: Renmin jiaoyu chubanshe, 1987 and 1988), pp. 189–95.

the level of their teachers and quality of their education."[49] The corollary to the neighborhood enrollment principle, therefore, is the promise now being made by many localities either "to abolish progressively" the key junior secondaries or "to reduce gradually" the qualitative difference between these and the non-key schools.[50]

Meanwhile, elaborate quota systems are being devised to tide everyone over the "transition." The 1986 circular authorized schools to use recommendations, oral examinations, or "other enrollment methods" during this uncertain period of indefinite duration, leaving it to the local authorities themselves to decide. Except in the case of truly outstanding students, however, such methods naturally leave open much room for maneuver—especially given the common assumption expressed by Chinese educators everywhere that children from "established" or intellectually and economically secure families will perform better in school overall and therefore deserve access to better facilities. Stories also abound as regards the exchange of favors and money that occur at this point.

Among the new locally authorized methods, one model county in Hebei Province allows each primary school to recommend a certain number of its best graduates for admission to the key junior secondaries. The county education bureau has also issued strict regulations to control student transfers and repeating grades, especially the final year of primary or junior middle school. Both are common methods for lateral entry into key schools and for trying to boost pass rates onto the next level.[51] The districts and counties within the Beijing Municipality are now using a variety of methods to enroll at the junior secondary level. But about 70 percent of all primary school graduates are entering non-key neighborhood schools. Key schools must enroll half their students from the neighborhood; the other half are recommended via a system of quotas granted to the primary schools to accommodate their "best" graduates.[52]

---

[49] *Guangming ribao*, Aug. 12, 1987.

[50] Such localities include Shanghai (*Wenhuibao*, May 7, 1986; *Zhongguo jiaoyu bao*, April 26, 1986; Feb. 24, 1987; *Guangming ribao*, Nov. 10, 1987); Guangzhou (*Yangcheng wanbao*, May 11, 1988); Dalian (*Guangming ribao*, Aug. 12, 1987); Shenyang (*Liaoning ribao*, March 6, 1987); Yingkou (*Guangming ribao*, Feb. 13, 1989); Xiamen (*Zhongguo jiaoyu bao*, June 13, 1987); and Henan Province (*Jiaoyu shibao* [Education Times] [Xinxiang City, Henan], May 5, 1988).

[51] *Zhongguo jiaoyu bao*, Feb. 26, 1987.

[52] *Beijing ribao*, March 7, 1988; June 14, 1988. In Shanghai, many school principals are not satisfied with the unified enrollment procedure which still permits a cer-

The city of Guangzhou has devised a modified version of its old system but seems, on paper at least, to give more substance than many other localities to the aim of "progressively abolishing" its junior secondary key schools. Substituted for the unified all-city entrance exam are separate exams given by each of the eight districts in the city. One such district exam serves both as the elementary school graduation exam and the junior middle entrance exam. Each city district is further divided into two or three school districts, and students are assigned to junior middle schools in their own districts on the basis of their written preference and examination scores. In 1988, the city's six key middle schools also had to enroll 90 percent of their students on this same school district basis at the junior secondary level. Only 10 percent were allowed to enroll preferentially from elsewhere, but the regulations required them to be selected on the basis of their grades and examination scores rather than by recommendations.[53]

Obviously, central policy makers have made concessions in principle and practice to the critical opinions in society that have been demanding the abolition of the keypoint stream at the lower levels since 1981, and probably never accepted its reimposition in the first place. But whether the key schools themselves actually disappear is another matter. The next immediate problem in this regard, moreover, is the senior secondary level, where mass pressures from below are also beginning to erode the carefully restructured apex of the keypoint stream. At this level, however, the official "forces of regularization" have fewer critics and are not yet willing to compromise, so localities are working out accommodations on their own. The two examples cited below illustrate (1) an ideal-type solution designed by authorities in the city of Yingkou to maximize equal opportunities for the new-style neighborhood junior middle graduates and (2) the reality of the pressures from below that have built up within the college-preparatory stream in Shaanxi Province.

---

tain degree of preferential selection. Hence individual key junior middle schools are conducting their own talent search by sponsoring examinations and competitions in different subjects. Principals reportedly argue that "since students' intelligence is opened up at the junior secondary stage of education, it is a crucial time for developing talent, so keypoint junior middle schools cannot be abolished and a few students should be selectively chosen for keypoint training" (*Wenhuibao,* Shanghai, June 30, 1989).

[53] *Nanfang ribao,* June 11, 20, and 21, 1987; July 12, 1988; *Yangcheng wanbao,* May 11, 1988.

Yingkou authorities decided that abolishing the unified entrance examinations at the junior secondary level, which they did in 1985, was not enough. They are currently in the process of changing admissions procedures at the senior secondary level as well. Because its key Senior Middle School No. 1 maintains a pass rate of over 90 percent, local people regard admission to this school as "having one leg already on the way to college." In the past, students from all of the city's fifteen junior middle schools regularly applied for admission, but usually only those in the two key junior middle schools among them succeeded. The failure of everyone else did little to promote acceptance of the neighborhood school idea. City education authorities therefore introduced a new plan in 1988, whereby each of the junior middle schools would be assigned an enrollment quota for admission to the key senior middle school, the size of the quota to be determined by the size of the graduating class and its overall grade average. Candidates still have to take an all-city unified entrance exam. But the key senior middle school is now obliged to take the best students from each junior middle school, rather than the highest-scoring candidates from the city as a whole. The city education bureau will determine the minimum passing score overall, in order to "guarantee quality."[54]

By contrast, in a 1987 report, the Shaanxi provincial education bureau highlighted the problem of excess demand over supply in the province's key schools. Parents were blamed for believing that their childrens' future depended solely on admission to college. As a result, so many students were using the lateral entry or transfer method of gaining access to the college-preparatory stream that those schools' task of maintaining quality was being seriously undermined. Within the province generally, classes in ordinary and vocational secondary schools were often not even full, while those in the key schools were full to overflowing. As of 1987, classes in such schools averaged over seventy students each, well in excess of the stipulated standard.

The case of Rui Quan Middle School in the city of Weinan, near Xian, was cited as a case in point. There were in 1987 six classes of graduating seniors, that is, students in the third year at the senior secondary level. They numbered 534 in all with an average of 89 per class. Yet three years earlier, only 300 had been enrolled in these same six classes. Of the new students, only 70 were deemed

---

[54] *Guangming ribao*, Feb. 13, 1989.

to have transferred for legitimate reasons. The others had used "various kinds of connections" and "pressure from higher Party and government departments" to achieve their aim. Of the 234 transfer students, only 5 were of superior academic standing, 121 were average, and the rest were below average.[55]

Clearly, the ambivalence entertained by both critics and advocates of "regular" education in the past is still operative among their successors today. State Education Commission Vice-Chairman Wang Mingda identified the contradiction in remarks at a meeting of non-Communist Party intellectuals called to discuss education problems at the start of the 1986–87 academic year. Wang told the gathering that "on the problem of keypoint middle schools, we have already given notice that they should be eliminated at the junior secondary level. But in actually doing that, the larger the city, the greater the obstacles, and the main one is the opinion of cadres and intellectuals since they all hope their own children will attend keypoint middle schools."[56]

Thus China's education system has, in a sense, turned a full circle. The mass base may be very different from what it was half a century ago. But the regularization patterns reimposed within it are clearly identifiable both in the precedents they evoke and the ambivalence they arouse. Because of the potential the regularized keypoint stream represents, parents want their children to enter it. But at the same time, the critical consensus is such that everyone can also recite the system's defects by heart—including many of the same people whose interests are tied most closely to it.

Postscript: The Economic Crises of 1988

Ironically, given the history of the tensions surrounding it, senior secondary education suffered a blow from an entirely unexpected source in 1988. The challenge emerged from the cumulative

---

55 *Shaanxi ribao* (Xian), Nov. 1, 1987.

56 *Renmin zhengxie bao*, Oct. 24, 1986. On what has become a continuing debate over the pros and cons of keypoint schools, see for example: ibid., July 21, 1987; Cao Sibin, "Zhong xiao xue buyi she zhongdian chuyi" (My Humble Opinion on the Impropriety of Running Keypoint Middle and Elementary Schools), *Xiandairen bao* (Modern Mankind) (Guangzhou), no. 91 (Dec. 15, 1987), p. 1; Lin Shuangchuan, "Zhongdian zhongxue deshi tan," pp. 4–5; Gou Guoxi and Li Yaoming, "Zhongdian zhongxue banxue moshi de tansuo yu sikao" (Explorations and Reflections on the Keypoint Way of Running Middle Schools), *Jiaoyu lilun yu shijian* (Theory and Practice of Education) (Taiyuan) 8:2 (1988):5–9; and *Wenhuibao* (Shanghai), June 30, 1989 (quoted above in n. 52).

direct and indirect impact on tertiary education of the Chinese government's market-oriented economic reforms. Those consequences, which will be discussed more fully in chapter 7 below, can be summarized as follows: the inflationary erosion of university budgets and academic salaries; the rising cost of education for students and parents, including the introduction of tuition; new job-assignment reforms that mean an end to "iron rice bowl" guaranteed state jobs; and the consequent devaluation of higher education.

A *People's Daily* article timed to coincide with the 1988 fall semester quoted college teachers and students as blaming the heightened sense of demoralization on the uncertain prospects of college graduates in an economy where the "remuneration for mental and manual labor has been reversed." A second source of frustration was the new free-market approach to employment and the "unhealthy practices" associated with it.[57] The result was a quickening of the "wind of revulsion against study" or the new "study is useless" attitude that had been evident throughout the system in recent years.

Until 1988, this trend had been registered primarily in rising student and teacher dropout rates at the lower levels and a generalized intellectual lethargy among college students. That year, in addition, many cities and suburban districts reported a sharp drop in applicants at the senior secondary level for the first time since 1976. Press commentators reported uniformly that the major reasons for the drop were the low remuneration for jobs filled by college graduates, plus the new regulations announced in early 1988 abolishing tuition-free higher education and guaranteed job assignments for college graduates. "This year," noted one correspondent, "in order to find work, many university and graduate students and their parents are going everywhere establishing connections and seeking the help of influential people, which has had a great influence on the parents of secondary school students. They feel that the burdens of sending their children to senior middle school and on to college are too great...and the monetary rewards too small."[58] "Some say," wrote another commentator, "that this year the specialized technical middle school has become the last iron rice bowl."[59]

[57] *Renmin ribao*, Aug. 27, 1988.
[58] Ibid., July 25, 1988.
[59] Ibid., July 8, 1988.

Beijing had planned to enroll 25,077 students in 1988, but only 13,779 wrote first-preference applications for ordinary senior middle schools there, a drop of 45 percent over the year before. The beneficiaries were the previously unpopular secondary technical and vocational schools, which had 59,683 first-preference applications in 1988, for only 10,354 places. Even key schools were affected. Some 48 percent of the students graduating from Beijing's district-level keypoint junior middle schools applied to enter technical or vocational schools.[60]

Most urban areas in Jiangsu Province reported the same phenomenon. Nanjing had planned to enroll 7,000 into its ordinary senior middle schools, but only 5,000 applied; Suzhou had planned to enroll 1,700, but only 1,500 applied.[61] Similarly, the enrollment plan in Wuhan had called for 11,000 new students at the senior secondary level, but only 9,000 applied. Here, too, the trend was strong enough to influence applications for the keypoint stream. Whereas in 1987 there had been 5 applicants for every place in Wuhan's key senior middle schools, in 1988 there were only 3. By contrast, specialized technical secondary schools had an enrollment plan for 1,997 people and 7,872 applied, while vocational schools had 4,112 places for 8,547 applicants.[62]

The change was sharpest in the cities. Rural districts seemed more familiar with the symptoms of the new trend because of their typically low promotion rates to the tertiary level. A county in Hebei's Shijiazhuang Prefecture reported that its two ordinary middle schools had planned to admit 500 new students in 1988, but a week after the fall semester began, only half that number had enrolled. Local officials identified four reasons, including both new and old.

(1) Parents already knew that few local secondary school graduates could compete successfully for a place in college and, even if they could, henceforth college graduates would not be guaranteed state employment. Entering a technical school would therefore be the wiser strategy.

(2) Rising costs also entered into the calculation. In that locality, the monthly expenses of keeping a child in middle school, including tuition, books, and living expenses, had risen to about 40 rmb, while the monthly cost of supporting a college student ranged

---

[60] *Guangming ribao*, July 8, 1988.
[61] *Renmin ribao*, July 25, 1988.
[62] Ibid., July 8, 1988.

from 50 to 100 rmb. Such outlays were more than many local people could afford. If they could afford middle school but not college, the middle school graduate would be left with only a diploma and no guarantee of employment.

(3) "Not a few" people also calculated financial costs against benefits and concluded that, all things considered, a college education cost more, took longer, and yielded lower returns than technical training. An estimated 20 percent of the local senior secondary school dropouts did so because they could earn as much or more money without continuing their education.

(4) Finally, some parents who wanted to keep their children close to home harbored the "feudal" idea that the more schooling young people received, the more likely they were to seek their fortunes elsewhere. This phenomenon accounted for about 10 percent of the local senior middle school dropouts.[63]

Education authorities both urban and rural seemed surprised by the sudden change in 1988 and could not decide whether it was good or bad. "Many" worried about the shrinking pool of college talent. Others argued that if the new pattern continued, it could actually be a boon to the government's strategy of educational development. Ordinary non-key senior secondary schools could then be further reduced, an aim not yet sufficiently realized; the key schools alone could produce enough college candidates; and the divided system could be run more efficiently than had hitherto been possible.[64]

---

[63] *Zhongguo jiaoyu bao*, Oct. 18, 1988; and a similar story from suburban Shanghai (*Wenhuibao*, June 27, 1988).

[64] On the latter positive view, see especially *Renmin ribao*, July 8, 1988.

CHAPTER SEVEN

Higher Education

In the early decades of the century, the habit of copying Western course materials in toto, no matter how inappropriate, was a favorite target of those critics who deplored the mechanical transplant of foreign models. The critics did not necessarily object to the materials themselves but rather to the failure of Chinese educators to adapt the lessons for use in Chinese classrooms. Science teachers, in those early days, would use examples of flora and fauna for which no specimens were available and that neither teacher nor students had ever seen because they did not exist in China.

That past experience with foreign borrowing, repeated as late as the 1950s when China was learning from the Soviet Union, could not but inspire a similar reservation in 1980 when Chinese leaders were announcing the full range of reforms they were planning for higher education. The question then was whether American branches could be effectively grafted on a Soviet tree planted in a Chinese garden.[1] By 1989 the answer was clear. Such an exercise might yet succeed, but to do so will require far greater care and skill in adapting the logic of the reforms to the reality of the Chinese environment than Chinese leaders demonstrated in the 1980s. Much has been achieved and many lessons learned since the 1920s. But the desire for wealth and power in the face of poverty

---

[1] General references in this section to conditions in 1980 are based on extended interviews I conducted with Chinese university administrators at fifteen institutions of higher learning during the spring and fall semesters of 1980. This three-month survey was sponsored by the Committee on Scholarly Communication with the People's Republic of China. Portions of the data from those interviews have been published in Suzanne Pepper, "China's Universities: New Experiments in Socialist Democracy and Administrative Reform—a Research Report," *Modern China* 8:2 (April 1982):147–204; and idem, *China's Universities: Post-Mao Enrollment Policies* (Ann Arbor: Center for Chinese Studies Monograph No. 46, University of Michigan). The question on foreign borrowing was raised in the *Modern China* article.

and weakness remains, and with it the assumption that quick-fix solutions can be sought in foreign models.

At the elementary level and even more so at the secondary, the dominant tensions in the 1980s came from the initial attempt to reimpose the "regular" patterns of China's education tradition without much regard for the underlying popular critique in either its old or new manifestations. Both before and after 1949, the populist and mass-based concerns deriving from the critique revolved essentially around the question of whose children should receive how much of what kind of education. At the tertiary level, similar tensions are also evident. But they have been overshadowed in the 1980s by the new rush of outside influences from the West, as Chinese political and intellectual leaders abandoned the appropriate technology arguments of the Maoist era to revive their quest for "advanced international standards." In the process they have also revived, in appropriately updated form, the concerns associated with foreign borrowing and mechanical copying that were first articulated by critics during the early decades of the century. In the 1980s, of course, the old contest between Chinese foundations and foreign imports was further complicated as a clash between Chinese socialist ways and Western capitalist means.

The result as of 1987—when Wang Meng published his prophetic warning about superficial foreign borrowing, the one-sided obsession with wealth, and a need for real alternatives to iron rice bowl egalitarianism—looked like overall stalemate. With the multiple economic and political crises of 1988 and 1989, the consequences of Deng Xiaoping's decade of reform for higher education, at least, might better be categorized as a major tragedy for all concerned.[2]

---

[2] Wang Meng's views are elaborated in chap. 4. Assuming that those views as published in 1987 were his own, Wang's attempt to define a position between "the two lines" by identifying them as such and criticizing both was rare in the official public discourse of the 1980s. Unfortunately, given the ever-polarized Chinese political environment, such a position does not enjoy sufficient backing among the top power brokers to make a decisive impact in terms of policy, practice, or even public debate.

Wang Meng's recent fate would seem to confirm these impressions. After he was appointed Minister of Culture in the wake of the antibourgeois liberalization drive in 1987, he is said to have tried to protect liberal intellectuals like Liu Binyan while avoiding direct association with their critical ideas. But he has not been able to escape the backlash following the May 1989 student demonstrations. He was reported in July to be "on sick leave" and forbidden to return to work. Hong Kong observers concluded that Wang Meng had "played a very clever game" that for the time being, at least, was probably over (*South China Morning Post* [Hong Kong], July 27, 1989). His resignation as Minister of Culture was officially announced in early September

Deng's decade had begun with great fanfare, high hopes, and the total reversal of Cultural Revolution priorities. Those priorities, as noted, included quantitative expansion at the mass level and vocationalization of the entire system. Higher education was similarly vocationalized but without the quantitative growth. Lower-level schools also reopened much earlier, in 1968–69, after the Red Guard phase of the Cultural Revolution ended. Institutions of higher learning did not begin enrolling new students on anything like a regular basis until the early 1970s. By 1976, enrollments were growing again but had not yet reached even their pre-1966 levels. Qualitatively, according to interviewees, college curricula were essentially cut in half during the early 1970s. Socially and politically, the objective was to make "intellectuals" of workers and peasants (by building mass secondary enrollments and using nonacademic criteria for college admission) and to "proletarianize" existing intellectuals as well (by recasting them as peasants and workers after a stint of farm labor or factory work).

Following the logic of the post-1976 era, all of these priorities were reversed. The regularization patterns reimposed upon the system may have derived from old-fashioned assumptions among Chinese educators about how best to supply a quality product, but Deng Xiaoping's modernization strategy provided the demand and justification. Deng argued that China had to catch up with the rest of the world. Its first objective would be economic development, and it would once more measure itself by international standards. Because science and technology were the keys to economic modernization, and because education in turn held the key to their development, education should be reconstituted to fulfill these tasks.

Returning to China for the first time in thirty years, however, Western development experts advised, among other things, that a country China's size should have a college enrollment of about two million. Chinese leaders readily accepted this advice in the early 1980s and fixed 1990 as the target date for achieving it. As the following figures show—and subsequent discussion will indicate—this is one target that probably should not have been met on schedule.[3]

(*Wenhuibao* [Wen Wei Po] [Hong Kong], Sept. 5, 1989).

[3] Tertiary level statistics are from Guojia tongji ju (State Statistical Bureau), ed., *Zhongguo tongji nianjian, 1986* (Statistical Yearbook of China, 1986) (Beijing: Zhongguo tongji chubanshe, 1986), pp. 723, 726; *Renmin ribao,* March 1, 1989.

Year	Institutions	Students
1965	434	674,000
1977	404	625,000
1985	1,016	1,703,000
1988		2,066,000

Deng Xiaoping also, in the late 1970s, declared class struggle and mass movements to be at an end. Political labels from the past, like "rightist" and "historical counterrevolutionary" were removed. The use of family or class background as criteria for college admissions, job assignments, and other benefits was ended. Indeed, all the social consequences and implications of different kinds of education for different kinds of people were declared irrelevant to the overriding aim of education for modernization. In this respect, the system was freer of social and political constraints than it had been at any time since the founding of the People's Republic. All the suspicions that had formerly accumulated around intellectuals as a group because of their "complex" class and political backgrounds were officially erased. Mental and manual labor were declared to be of equal status if performed in the service of socialism, and intellectuals were formally defined as mental laborers so occupied (without actually having to become workers or peasants as before). The new aim was to rebuild tertiary education by deliberately exploiting the social division of labor thus redesignated. The older generation of university intellectuals referred openly to Deng Xiaoping as their "liberator" for the changes this reversal of priorities wrought in their lives.

In all other respects, the university system that was reestablished between 1977 and 1980 essentially replicated the antebellum model of the 1960s, which was essentially the same as the Sino-Soviet compromise variation that had emerged from the early 1950s pro-Soviet period. Hence, all of that system's centralized features abolished during the 1966–76 decade were restored. These included the national unified college entrance examinations, unified enrollment and job assignment plans, unified curricula, and systematized rules and regulations for everything.

Probably, if left entirely as an island unto itself thereafter, China's university system would have settled back more or less comfortably into this mold. From it, the worker-peasant-solider students, Cultural Revolution radical intellectuals, and other nonprofessionals were being purged or at least disempowered. Elementary and secondary education was being appropriately tracked and streamed all with the single-minded aim of producing talent for the tertiary sector. The system was recentralized, albeit in accordance with regular standards that minimized "irregular" and nonacademic intrusions. Educators consequently found themselves with greater freedom to pursue "quality" than at any time since 1949, and the value of a college education was also similarly enhanced.

Finally, in the late 1970s the cushion of socialist security was further inflated for university intellectuals as if to compensate for the deprivations of previous years. They continued to enjoy lifetime tenure, and cradle-to-grave security was also enhanced. For example, the special schools attended by and maintained for their children were exonerated and restored. College students, for their part, continued to enjoy free tuition, room, and board. They graduated into similarly secure state-assigned jobs, which now promised better prospects than ever before. Little wonder that in 1980 university intellectuals felt themselves on the threshold of a new "golden age" of peace and security, while parents could think of no better guarantee for their children's future than admission to college.

In fact, Deng Xiaoping's plans for everyone were just beginning. Not only did he, just prior to his own trip to the United States in 1978, order 10,000 students to follow him as quickly as possible. He also is said to have ordered all leading cadres to make at least one trip abroad. His aim was not just to give them a glimpse of the outside world or even to import Western capital and technology, but to try and graft the ways and means of capitalism onto China's socialist system in the hope of making it work more effectively. He aimed further to include China's institutions of higher learning in that experiment. Already aware of the new orientation, although not the extent to which they would be pushed to achieve it, university educators said in 1980 that China was now looking especially to the United States as a source of expertise precisely because of the latter's status as the most successful example of Western capitalism. They also discussed specific ways in which China's universities might learn from their American counterparts.

It is not clear who else besides Deng Xiaoping was promoting this discussion, but the points were the same everywhere. Beijing University president Zhou Peiyuan summarized them after his own trip to North America in 1980. He wrote that because of leftist errors since 1957, China's higher education was backward and out-of-date. The American example would show the way forward in several areas.

Zhou first emphasized faculty selection procedures. In America, universities enjoyed the freedom to hire talented people and remove the unqualified. Such circulation was necessary to prevent the former from being "stifled in a pond of stagnant water," as in China's institutions of higher learning. Apparently because the life tenure custom in American universities contradicted the point he wanted to emphasize about hiring and firing, Zhou glossed over the custom, concentrating instead on the long years of testing that the tenure process entailed.

Second, American students did not begin specializing as soon as they entered college, and they were free to change their majors. Students in China should also be able to chose from a range of electives, and they should be required to study a range of courses outside those taught by their own departments. The division between science and technology, on the one hand, and the social sciences and humanities, on the other, should not be absolute as it was in Chinese universities. Furthermore, Chinese universities, in comparison with their American counterparts, lacked interdisciplinary courses and training in the frontier sciences. Entire branches of learning, such as sociology and psychology, had disappeared from college curricula for political reasons.

Professor Zhou stated that his one consolation was China's students, whom he regarded as superior to Americans in their moral standards, values, and attitude toward study. Yet he worried about the confusion of China's youth and their loss of direction due to the abrupt political changes. For this problem, he counseled better ideological and political education.

Noting that the founders of America's famous universities were all people of academic standing, Zhou demanded that administrative leadership within China's universities be returned to the academic professionals. The practice of "laymen leading professionals" was a leftist error, which had led to "bureaucratism." New formulas had to be found for dividing labor in a university, leaving political and ideological work to its Party organization while allowing the professionals to assume responsibility for academic affairs and routine administration.[4]

Zhou Peiyuan's agenda for academic reform nevertheless represented only about half the total package being unwrapped in 1979–80. Deng Xiaoping's economic and political reforms consti-

---

[4] *Renmin ribao*, April 2, 1981.

tuted the remainder. When translated into the world of China's universities, of course, even Zhou Peiyuan's proposals encountered obstacles at just about every turn. But these "contradictions," despite their origins in the clash of Soviet and American academic cultures, have been relatively benign. They have also been moderated by the obvious enthusiasm with which Chinese educators have joined their Western colleagues in reestablishing academic ties. Thus, despite the challenges to their newly restored "Sino-Soviet" academic model so soon after the radical disruptions of the Maoist past, Chinese educators could accept the academic reforms as being more or less convergent with their own interests. Two examples of such academic reforms are the efforts to "decentralize" the unified curricula and the unified college entrance examinations, both described below.

The same could not be said for the other half of the reform package, however, and it was with the intrusion of Deng Xiaoping's economic and political reforms into China's universities—examples of which are also described below—that academics saw their interests begin to diverge from those of their erstwhile liberator. Initially, these contradictions too seemed relatively benign. The economic reforms aimed to break up the over-centralization of economic power and socialist distribution. Universities and teachers had already been told in 1980 that as a preliminary application of the economic reforms in their realm, they should supplement modest budgets and low incomes with their own profit-making endeavors. Universities had also been told that free state-subsidized higher education would be phased out and were, in 1980, already engaged in changing the distribution of student stipends as a preliminary step toward that end. Previously these stipends had been allocated to all on an equal basis. A scholarship system was introduced at the same time to introduce the "Western" concept of linking material rewards with academic performance.

Then Deng Xiaoping himself announced, also in 1980, a series of political/administrative reforms for the society as whole without which, it was argued, the economic reforms could not succeed. These "reforms of 1980" were designed to correct the overconcentration of political power and other evils of bureaucratism. The goals included (1) reforming the cadre or personnel system by abolishing life tenure, smashing iron rice bowls, and tying job performance to rewards, punishments, and dismissals; (2) democratic management and popular participation in local government and enterprise administration; (3) the separation of political and Party functions from professional and administrative work; and (4) decentralization, or expanding local autonomy and the decision-making powers of individual institutions. And over all was the injunction to look to the capitalist West for inspiration and applicable solutions.[5]

The universities were told that their academic reform agenda, as outlined by Zhou Peiyuan, must proceed simultaneously with the other economic and political reforms as specified for the education sector. Indeed, success with academic reform would depend on success in completing the economic and political tasks. In 1980, university personnel were just beginning to understand that the new pressures had the potential to disrupt their academic way of life almost as profoundly, if not as destructively, as those introduced during the recent radical past.

Undoubtedly, one major fault was simply a surfeit of reforms. No other sector of Chinese society has been quite so overloaded as higher education—ordered to introduce simultaneously major academic, economic, and political innovations as well as absorb the sudden impact of direct contact with the West. By the mid-1980s, the universities were so bombarded by demands for change that a state of overall gridlock seemed to be setting in. "Because of pressure from critics, social inertia, and other reasons," noted one report in late 1984, "most institutions of higher learning have not been able to carry out reform even though they wanted to do so."[6] The commentator was Zheng Xuchu, party secretary of Shanghai's Jiaotong (Communications) University, discussing the past five years of reform efforts in China's universities. To break the impasse, Deng Xiaoping, Wan Li, Wang Zhen, and Zhao Ziyang all lent their names to the 1983–84 publicity campaign to promote Jiaotong's experiments in economic and administrative reform as a national model for others to emulate. But in 1985 and 1986, such experiments both in academia and in the society as a whole helped provoke the first unauthorized nationwide student protests of the

---

[5] "Deng Xiaoping zai zhongyang zhengzhiju kuoda huiyishang de jianghua" (Deng Xiaoping's Speech at the Enlarged Meeting of the Central Political Bureau), Aug. 18, 1980, *Zhanwang* (Prospect) (Hong Kong), April 16, 1981, pp. 24–30; Liao Gailong, "Zhonggong 'geng shen gaige' fang'an" (The Chinese Communist Party's "Reform of 1980" Program), *Qishi niandai* (The Seventies) (Hong Kong), March 1981, pp. 38–48; and a two-part article by Feng Wenbin in *Renmin ribao,* Nov. 24 and 25, 1980. Deng's 1980 speech was not officially published until 1987 (*Renmin ribao,* July 1, 1987).

[6] *Guangming ribao,* Nov. 14, 1984.

post-Mao era and set in motion the chain of events that led directly to Tiananmen Square, 1989.

Amid all the economic and political excitement, meanwhile, education reform in the sense of improving the content and quality of what is taught and learned appears to have been all but eclipsed. This is perhaps the greatest irony of all, after the entire education system from kindergarten upward was restructured ostensibly to concentrate the nation's best talents for the pursuit of higher learning, unhindered by any other concern. However important any given reform may have seemed, then, and however well-meaning its individual promoters, one can only wonder at the wisdom of national policy makers who turned higher education into a laboratory for virtually every innovation that caught their fancy. From this perspective, the military crackdown against the students and their supporters in June 1989 was only the climax of the tragedy. Its architects were those central decision makers, with Deng Xiaoping certainly foremost among them, who persisted in promoting all the major components of the reform strategy at once within China's institutions of higher learning.

Academic Reforms: Curriculum and Teaching Plans

One of the most interesting areas of academic reform, due to the clash of academic cultures it represents, is that of curriculum development and use. After the extreme decentralization of the early 1970s when universities prepared their own curricula and teaching materials—albeit on the basis of guidelines from above—the system was recentralized, standardized, and unified. The unified curricula specify which courses, both compulsory and elective, must be taught for each major; the sequence in which they are to be taught; and the number of hours per course. Syllabi further prescribe the content of each course. University administrators insisted in 1980 that these teaching plans, which were just then being reissued, would be used more flexibly than in the 1950s, when they were enforced "like the law."

The structure of Chinese higher education is still based on the Soviet pattern in which the arts and sciences are taught at the comprehensive universities with separate institutions responsible for other fields. Academic departments within each institution, in the early 1980s, still followed the Soviet pattern by offering a host of narrow specialties or majors. All of these were designed to fit specific job requirements and achieve ultimate fulfillment in the unified job assignment plan for college graduates.

No sooner had all the pieces of the old system been put back in place, however, than academic opinion makers such as Zhou Peiyuan began returning from their trips abroad with the news that China's system was too centralized and its curricula too dated, while courses were too narrowly defined and too rigidly presented. One possible solution being discussed in 1980 was to bring some of the specialized institutes back into the universities to create an American-style comprehensive university, which was the original model for many of China's pre-1949 institutions. But university administrators immediately vetoed this suggestion, protesting that any major expansion or merger was not feasible because of the logistical burdens caused by the self-contained cradle-to-grave services that China's socialist universities provided for the entire campus community. As a result, the merger idea could not be implemented.

The American credit system, previously criticized as a capitalist-style invention that reduces course work to commodity status, became an officially recommended antidote for the "fixed" and "dead" features of unified curricula and study plans. But in the early 1980s, the credit system was simply superimposed upon the fixed teaching plan, and students still had little freedom of choice among courses. About 70 percent of all courses in any given major remained compulsory as before, and some of the electives could be selected only from among a few fixed choices. Students were granted some new freedom to select a limited number of courses outside of their majors and even their own departments. But they could not study at their own pace, another declared aim, because to graduate out of turn would disrupt the predetermined enrollment and job assignment plans. Administrators at three universities where the credit system had been introduced by 1980 acknowledged that it could not fulfill its promise so long as the unified curricula, enrollment, and job assignment plans remained basically unchanged.

Another example of clashing academic cultures occurred when institutions were urged to exercise autonomy in upgrading their curricula. Faculty members at one medical school returned from their stay abroad in the mid-1980s with plans to improve the quality of diagnostic training, a well-known weak point in China's medical education. They set about introducing the necessary changes only to find that when the unified internal assessment examinations were given, based on the national unified medical college curriculum, their school plummeted from the top to the bottom of the national medical school rankings.

The Party's 1985 decision on education reform specifically granted to individual institutions "the power to readjust the objectives of various disciplines, formulate teaching plans and programs, and compile teaching materials."[7] But the decision did not suggest how contradictions between the institutions new powers and the centralized, planned system should be resolved. In fact, the solutions are being worked out on an ongoing trial-and-error basis.

A State Education Commission (SEDC) spokesman confirmed in an interview in late 1988 that the unified curricula had been abandoned "in principle" with the 1985 decision.[8] But he also confirmed that the narrow scope of all academic specialties or majors had been uniformly expanded and the number of specializations reduced, in deference to the criticism based on American experience that the old Soviet-style divisions were too limited in content. For example, the 740 engineering specialties in existence in 1985 have been expanded in scope and reduced in number to the present 255. Such details suggest that curriculum reform has been extensive but that it is still governed by central fiat.

The spokesman explained further that the overall structure of the national tertiary-level curriculum continues to be fixed by the center with particular attention paid to: the ratio of applied versus academic courses; the ratio of compulsory versus elective subjects

[7] *Renmin ribao,* May 29, 1985.

[8] References in this chapter to information from interviews in late 1988 or the winter of 1988–89 refer to a series of formal interviews and informal discussions I conducted during that time in Hong Kong, Beijing, and Guangzhou with Chinese university and education administrators and foreign academic consultants in China. Most interviewees spoke on the record for attribution at that time. But because of possible repercussions for these individuals in the post–June 4, 1989 Chinese political environment, which is very different from the one in which they spoke, I quote them throughout the chapter without, for the most part, identifying either the individuals or their work units. The exceptions are two interviews conducted in early December 1988 with the State Education Commission spokesman and members of the Guangdong Higher Education Bureau. Both were very formal, with questions and answers prepared in advance, and the resulting information was entirely uncontroversial. I also cite by name Beijing University President Ding Shisun, whom I interviewed in Hong Kong in October, because he only elaborated views already widely attributed to him in the Chinese press (as indicated in the notes below). I conducted these interviews and discussions while on temporary assignment for *The Chronicle of Higher Education* (Washington, D.C.). The *Chronicle,* of course, is not responsible for the way the material is presented in this monograph.

within courses; the content of politics courses; and the new extra-curricular "social practice" requirement introduced in 1987. Another interviewee described how a new economics syllabus intended for use in more than just one university was recently developed in the old way (but with new content) through coordinated planning, meetings, and consultations among leading economists.

Hence the nature of the autonomy actually enjoyed by the individual university, department, and faculty member responsible for offering the economics course or the prescribed and expanded engineering majors remains to be clarified. An administrator at one leading university insisted, in late 1988, that since 1979–80, when the unified curricula began to be reintroduced, his institution had not been subjected to any internal monitoring examinations designed to enforce uniform curricular requirements, such as that described for the medical school above. An administrator at another leading university said there was an SEDC evaluations committee but that he knew little of its work. Both claimed that their universities were devising their own curricula, coordinated by the individual academic departments and the faculty teaching-research groups within them. But both men also indicated that the national centralized curricula for different courses were being used "for reference"; that in the sciences much of the content was "required and essential" anyway, leaving little scope for individual input; and that the Soviet Union's contemporary natural sciences curricula should be adapted for use because they were "more rigorous" than their American counterparts.

Administrators at another provincial university noted that specialties could not be offered without SEDC approval, however great the local demand and profitability for the school. Also, they said, a large number of "basic" or required courses still had to be offered according to central specifications. The unified curriculum and teaching plans were still followed for such courses; schools were supposed to use them; and indeed, they were necessary to maintain quality and content requirements. However, the schools were also expected to supplement and update content as necessary. Such revisions were always coordinated by the departmental teaching-research groups and were something of a "problem" because they required extra training and additional work for the teachers. In recent years, said these administrators, many courses had also been added and subtracted, following SEDC demands to "modernize" the curriculum, all of which had entailed a similar kind of accom-

modation between central requirements and local effort. Such are
the current compromises, being worked out in practice, between the
"fixed," Soviet-style centralized curricula restored in 1980 and
some more flexible yet-to-be-determined alternative inspired by the
American example.

**Academic Reforms: The Unified College Entrance
Examinations**

The attempt to "decentralize" the national unified college entrance examinations has so far achieved equally uncertain results.
No sooner had these examinations been restored, in 1977, than the
critics moved into action. In this case, the critical impulses were as
much indigenous as externally inspired. From the latter came the
knowledge that China's examinations, with all their ponderous administrative procedures and old-fashioned methods, were an
anachronism in the modern world. Exchanges accordingly soon
commenced between the Education Ministry and the U.S. National
Testing Service in Princeton, New Jersey. But the strongest arguments were tied to the backlash against all the associated faults of
the keypoint stream—since passing the college entrance exams was
in practice its chief reason for existence.

So strong was the criticism by 1980 that educators in Fujian
Province refused to entertain any questions concerning the examinations. Fujian was then under investigation by the Ministry of
Education for having achieved the highest scores nationwide immediately after the examinations were restored. These scores raised
doubts about the efficacy of the exams, because the province was
not otherwise known for its educational attainments. The internal
chagrin deepened after the investigation concluded what Fujian
middle school teachers knew all along. The province had a relatively small number of keypoint middle schools located mainly in the
coastal towns. Cramming methods, conscientiously developed
along with the system itself in the early 1960s, were among the
most intense in the country. Given the small size of the system, its
methods were able to revive quickly as soon as the bans against
them lifted in 1976. And such methods were judged by Education
Ministry investigators to be responsible for the high scores achieved
by Fujian candidates, since their subsequent performance in college
was found to be no better than that of other students.

Education officials in Shanghai also tried to discourage questions
on the subject arguing that, as the national college entrance examinations were about to be abolished once more, any questions would

be of "historical" interest only. In fact, the questions are still relevant ten years later. But Shanghai officials also knew whereof they spoke. In 1984, it was announced that Shanghai would take the lead in an experiment aimed at decentralizing the process by allowing Shanghai students to take a set of locally prepared examinations. But the scores would then be used for the enrollment of the city's successful candidates not only in Shanghai institutions but in those throughout the country, as Shanghai candidates were assigned their places in accordance with the still unified national enrollment plans.[9]

The advantages of this reform were not immediately clear when the Shanghai experiment began in 1985, given the extensive examination procedure still involved. It has since been declared a success, however, and was scheduled as of early 1989 for extension nationwide "within three years more or less." The SEDC has announced that a new "examination yuan," or department, is to be established nationally with counterparts in each province to oversee implementation of this reform.[10]

The Shanghai experiment has progressed through several variations, and has yet to assume its final definitive form. By 1987, the procedure entailed a preliminary unified examination (*huikao*) for all graduating seniors in the city over a three-day period, during which they were examined in the usual subjects: politics, physics, chemistry, biology, history, and geography. Chinese, math, and a foreign language were still tested as part of the regular college entrance examinations (*gaokao*). A combined *huikao* and *gaokao* score was then used to determine enrollment. The ultimate aim, however, is to administer locally unified secondary school examinations as students complete the syllabus for each subject, rather than all at once at the end of the senior year. All students would be examined in all subjects, rendering unnecessary the current practice of dividing senior high school students into liberal arts and science streams in order to prepare for the college entrance examinations which are also divided in that way. This change is intended to promote all-around learning and discourage cramming. The scores from these locally prepared subject examinations are to be used for reference only. According to current thinking, the formal entrance

---

[9] See, for example, *Wenhuibao* (Shanghai), Sept. 28, 1984.

[10] *Zhongguo jiaoyu bao* (China Education News) (Beijing), Feb. 28, 1989; *Renmin ribao,* Nov. 21, 1988. These plans were reiterated by the SEDC in early 1990 (*Wenhuibao,* Hong Kong, Mar. 25, 1990, and *China Daily,* Mar. 26, 1990).

exam itself should ultimately include no more than three mandatory subjects (Chinese, math, foreign language) plus one or two subjects which candidates will select in accordance with their chosen future fields of study.

Educators in Guangzhou and Beijing were not optimistic about extending the Shanghai experiment nationwide, however, despite instructions they said the SEDC had issued to begin working toward that aim. The Shanghai experiment could succeed there, they explained, because the standards of its senior secondary schools are uniformly high. This they attributed to the city's unique environment as a compact, economically developed urban area. Elsewhere, teachers and methods vary widely, despite the unified national secondary school curriculum used by all. According to the conventional Chinese educator's way of thinking, these local variations necessitate the unification of standards at the elite level that only a national entrance examination containing exactly the same questions for everyone can provide. Yet whether the guarantee of quality is more important than the appearance of fairness is uncertain. In any event, the national examination is also regarded as a safeguard against the unfair advantages that favoritism and connections inevitably bring to the enrollment process. And even for Shanghai, the official interim assessment of the decentralization experiment could not help but cite the costs including the "relative disorder" it had introduced into the carefully restructured college preparatory regimen.[11]

Economic and Personnel Reforms

If effectively reforming the centralized system in matters such as curricula and entrance examinations has proved so complicated, then changes that touch people's economic and social interests directly in terms of incomes and careers must be even more so. The main reform-related issues, which were moving together onto a collision course by the mid-1980s, concerned: budgetary priorities; university financing; faculty incomes; the structure of the hastily expanded tertiary system; unified student enrollment and job assignment; free, state-subsidized higher education; and study abroad.

---

[11] According to a good summary of the experiment in *Zhongguo jiaoyu bao,* May 9, 1989; see also *Wenhuibao* (Shanghai), Aug. 5, 1985; Sept. 18, 1986; Dec. 27, 1986; April 19, 1987; May 19 and 31, 1987; and Aug. 15, 1987. *Zhongguo jiaoyu bao,* Dec. 27, 1986; and July 9, 1987.

Interwoven with almost all of these issues, moreover, was not so much an ideologically "conservative" undercurrent of resistance as a growing awareness in all quarters that at the tertiary level, too, the initial attempt to exclude the "interests" represented by the old critique of the regular system was creating tensions serious enough at some points to threaten the successful implementation of the reforms themselves. Also undermining that success, of course, was the overall impact of the economic reforms on the society as a whole.

Budgetary Priorities

After a 1983 tour of educational facilities in Jiangsu and Shanghai, Deng Xiaoping was quoted as saying that more money should be allocated to institutions of higher learning, "even at the expense of less distribution to the people."[12] The battle over budgetary priorities reflected in his comment erupted briefly into public view at the concurrent meetings of the National People's Congress (NPC) and the Chinese People's Political Consultative Congress (CPPCC) in 1987 and 1988. Conservative forces may have been rising within the CCP in 1987, but from the perspective of history, some of the speakers sounded more like latter-day successors of Liang Shuming and others who worried about an education system designed to promote the growth of an urban-based elite.

Beijing delegate Zhang Guoji, for example, complained at the April 1987 meeting of the NPC that the government's education budget was mostly spent in the urban areas. As a result of poor facilities and the lack of good teachers, students in the countryside had little access to schools of higher learning. Other delegates were also critical of the government's spending priorities, which they said favored the tertiary level.[13]

World Bank data for 1979 had shown China's spending proportionally low for primary and secondary education and high at the tertiary level, by comparison with other countries. This reproduced a spending pattern similar to that found by the League of Nations' Mission in 1931. But in the mid-1980s, that pattern fueled provin-

---

[12] Li Shangzhi, "Kaifa shiyi ren zhili de weida shiye" (The Great Enterprise of Developing the Intellectual Capacities of One Billion People), *Liaowang* (Outlook) (Beijing), June 20, 1983, p. 4; also *Beijing ribao,* June 16, 1983.

[13] Xinhua, English service, Beijing, April 3, 1987 in Foreign Broadcast Information Service (Washington D.C.), *Daily Report: China* (hereafter, FBIS, *Daily Report*), no. 064 (April 3, 1987), p. K-15; similar comments from other delegates are also summarized in *Renmin ribao,* April 2 and 3, 1987.

cial educators' complaints about specific investment priorities. Data compiled at the end of the Sixth Plan showed that for every 100 rmb spent on a college student in China, only 12 rmb was spent per student at the elementary and secondary levels combined. The allocation ratios of Japan, the United States, and the Soviet Union would have produced expenditures of 69, 39, or 30 rmb, respectively per student at the lower levels. Stated another way, Japan allocated 42 percent of its education budget for elementary schooling and only 13 percent to tertiary education. In Western European countries (Britain, West Germany, and France), the proportion was roughly 50 percent to 10 percent. In China, 31 percent of the education budget was spent at the lower level and 33 percent at the higher.[14]

In addition to spending patterns within the education sector, of course, delegates were also critical about the low level of funding overall. They pointed out that according to the Finance Minister's just issued budget report, state investment for education, health, and culture combined had increased at an annual rate of 15.2 percent during the Sixth Five-Year Plan, 1981–85. In 1986, investment in these areas had increased by 20 percent. But in 1987, because of financial difficulties, the increase (both combined and for education alone) was just over 2 percent, by comparison with the preceding year. Delegates complained that the increase was just sufficient to cover rising prices and support the additional numbers of college students due to be enrolled in 1987, which meant no real increases at all for the sector as a whole.[15]

As a measure of the limited increase in educational spending, the World Bank had found in 1979 that education accounted for only 6.6 percent of the central government's total expenditure (by comparison with about 15 percent in other countries generally, whether more or less developed). The projected increase for the Seventh Five-Year Plan, 1986–90, would bring the state education

---

[14] *China: Socialist Economic Development* (Washington, D.C.: The World Bank, 1983), 3:180–85; Yang Jinfa, "Woguo puji jiunianzhi yiwu jiaoyu de youli tiaojian, buli yinsu ji duice chuyi" (My Humble Opinion Concerning Our Country's Beneficial Conditions for Universalizing Nine-Year Compulsory Education and Ways to Deal with the Nonbeneficial Factors), *Jiaoyu lilun yu shijian* (Theory and Practice of Education) (Taiyuan, Shanxi), 7:2 (1987):27.

[15] Xinhua, English (Beijing), April 3, 1987; Xinhua, English, March 28, 1987, in *Summary of World Broadcasts* (hereafter, *SWB*), British Broadcasting Corporation, Reading, England, FE/8538/BII/8, April 9, 1987; on the budget report itself, see *Renmin ribao*, March 27, 1987.

budget up to 10.40 percent of its total expenditure. Such comparative development figures have been used repeatedly by Chinese educators throughout the 1980s to bolster their general demands for greater public investment in education.[16]

Taking cover under the demand for a more generous state education budget overall, the tertiary level struck back in 1988 as if to rebut the 1987 arguments against spending priorities that were short-changing the lower levels. Delegates turned the question of education budgets and especially financing for higher education into one of the main issues discussed at the NPC and CPPCC meetings. Commenting on the ensuing wave of publicity, a Beijing professor active in CPPCC affairs said during an interview the following winter that academic delegates had decided in advance to make an issue of education funding at the 1988 meetings. The aim was "to change attitudes in society and among the leaders," since many were not in favor of more money for education.

During the spring 1988 meetings, the comments of Beijing University President Ding Shisun in particular created something of a sensation both because of their candor in criticizing official policies and because of the unusually widespread coverage his remarks received in the official press. "Some people ask me whether as Beijing University president I fear student protests," he said, "but I answer that what I fear most is not having enough money." He lashed out, among other things, at the recent "blind" effort to increase tertiary enrollments, saying it was one reason for the shortage of funds. He argued that billions of dollars used to build new colleges and universities would have produced better results had they been allocated instead to existing institutions.[17]

---

[16] *China: Socialist Economic Development,* pp. 180–85; Yang Jinfa, "Woguo puji jiunianzhi yiwu jiaoyu de youli tiaojian," pp. 25–29; also, for example, Qian Jiaju, "Ba zhili touzi fang zai diyiwei" (Place Investment in Intelligence in First Place), *Jiaoyu yanjiu* (Education Research), no. 11 (1982), pp. 24–28; Liu Rongcang, "Shilun woguo de jiaoyu touzi zhanlue" (A Discussion of Our Country's Educational Investment Strategy), *Fujian luntan* (Fujian Forum), no. 5 (1982), pp. 18–22; Wang Shanmai, "Woguo jiaoyu touzi bili de lishi fenxi" (A Historical Analysis of Our Country's Educational Investment Ratios), *Beijing shifan daxue xuebao* (Beijing Teachers Training University Journal), no. 5 (1987), pp. 66–75.

[17] *Zhongguo qingnian bao* (China Youth News) (Beijing), April 5, 1988. Professor Ding's comments at this time were also reported in *Guangming ribao,* March 29, 1988; Zhongguo xinwen she (China News Service) (Beijing), April 5, 1988, in *Zhongguo xinwen* (China News) (daily bulletin edited by China News Service, Hong Kong branch), April 6, 1988, p. 4; Xinhua, English, March 20, 1988, in *SWB,* FE/0110 B2/7, March 26, 1988; *China Daily,* April 13, 1988.

The 1987 and 1988 offensives together with their claims and
counterclaims raise more questions than they answer. Were institutions of higher learning, especially the elite schools among them,
merely trying to hold on to their gains against the 1987 challenge?
Or did President Ding and his allies really expect to win substantial
increases in their state-allocated budgets?

Several months later Ding Shisun explained, during an interview
in Hong Kong, that he was an active proponent of increased
government funding, which he viewed as the only real way of solving the problems he faced. To support his case, he pointed out that
all 36 of the universities under the direct control of the
SEDC—which include the most important of China's 90-plus formally designated keypoint institutions of higher learning—are allocated funds at the same rate of 1,800 rmb per student, per year.
Yet some provincial universities, he said, receive annual allocations
as well as supplements from their localities that bring their total as
high as 2,300 rmb per student. Professor Ding argued that this was
unfair. Hence his demand that the centrally controlled key institutions be granted larger state appropriations in order to support the
higher standards they were supposed to maintain. He said, with
reference to the proposed introduction of tuition fees, that Chinese
students would not be able to pay at rates high enough to do more
than supplement university funds. He regarded the university's
self-earned income in the same light.

He also indicated, however, that the efforts of the education lobby were beginning to bear fruit. He told Hong Kong journalists
that central leaders were now thinking more realistically about education and its budgetary constraints. He also revealed that a top-
level working group was set up after the spring NPC meetings. The
new group, headed by SEDC Minister Li Tieying, was preparing a
comprehensive ten-year development plan for education to cover all
levels, including teachers' working conditions, salaries, and possible
legislation to guarantee funding. The plan was to be debated at the
next plenary session of the Party's Central Committee in 1989.[18]
The SEDC spokesman interviewed in December 1988 confirmed all
of these developments. But he denied the accuracy of the above-
cited 1987 figures that showed a continuation of traditional spending patterns favoring the tertiary level. He reiterated the official

[18] *Hong Kong Standard,* Oct. 22 and 29, 1988; *South China Morning Post,* Oct.
25, 1988; *Mingbao (Ming Pao Daily News)* (Hong Kong), Oct. 27, 1988.

figures, insisting that higher education's share of the total education budget was no more than 20 percent.

Yet when the new budget for 1989 was announced, the increase in education expenditure over the preceding year was only a modest 15.4 percent, probably not sufficient to cover the cost of inflation. Nor was there any indication of a larger share for the tertiary sector. Austerity measures necessary to curb inflation meant across-the-board reductions in expenditure, noted Premier Li Peng, in his annual government work report. His message to the education lobby was clear: their sector had been favored in 1989 as one of the few not to suffer cutbacks. "Under the current circumstances where state finance is short of funds," said Li, "the government has done its best."[19] And by the time the next CCP plenum finally met in June, the education development plan was the last thing on anyone's mind. The main concerns instead were the latest round in the Party power struggle and the suppression of "counter-revolutionary" student rebels.

University Funding and Faculty Incomes

The rhetoric over budgetary priorities also obscured certain questions about university financing and faculty incomes. Only one point was clear by the end of the 1980s, namely, the general resentment within the academic community against the direct and indirect impact of the market-oriented economic reforms on the academic community's way of life and work.

Despite the initial excitement at the prospect of trying to reform China's socialist economy by mixing it with elements of Western capitalism, public confidence in the ability of the experiment to produce positive results was badly shaken by 1988. Inflation was then officially estimated at about 20 percent. In addition, pervasive corruption, food hoarding including that of rice and salt, panic buying of consumer durables, industrial and rural unrest, bank runs, and student discontent were all acknowledged in the official Chinese news media during 1988. This particular combination of the indicators associated with political and economic collapse had not occurred in so concentrated a form since the last years of Guomindang rule in the late 1940s. Although not comparable in degree, the similarities in kind with that gone-but-not-forgotten era probably did as much to undermine confidence as the problems themselves. In October, a two-year austerity program aimed at curbing

---

[19] Beijing radio, March 20, 1989, in *SWB*, FE/0416 C1/9, March 23, 1989.

the worst consequences of economic mismanagement was announced. This was the context within which Li Peng's above-cited
advice to the education lobby was made in early 1989, and the
shoals against which its escalating demands for more funds were
dashed.

Education Minister Li Tieying had been more forthright in his
remarks to a gathering of university leaders held at Beidaihe the
previous summer in the midst of the developing economic crisis.
Li was reported to have said that "all the contradictions in developing education are closely related with changes in the economic system," and that "we must extricate education from the influence of
the commodity economy." Li mentioned specifically the problems
of funding and low teachers' salaries.[20]

The most important indirect impact of the economic changes on
education came in the form of inflation—causing some to claim
that the real value of budgets and incomes had actually declined as
a result. One report from Shaanxi illustrates the problem. Speaking at a provincial higher education conference in July, Governor
Hou Zongbin said that investment at the tertiary level had risen
each year throughout the past decade. But calculated against the
provincial price index, 42.8 percent of the increase was written off
to rising costs. This inflation plus the quantitative growth of higher
education meant that actual spending per student had declined over
that time.[21]

Educators throughout the country were voicing the same complaint. But in order to make ends meet, they must rely on their
own money-making endeavors. As one of the direct applications to
academia of the market-oriented economic reforms, universities are
encouraged to supplement their state budgets in this way, with the
proceeds shared out in the form of individual and collective
benefits. In 1980, shortly after it was first raised, this suggestion
seemed to be regarded indulgently as a marginal means of bolster-
ing welfare and bonus funds. A few years later, Shanghai's Jiaotong
University was promoted as a national model for tertiary-level
economic reform especially, in order to overcome just such "inertia." The university's teachers, students, and foreign professors were

[20] Xinhua, Chinese, Aug. 23, 1988, in ibid., FE/0241 B2/5, Aug. 27, 1988. Li
Tieying's remarks were reported rather differently in the *People's Daily* version (*Renmin ribao*, Aug. 24, 1988).

[21] Xian, Shaanxi, provincial radio, July 15, 1988, in *SWB*, FE/0211 B2/3, July
23, 1988.

praised for being "all full of enthusiasm in their pursuit of the profit motive."[22] By 1988–89, prices had risen so dramatically that universities could not survive without added sources of income, since their budgets had not increased proportionally with inflation. Under these circumstances, the profit motive became a necessity but enthusiasm did not develop accordingly.

Beijing University, for example, was making up about one-fourth the cost of educating each undergraduate from its own earnings but still lacked enough funds to improve austere campus facilities. Income-earning activities included research services and consulting, sponsored mainly by individual academic departments. The proceeds were being used to supplement faculty salaries.[23]

What has aroused the most ire, however, is the government's continuing insistence that individuals must augment their inflation-eroded personal incomes in this way as well. Educators everywhere have responded that taking a second job cannot but damage the main tasks of teaching and research. Nevertheless, the call to perform "paid services for society" was reiterated in Premier Li Peng's formal government work report to the 1988 NPC and personally endorsed by Party leader Zhao Ziyang as well. This provoked "heated discussions" among delegates and a satirical demonstration by a handful of student protestors who gathered outside the congress meeting hall in Tiananmen Square offering to shine delegates' shoes.

One Beijing professor declared emphatically during an interview that "people outside academia raised moonlighting" as a solution and maintained that few teachers favored the practice. President Ding agreed that most faculty members were against it and concurred with the majority opinion. He was therefore experimenting

---

[22] Wu Jiayu, "Shanghai jiaotong daxue de gaige" (The Reform of Shanghai Jiaotong University), *Zhengming* (Contending) (Hong Kong), no. 79 (May 1984), pp. 29–31. Jiaotong's experience was extensively publicized in the Chinese press during 1983 and 1984 and compiled in Shanghai jiaotong daxue dangwei bangongshi (Shanghai Jiaotong University Party Committee Office), ed., *Shanghai jiaotong daxue guanli gaige chutan* (Preliminary Inquiry into the Management Reforms at Shanghai Jiaotong University) (Shanghai: Shanghai Jiaotong daxue chubanshe, 1984).

[23] For some detailed figures on state allocation and self-earned income at Beijing Agricultural University, see Robert Delfs, "Brighter Means Poorer," *Far Eastern Economic Review,* June 16, 1988, pp. 34, 36. The Beijing University figure was cited by Ding Shisun during the October interview in Hong Kong and also by the university's Party secretary (*Guangming ribao,* March 24, 1988).

with a more rational division of labor whereby some teachers, if willing, can stop teaching and devote themselves full-time to financial management for the university or the various income-earning activities at the departmental level.

While many share his sentiments, not everyone can follow his example, however, due to the different kinds of money-making expedients to which they have turned. One university official in Guangzhou explained that, unlike Qinghua, which is now running its factories for profit, or Beijing University, which can rely on contracted research, some 70 percent of his school's extra income had to come from selling its teaching services. These profit-making projects included correspondence courses, refresher courses, adult evening classes, a two-year technical training program, and programs enrolling different kinds of tuition-paying, enterprise-sponsored students. Hence it would be impossible to apply Ding Shisun's division of labor principle to the faculty's various endeavors.

Ironically, given all the talk about money, the question people seem least willing to answer is how much they actually earn. This question is related to a second, concerning whether the academic community's grievances are relative or absolute. One university spokesman in Beijing claimed he could not answer these questions on grounds that the information was "like a state secret" and "not for outsiders." He scoffed when he heard that a Qinghua University briefing had provided figures claiming 120 rmb per month as the average teacher's salary, to which was added an average monthly bonus supplement of 66 rmb for 1988. The bonus represents the share-out from the university and departmental ventures. "They're lying," he said. "That's just what they tell outsiders!" And how did he know? "Because that bonus figure is the same as ours, and they must be earning more than we do!"

For Beijing University, however, President Ding provided similar figures. In 1987, the average annual bonus supplement was 600 rmb per person. The actual amount varies from department to department. The highest annual supplement in 1987 was over 1,000 rmb per person in Computer Sciences and the lowest, only 200 rmb in the History Department. Independent academic visitors to Beijing University reported similar figures. One estimated a 100-rmb monthly bonus supplement in the Economics Department for 1987. Another visitor reported half that amount in geography.

A third visitor with knowledge of Beijing University's nonteaching research personnel—the university has a total of sixteen research institutes—told a different story. She reported that as of 1988 staff in areas of research with little practical application, and therefore little extra earning power, were actually borrowing money regularly from the university to make ends meet, without expectation on either side that the money would ever be returned. She described the economic problems of Beida's research personnel as great and their situation as "very bitter." Because of it, she said, the university was now blaming the old Soviet model that had separated teaching from research. A plan was therefore being considered to give the research institutes some teaching responsibilities. Some of Beijng University's budgetary allocation from the state of 1,800 rmb per student per year could then be shared with the research institutes.

The above-cited provincial university in Guangzhou, which earned most of its extra income from tuition and fees for its teaching services, was able to guarantee its faculty members an average monthly bonus of at least 50 rmb in 1988, and some departments were able to pay over 80 rmb. Nonteaching administrative staff received 40- to 50-rmb monthly bonuses. But bonus figures that can be aggregated in this way represent remunerated work either organized by the university or at least reported by the individual. Rules require that a specified percentage of the income earned for work done primarily by individuals is supposed to be turned over to the university or department to become part of the collective distribution fund. For this reason, explained the Guangzhou official, actual income figures on his campus really are a "secret," because much of the moonlighting done independently by faculty members goes unreported.

To the question of whether the academic community's grievances are relative or absolute, he replied that "the standard of living for teachers is not lower than before, but it is not necessarily better either." He went on to explain that the livelihood of a few had definitely improved, but, customs being what they are, such people hated to admit it and continued to complain about their poverty. And everyone, of course, resented the inflation. Someone else answered this question by describing the lives of academic friends in Beijing. A middle-aged middle-income lecturer there earning 122 rmb per month with a 50-rmb supplement would not be able to support a family of three at today's prices without a second income in the family, he said. Faculty pay scales in Beijing range from 70 rmb per moth for a beginning assistant lecturer to 360 rmb for a full professor.

Probably as much as absolute hardship or rising prices, however, university intellectuals resent the relative devaluation of their status in an increasingly materialistic society. Comparative pay scales are a favorite topic of conversation, and everyone has a favorite example. One Beijing college teacher explained how a secondary school dropout working as a waiter in a joint-venture hotel—where the 40-rmb basic wage can be supplemented by up to 200 rmb in bonuses per month—earns as much as a middle-aged college teacher with over ten years' seniority. A university vice-president in Beijing also acknowledged that his grievance was relative. He said he thought it was wrong that both he and his driver earned the same, approximately 400 rmb per month. A Shenzhen University full professor felt similarly chagrined to learn that his salary was the same as that of his son, who was just out of college and working at his first job with a joint venture company in the Special Economic Zone.

Scarcity and the Structure of Higher Education

Whether the deprivations are relative or absolute, higher education lobbyists have grown ever more insistent in demanding more funds. Their determination led them ultimately to a natural target in the quantitative growth of the tertiary level during the past decade. Ding Shisun thus slipped easily into the old regularization mode as he elaborated his arguments calling for more funding at the top of the pyramid while criticizing the quantitative expansion of higher education as a whole. He said he no longer agrees with the advice China received a decade ago about maintaining a national college enrollment of two million. He changed his view on this question only in recent years, after he saw the inappropriate fit between the large numbers of college graduates being produced at a time when the greatest economic growth was occurring in small-scale county enterprises. "Such industries," said Professor Ding, "need intermediate-level technicians, not university graduates." Having rediscovered the classic dilemma between economic and educational development, he began advocating a smaller cohort of college students and arguing at the same time that funds saved on quantity could be used to improve quality at the keypoint level.

The political cost of this solution, however, is the admission of having too precipitously accepted the advice of Western development experts back in 1980, without adequately adapting it to Chinese conditions. Perhaps this is one reason why Chinese education leaders have recently grown much more circumspect, as some consultants observed in late 1988, about accepting direct foreign advice. Without acknowledging these costs, the Education Commission spokesman interviewed at the same time nevertheless emphasized the need to adapt higher education more closely to the developing needs of Chinese society. He recalled that this problem was first formally recognized at the 1983 national higher education work conference and had been the subject of increasing reform efforts since 1985.[24] The structure of the newly restored system of higher education was inappropriately designed, he explained, producing too many four-year graduates in the general sciences, both social and natural, and not enough of the intermediate-level technicians for which there was the greatest need. According to the statistics he provided, China's tertiary institutions totaled 1,063 by the end of 1988. Of that number, 695 offered primarily four- or five-year regular undergraduate programs. The remainder specialized in shorter courses at the junior college level. The new aim being promoted by the SEDC was to continue restructuring higher education until a one-to-one ratio had been achieved, that is, until the number of regular four-year college students was at least equaled by those in two-year post-secondary programs.

Underlying the spokesman's detached assessment, of course, lay all the endemic strains of twentieth-century China's educational development—banished from consideration when the system was being rebuilt in the late 1970s, but now returning inexorably to haunt everyone once more. University administrators, on the frontline as they are of this reemerging dilemma, have been considerably less clinical. For them the dilemma translates not only into insufficient funds, but also into the increasing difficulties they face each summer in placing the annual crop of graduating seniors. These difficulties have, moreover, now been exacerbated by the additional reform, described below, aimed at "allowing" graduates to find their own jobs.

At a Beijing college in December 1988, one elderly vice-president elaborated on the now universally acknowledged "contradiction between supply and demand," or the surfeit of college graduates trained for jobs that do not exist, while the needs of "basic level" and rural work units for trained personnel go unmet. But he ignored the official explanation of too many college students

---

[24] Coincidentally, it was also in 1985 that the SEDC was formed and the current premier, "conservative" Li Peng, began his two-year term as the commission's first head.

in an improperly structured tertiary system. Instead, he blamed the restructured system at the secondary level and the social origins of the students it is designed to serve. "This problem of job assignments for students is directly related to the problem of students' background and origins," he said. "All college students now originate from urban senior middle schools, and it is only the children of cadres and intellectuals who can go to college." Because of their origins, he said, his students all wanted provincial jobs at least and were not interested in openings at the county level or below, where needs were now greatest.

On the Beijing University campus itself, one middle-ranking official eschewed this controversial view with all its ties to the radical critique of the past. But she still, in effect, threw up her hands over the related headaches. "We can no longer keep up with the state's reforms," she said, explaining how difficult it had become to place their graduates in philosophy, history, and Chinese especially. After 1978, Beijing University graduates could realistically expect the best job assignments in the country. Today, she continued, such jobs are already taken. Meanwhile, "basic level" work units such as factories, middle schools, and county offices all needed trained people but Beijing University graduates still maintained the old expectations. Chinese majors were naturally dissatisfied at the prospect of a clerical job in some county enterprise office for which they lacked the necessary secretarial skills in any case.

The universities had therefore been ordered to reduce enrollments in specialties for which there were fewer job openings and to improve their graduates' "adaptability." As a result, Beijing University in 1988 was trying once again to "meet the needs of society." Officials had decided against the controversial decision announced during the fall semester, 1988, by Zhongshan University in Guangzhou to make all undergraduates take a qualifying examination at the end of their second year. Those who "fail" are to be mustered out as two-year post-secondary graduates. Anticipating too great a protest from parents, Beijing University has been searching for other expedients. One is a new "secretarial class" run by the Chinese Department to produce graduates with clerical skills. Another is to require students majoring in foreign languages such as Spanish and Japanese to study English as well in order to enhance their "adaptability."

Enrollment, Tuition, and Job Assignment Reforms

Guangdong's institutions of higher learning were thrust into the unaccustomed glare of national publicity in early 1988, when the SEDC gave them a specific pioneering task. They were assigned to introduce the new package of enrollment, tuition, and job assignment reforms from the beginning of the 1988–89 academic year. Few reforms illustrate better than these the complexities involved in trying to introduce elements of Western-style capitalism into China's centralized socialist system. Following the general trends in the economy, the aims of this package of reforms are (1) to abolish free higher education; (2) to change the centralized system of enrollment whereby students are admitted to all institutions of higher learning throughout the country each year in accordance with a unified plan drawn up by the central and provincial governments, which stipulates in minute detail the number of students to be enrolled from each province, into each school, and into every academic major within it; and (3) to break the job assignment plans whereby all college students are assigned jobs by the state upon graduation.

That a full decade has passed since the old Ministry of Education first announced, in 1979–80, the intention to implement these reforms is testimony to the obstacles that have prolonged their introduction. Higher education has been wholly state-supported since the early 1950s, when the enrollment and job assignment plans also went into effect. Enrollment and job assignment procedures underwent radical change in the early 1970s, but some version of the plans themselves remained. The entire system was then restored in the late 1970s. Guangdong was selected to lead the way in 1988 because the task represented another direct application to the tertiary sector of the market-oriented economic reforms, tolerance for which is reputedly greatest in that province.

According to officials interviewed at the Guangdong bureau of Higher Education in late 1988, the province's tertiary institutions had been directed to begin collecting tuition from freshmen students for the fall semester that year. When these same students graduated, two to four years later depending on their study programs, the state job assignment plan would not apply to them. They would be responsible for finding employment on their own. These changes would then be applied to each new entering class until they were extended to all college students in Guangdong Province by the 1991–92 academic year. This same set of reforms would then be extended in the autumn of 1989 to freshmen in the

36 institutions administered directly by the SEDC. All other terti- ary institutions throughout the country were to introduce these re- forms for their first-year students by the start of the 1990–91 academic year.[25] As of fall semester 1989, the introduction of tui- tion was still proceeding on schedule despite the economic and pol- itical crises that had intervened since it was announced in early 1988. Job assignment reform appears not to have survived so well, as will be indicated below, but its fate remains unclear in part due to the phased timetable for the package as a whole.

Thus with the job assignment phase still two to four years dis- tant, tuition was the chief concern in Guangdong during the 1988 fall semester. The province introduced tuition at the rate of 100 rmb to 150 rmb per semester per student (at the late-1988 official exchange rate: US$1 = 3.72 rmb). The actual amount charged varies depending on the academic major. Guangdong institutions of higher learning have also begun charging incidental fees to help defray dormitory and utility costs at the rate of 20 rmb to 30 rmb per semester per student. Tuition and fees are retained by the insti- tution. These expenses are added to those for food, books, and in- cidentals, which in Guangdong amount to about 100 rmb per stu- dent per month.

The national student-stipend scheme began to be phased out in 1979–80 (when the cost of food per month for one student was less than 20 rmb). University officials at that time explained this as a preliminary step intended to prepare the public concerned for the eventual end of free higher education. Nevertheless, that step—changing the egalitarian distribution system and introducing merit scholarships—provoked anger as a move inspired by "foreign" ways that would add to the burdens of poorer students. Even in Guangdong, students were still debating the inequities of this reform when its next phase, the student loan program, was in- troduced in the mid-1980s. The subsidies were replaced for most students in 1986–87 by state-financed loans, which in Guangdong Province are currently limited to 400 rmb per student per year.

---

[25] The public announcement of this timetable appeared in *Zhongguo qingnian bao,* Jan. 2, 1988, for the nation as a whole; *Nanfang ribao* (Southern Daily) (Guang- zhou), April 18, May 13, 1988, and June 23, 1988, for Guangdong province; *Wenhuibao* (Shanghai) April 27, 1988, for Guangdong and Shanghai. This timetable was confirmed by the officials interviewed at the Guangdong Bureau of Higher Edu- cation in early December, 1988. The following discussion of tuition reform is based primarily on that interview.

Among those exempt are students at teacher training and national minorities institutes, who continue to receive a monthly cost-of-living allowance.[26]

The Guangdong officials claimed that as the tuition rates were low, everyone could afford them without too much difficulty. They had been concerned, they said, about a possible negative reaction from students and parents. But their fears did not materialize. They cited comparative provincial application statistics for 1987 and 1988 to support the conclusion that "tuition reform has been accepted here."

One obstacle Guangdong had to overcome, however, was that presented by "out-of-state" students. The initial apprehension among Guangdong educators was reinforced by the hue and cry raised in other parts of the country after the SEDC announced the reform timetable. As noted in the preceding chapter, that reaction led to substantially reduced applications at the senior secondary level in many places, including Beijing. The Guangdong officials claimed that adverse reaction had been due to a "misunderstanding" about how much money parents would have to pay. Many thought they would be responsible for full tuition fees, which are 500 rmb or more per semester. In recent years, tertiary institutions everywhere have been allowed to enroll a small proportion of "self-financed" (*zifei*) students, who can pay at that full rate in return for admission with somewhat lower examinations scores than the norm. Fees paid for students by their future work units (called *daipei,* or sponsored students) are even higher, and both categories are often said to be enrolled "outside the plan," although there are restrictions limiting the size of each category. The initial announce-

---

[26] This paragraph on the ten-year effort to begin phasing out free tertiary education is based on my own conversations with university officials in 1980 (see n. 1) and at Zhongshan University, Guangzhou, in October 1985; plus, *Yangcheng wanbao* (Guangzhou Evening News), May 17, 1985; *Zhongguo jiaoyu bao,* Feb. 22, 1986; *Jiaoyu wenzhai* (Education Digest) (Beijing), Aug. 20, 1984, and April 13, 1986; Li Yongzeng, "Zhongguo gaodengjiaoyu de yixiang zhongyao gaige" (An Important Reform for China's Higher Education), *Liaowang zhoukan* (Outlook Weekly), overseas edition, no. 33 (Aug. 18, 1986), pp. 16–17; *Zhejiang ribao* (Zhejian Daily News) (Hangzhou), Jan. 27, 1987; *Beijing ribao,* May 18, 1987; *Liangyong rencai bao* (Dual Purpose Personnel News), (Chengdu Military District, Political Department), April 21, 1987; *Guangming ribao,* Aug. 8, 1987; Liu Zhongde, "Jiji erh wentuo di tuijin renmin zhuxuejin zhidu de gaige" (Carry Out the Reform of the Peoples Stipend System Actively But Reasonably), *Zhongguo gaodeng jiaoyu* (Chinese Higher Education) (Beijing), no. 9 (1987), pp. 2–3.

ments from the SEDC used the same "outside the plan" terminology without specifying what rates regular students would have to pay under the new rules.

Concern about the outside reaction was so great that Guangdong exempted ordinary out-of-province freshmen from the tuition reform in 1988. According to official statistics, of the total 42,739 freshmen who entered tertiary institutions in Guangdong for the fall semester 1988, 17,810 were enrolled from other provinces. In addition to this group, 13,332 or 53 percent of the total 24,929 in-state freshmen also fell into a variety of tuition-exempt categories. These last, which reflect the priorities and prejudices of Chinese society, represent a second major obstacle to the full implementation of the new tuition and job assingment reforms.

In recognition of this obstacle, the SEDC has directed that college students should, for the purpose of these reforms, be divided into two basic enrollment categories. One is the "directed" or state-assigned plan (*zhilingxing jihua*). The other is the more flexible "guided" plan (*zhidaoxing jihua*). Students enrolled under the state-directed plan will generally be exempt from paying tuition, and their other expenses will be largely state-subsidized. But in return, they must agree to major in one of several unpopular specialties, enrollment plans for which are typically difficult to fill. They must also accept a state-assigned job in the area for which they have been trained. Other students, under the guided plan, will be responsible for their own tuition and living expenses and for repaying any loans incurred. But they will be free to apply for enrollment in more popular specialties that train for better-paying and more prestigious careers, and they will find employment on their own after graduation.

The division, in other words, tries to obtain the best of both worlds. The centralized socialist state plan fulfilled at least two functions that, for the time being at least, cannot be performed by the more flexible alternative. The two functions are (1) allowing students from poorer families to attend college and (2) guaranteeing enrollments in essential specialties that, admitted one Guangdong official, "no one wants to study."

At present, he explained, those fields include teacher training, agriculture, water conservancy, geology, petroleum engineering, and mining. Students in the nationalities institutes, which train for work among China's ethnic minorities, are also included in the state-directed plan. So too are a small number, about 5 percent of the total college enrollment in Guangdong, who are enrolled from border and mountain regions under contractual arrangements (called *dingxiang*) between the school and the locality, to which the students must return after graduation. All of these categories will be included in the "directed" plan. The numbers to be enrolled, the localities from which they are enrolled, and where they are to study will all continue to be fixed by central and provincial planners in essentially the same way as has been done for all students until now.

The formula for enrolling in other fields is still being worked out, but the aim is to allow individual institutions to devise their own enrollment plans based on their capabilities and the economy's needs. These plans they will determine by themselves, but in coordination with general guidelines drawn up by the central and provincial authorities. The example to be followed is that currently used to enroll the wholly self-financed students and those sponsored by their future work units. Guidelines limit the number of students that can be enrolled in these two categories. Guangdong Province also stipulates the annual minimum fees that must be charged for each (1,200 rmb for self-financed students and 3,000 rmb for *daipei* students). The aim is gradually to reduce the number of students enrolled under the directed plan and increase those in the more flexible category. And within the latter, the aim is further to increase the numbers of wholly self-financed and sponsored students.

The reasons for the ambivalent assessment of the experiment given by Guangdong officials at the end of its first semester seem clear. On the one hand, they were able to introduce "the idea," as they said, of tuition for ordinary college students without any great negative reaction. In addition, Guangdong boasts one of the highest proportions of wholly self-financed and sponsored students in the country. Yet even in Guangdong, this particular reform package was still in a very preliminary stage. Negative reaction elsewhere in combination with local needs meant that the majority of freshmen in Guangdong tertiary institutions were exempted from tuition for the 1988–89 year. In order to be accepted at all, the tuition rates also had to be kept so low that they could contribute but marginally to the overall costs of a college education calculated on the average at 24,000 rmb for a four-year undergraduate course in Guangdong.

The division of students into two separate enrollment plans was also just beginning. Hence, the distinctions that were, according to the new regulations, supposed to separate tuition-paying and tuition-exempt students were not yet clearly drawn. For example, some students in fields that belonged in the directed plan actually paid tuition, while others in the guided category did not. Administrators anticipated that "social contradictions" will appear when and if the distinctions between the categories are more precisely defined in practice. This is because the categories will exacerbate distinctions already evident between more and less advantaged students in terms of their study and employment opportunities. Guangdong officials were thus cautious in their conclusions that while they had succeeded in introducing tuition, any definitive verdict on their work was still "premature."

Similarly, in Beijing at one of the 36 universities scheduled to introduce tuition for freshmen in 1989, an official was openly negative. He declared that this reform had been forced upon them by the SEDC and that university personnel "were all against it," even after the clarification on the amounts to be paid. They calculated that since college students were primarily the children of intellectuals and cadres (a majority of whom were actually in the middle income category), most of one person's monthly income in such a family would be required to pay tuition and support a child in college. Beijing officials nevertheless indicated at the start of the 1989–90 academic year that the timetable for implementing the tuition reform would proceed as scheduled.[27]

Job Assignment in Transition

If the verdict on tuition was still premature at the end of 1988, that for job assignment reform was in a state of temporary suspension. The initial furor over tuition may have been due to a misunderstanding, but the same could not be said for that over job assignments, which comprised the other half of the package announced at the start of the year. Anxieties had, in fact, already been aroused by several years of experimental application.

Under the old job assignment system, as it was restored in the late 1970s, central and provincial authorities drew up the employment plans each year. Schools, and more specifically the CCP organizations within them, then assigned their graduates to fill the

---

[27] Although published details remain scarce, a SEDC spokesman in Beijing confirmed the continuation of this reform in a telephone interview with a Hong Kong newspaper on September 5 (*Hong Kong Standard*, Sept. 6, 1989); see also *Zhongguo jiaoyu bao*, Aug. 12, 1989; *Guangming ribao*, Aug. 15, 1989; *China Daily*, Aug. 16, 1989; and specifically for Shanghai, Zhongguo xinwen she (Shanghai), Aug. 10, 1989, in *Zhongguo xinwen* (Hong Kong), Aug. 11, 1989, p. 7.

slots, more-or-less sight unseen, although there was some margin for maneuver on both sides. The objective for the future, according to the SEDC's above-mentioned timetable, is that by the mid-1990s the state employment plan will be used to place only a minority of China's college students as necessary for the hard-to-fill occupational quotas. Most graduates will by then be responsible for finding their own employment, a change that it is hoped will mean a more rational allocation of talent. "In principle," that aim has been widely applauded by all concerned. The question is how to achieve it.

Qinghua University in Beijing was one of the first to pioneer this new approach a few years ago, according to the SEDC spokesman interviewed in December 1988. But what was a relatively smooth transition for graduates of the country's leading institute of science and technology has now developed into a nationwide experiment of great complexity, he said. The first indication of that complexity occurred in 1985, when only 24 percent of that year's graduating seniors were allocated jobs by the state according to the old system. The others were allowed to follow more flexible arrangements. College graduates immediately demonstrated that they would rather remain temporarily unemployed, which many chose to do, than accept some assignments. Or, as one account explained, the experiment "did not ensure that key industries and government units, especially those in remote and backward regions, receive much-needed graduates." The report did not indicate whether the outlying regions and unpopular professions had offered monetary incentives as authorized by the Party's 1985 education decision. But a majority of seniors (69 percent) graduating in 1986 had to accept state-assigned jobs to make up for the shortfall the year before.[28]

China's university students appear to have responded overwhelmingly to the new official line about developing one's talents and using them in good, well-paying jobs. Unfortunately, there are not enough such opportunities waiting each year for all the graduates who aspire to them. Chinese educators saw the new values and rising aspirations, checkmated by the lack of attractive job openings, as major reasons for the low student morale that became increasingly evident on many campuses including some of the nation's best during the 1980s. Cheating on examinations, without

---

[28] *China Daily,* July 23, 1986.

fear of reprimand, was commonly reported as a symptom of the new malaise. A division similar to that reported at the secondary level developed: between students who by reason of their personal circumstances (school, major, and family connections) could look forward to bright futures in terms of employment prospects or overseas study; and students in less favorable circumstances. Among the latter there arose the new "study is useless theory" (*dushu wuyong lun*), not heard on Chinese campuses since the pre-1976 era when the prevailing political criteria were blamed for the phenomenon. Students a decade later claimed they were doing just enough to get by because they knew their school performance would have little influence on their future prospects, which were not very bright in any case.

Against the background of this experience, the SEDC nevertheless pushed ahead with its tuition and job assignment reform package in early 1988. When the popular *China Youth News* printed a critical comment from a reader, it prompted 1,361 additional letters in response. The paper did not report how many were for and how many against. But the main argument against in those it selected for publication was that fair competition on the job market was not possible. "In finding employment," wrote one reader, "there is only equality on the surface but not underneath." Another demanded "legal guarantees of fair competition" as a condition for forcing graduates to find their own jobs. The consensus was that the best opportunities are reserved for male students from big cities whose parents have many "well-connected" friends and relations.[29]

On several campuses later in the year, administrators explained just how complex the experiment had become. The current transitional state, referred to as "two-way selection," is intended to ease the passage between past and future. The plans are still in effect, and most students continue to be assigned jobs in accordance with them. But potential employers are now given an opportunity to survey the field of prospective qualified college graduates, within the parameters fixed by the plan, and select as they prefer. Graduates can similarly shop around. Also within certain limits, all sides—employer, students, and their schools—can veto any proposed match.

Each university is still given its quota of jobs. A university in Beijing that enrolls nationally, for example, will be notified of how

---

[29] *Zhongguo qingnian bao*, April 19, 1988, and May 9, 1988.

many teachers or research workers Guangdong, Gansu, and other provinces can hire from among its graduating seniors. Within these limits as defined by the plan, and following the general principle that college graduates should return to their home provinces, students can proceed during their senior year to look for their own jobs. The "job fair" that many cities now hold for one or two days each year is designed as much to publicize the new approach as to assist in that actual search. But for students who fail to find a work unit within the choices given them by the plan, the school must make the assignment as before. The freest choices naturally go to the most popular and best-paying employers, on the one hand, and to the top students from the leading schools on the other. But such is the aim during this transitional stage, namely, to introduce everyone to the "competitive market mechanisms" that will govern job placement in the future.

One of the university vice-presidents interviewed in Beijing acknowledged that most students would probably prefer to have jobs assigned by the state. People have an assumption, he said, that the state will care for them in this way. But then the students compound the problem by demanding jobs to match their "ideals." One added difficulty for 1989 graduates, he said, was the government's economic rectification drive. The new austerity measures designed to combat inflation, although not affecting education budgets directly, had reduced the level of state investment and would mean fewer job openings in the summer of 1989. After spending the better part of two days with his students at the December 1988 Beijing job fair, he also acknowledged that the reform in this area was making life more difficult for college administrators responsible for student placement. His work was obviously cut out for him as a group of his students approached with the matter-of-fact conclusion that "nobody wants us," and one young man began elaborating the proposition: "We are like commodities here; our school is selling and the work unit is buying."

"Society's Needs" Revisited

Such is the climate that has fostered the new preoccupation—expressed by officials at all six universities visited in December 1988—with adapting higher education more closely to the developing needs of Chinese society. Not only are the needs themselves changing rapidly under the overall impact of the economic reforms, but so too are the conventional means for meeting them.

The responsibility for finding solutions is increasingly being shifted to the institutions themselves, as they are given greater autonomy over fund raising and school admissions, while being told to make their students more adaptable on the job market and to help them find the jobs as well. Central policy makers have hit upon the device of dual fixed and flexible plans to serve as an interim safeguard while everyone learns to live by the new rules. But for the time being, educators admit they are not quite sure how these rules should be formulated.

As the centralized plans recede, in other words, new ways must be found for performing the functions that everyone had learned to take for granted under the old socialist system. In the case of job assignment, the state plan also performed at least two such functions for which the new free market approach has yet to find viable substitutes. First, in providing secure iron rice bowl employment, it camouflaged the scarcity of good job opportunities and curbed the "unfair" practices used to gain access to those available. Second, the plan also ensured that jobs were filled that otherwise might not have been, camouflaging the inherited prejudices of university-educated intellectuals. Both the unfair practices and the old prejudices began to proliferate, therefore, once central planners began to phase out their central plans without first devising any countervailing mechanisms. As a result, the anticipated benefits of a free job market for college graduates have by and large been neutralized, and "society's needs" are not being adequately met either.

Thus concerns such as equity and social responsibility may have been banned from the field of public controversy, but they are inevitably re-emerging not just at the elementary and secondary levels but for higher education as well. And here, too, the concerns themselves did not actually disappear in the late 1970s, but only retreated inward. In early 1981, during the brief upsurge of protest against the newly restructured secondary school system, the president of Xian Jiaotong (Communications) University warned: "Mobility of human talent must be carried out under leadership and in a planned way. We must never encourage spontaneity. ...Otherwise, the flow will be concentrated in the direction of Beijing and Shanghai and along the coast, which will not be beneficial to building our country."[30] Xian Jiaotong would be an appropriate source of such a warning. In the late 1940s, Shanghai Jiaotong

---

30 *Guangming ribao,* Feb. 12, 1981.

University had gained national fame as a leader of the anti-Guomindang student movement, and in the mid-1950s, most of the campus was called upon to move inland to Xian. The move was part of the mission to break the coastal big city concentration of China's intellectual life that had been a favorite target of pre-1949 critics.

In 1988, a university vice-president in Guangzhou expressed the same concern as the free-market approach to job placement was making itself felt. Repeating the old reformers' axiom that "college-educated intellectuals concentrate where culture is high," he cited the example of Hainan Island, recently detached from Guangdong to become an independent province. Even within the island itself, he said, the "brain drain" is evident. "Students who graduate from Hainan Island senior secondary schools go to college on the mainland and do not return. The best leave, and the backwardness remains. If they return, they want to work in Haikou, while the counties in the hinterland have a difficult time getting teachers and doctors." Speaking of his own university, one of its student affairs officers commented on the considerable "thought education" that had to be applied to convince graduates to accept jobs even in neighboring counties, which are among the most prosperous in a prosperous province.

Officials at a provincial teachers' training institute also in Guangzhou repeated the story from the perspective of their own experience. In this case, because the entire institute trains for the unpopular career of secondary school teaching, almost all of its students fall under the new "directed plan" category. They will therefore continue to receive tuition-free state-subsidized education and accept state job assignments upon graduation. "The main problem," said one of the officials explaining the situation, "is that no one wants to be a teacher because the pay and status are too low." There was no solution for the status problem, he said, because the inferior status of the teacher was a tradition inherited from ancient times (when the successful became scholar-officials and the unsuccessful, teachers of children). And even though school teachers now receive about 10 percent more than college teachers—a deliberate national policy to encourage the former—teaching salaries still could not compete with incomes in Guangdong's new business sector.

As a result, the best students went elsewhere, and this institution had to settle for something less. Furthermore, "since the best students come from the cities, urban youth do not like to come here."

Some 70 to 80 percent of the university's students originated in county town middle schools. The university officials went on to describe the pattern of "rural" schooling today whereby the best students in a county are concentrated in its one key middle school. Such students could not compare with the graduates of similar big city key schools, of course. Yet once the university's own students graduated, they did not want to return to the counties from which they had come. They wanted to remain in the provincial capital or at least be assigned to one of Guangdong's larger towns. The state job assignment method was necessary, explained these officials, in order to guarantee a supply of teachers at the county level.

That China's institutions of higher learning are not currently doing a very good job of preparing students for life after graduation in Chinese society has thus become the "new" conventional wisdom among university personnel today. The challenge, they accept, is "to harmonize society's needs with the students' preferences." But there seems little consensus about the underlying causes of these problems, or how best to solve them, or the extent to which the institutions themselves can be held responsible for doing so.

Although no one would admit it in so many words, China's universities found themselves in 1988 debating again the very same question they were forced to address under different circumstances during the 1966–76 decade, namely, how to adapt higher learning to China's needs. Then it was imposed from above by the dictates of Mao Zedong's class-based radicalism. In 1988, it was being enforced by the exigencies of the economic reform drive itself. Yet the challenge was much the same throughout, as it has been for most of this century. The crux of the problem is how to counteract the commonly acknowledged tendency of college-educated people "to concentrate where culture is high," in the big cities and coastal areas and in the most socially rewarding jobs. The current brain drain abroad is only an extension of the same trend at home (or was, until the crackdown against the spring 1989 democracy movement created an additional political imperative). The dilemma, which many have deplored over the years but no one has ever successfully solved, is how to redirect that trend in ways that are both acceptable to Chinese intellectuals themselves and beneficial to everyone else.

For the individuals who staff China's universities, however, these dilemmas are perhaps best expressed in personal terms. A middle-aged Chinese college teacher summarized the spirit of the times during the spring of 1988:

The authorities tell us to find our own ways of earning more money, so teachers have become businessmen going everywhere in search of opportunities.... If there is money in it, they do it; if not they don't.... Under such conditions, how are we supposed to train the next generation to serve the people?... The students are dropping out half way through, and graduate students are quitting to go into business. Job assignments are also becoming problematic. The big cities are full and students are not willing to join basic-level work units. Those with ability do everything possible to go abroad. Parents pay high rates for the foreign currency necessary to send their children overseas. Those without ability just drift along aimlessly...

Study Abroad

The teacher's lament pointed also to one final issue that came together in the multiple crises of 1988, namely, overseas study. Again without anyone really articulating it as such, the spirit of the pre-1949 critique was reborn in the "new" concern about China's universities and study abroad, "educating people for another society."

The "crisis" that publicized the contemporary version of this concern was precipitated by protests among Chinese students in the United States against tightening Chinese government restrictions on the terms of their tenure abroad. The publicity grew from interviews with the *New York Times* and an "open letter to Li Peng," both published in March 1988.[31] Both protested the increasing restrictions and the Chinese government's alleged plan to reduce drastically the numbers of students that would in the future be allowed to study in the United States. In fact, Chinese authorities denied categorically that any drastic reduction in numbers was planned. The tightening restrictions, however, were part of a trend at least two years old, aimed at promoting the return home of Chinese students abroad as their inclinations to do otherwise became increasingly evident.

According to one of the more authoritative compilations of official Chinese government statistics on this question, China sent more than 50,000 students to some 70 countries between 1978 and early 1988. The figure includes both government-sponsored and

---

[31] *International Herald Tribune,* March 25, 1988; *Shijie ribao* (World Daily News) (New York), March 30, 1988.

privately funded students. Of that total number, about 20,000 had returned home. A majority of the returnees were from the older "visiting scholar" category, 90 percent of whom completed their studies as planned during relatively short stays abroad. At the opposite end of the spectrum were the 10,000 privately funded students. Virtually no one in this category had yet returned home, confirming the conventional wisdom about the inclinations of this group.

In between, and the cause of the greatest concern, were the younger "government-sponsored" scholars working for graduate degrees. Of the 12,000 in this category, only 200 to 300 had returned as of early 1988. Similarly, most of the thousand or so undergraduates returned home in the early 1980s only to resume their careers abroad as graduate students.[32] Because large numbers did not begin going overseas in the graduate student category until 1982 and most were enrolled in Ph.D. programs, it was still too early to determine the extent to which the increasing requests for study extensions would turn into applications for permanent residence. But the signals were sufficient by about 1986 to start alarm bells ringing in Beijing.

The initial response from the SEDC was a series of ad hoc proposals that had little effect in practice. On the contrary, the number of Chinese students enrolled in American universities rose dramatically between 1985–86 and 1988.[33] During the 1987–88

---

[32] Zhuang Yan, "Zhongguo liuxue renyuan gongzuo toushi" (A Thorough Explanation of Work Concerning Chinese Studying Overseas), *Liaowang zhoukan* (Outlook Weekly) (Beijing), overseas ed., March 21, 1988, pp. 5–6.

[33] A compilation of relevant statistics by the Institute of International Education, shows the number of students from China (the PRC) on U.S. campuses rising sharply from 14,000 in 1985–86 to 20,000 in 1986–87 to 30,000 in 1987–88. Jay Henderson and Glenn Shive, "Diversity and Dynamism in International Education: China, Hong Kong, and Thailand, 1988," briefing paper, March 1988.

In response to the March 1988 allegations of a proposed reduction in these figures, Chinese officials insisted that controls on publicly financed students were already being enforced and implied that any increases beyond the controlled numbers were occurring in the privately financed category. Chinese officials claim to have no accurate statistics on the number of students who are able to finance their studies abroad from private sources.

The controlled figures for state and publicly financed students were confirmed by SEDC spokesman Huang Xinbai in an April 5 interview in Beijing and by other SEDC officials in meetings and telephone conversations with U.S. Embassy officials in Beijing. According to the Huang interview (Xinhua, English, April 5, 1988, in *SWB*, FE/0121 B2/5, April 9, 1988), and two unclassified U.S. Embassy memos circulated in April and May, the quotas for study abroad were fixed as follows: The

academic year, however, official efforts to promote the return of Chinese students abroad were more systematically formulated and advertized. Chinese officials began openly identifying three areas where "adjustments" were already being concentrated.[34]

(1) Students were being encouraged to specialize in applied fields, and especially those needed for industrial and coastal region development.

(2) Based on recent rates of return, emphasis would in the future be placed on the "visiting scholar" category, meaning shorter stays by older people, and those working for advanced degrees in areas where China itself lacked facilities for training.

(3) Efforts were being made to diversify the destinations of Chinese students, the great majority of whom have gone to the United States in recent years.

The more specific regulations that had been introduced since the mid-1980s and now seemed destined for more systematic enforcement included the following:

Time limits. State-sponsored students were to complete M.A. degrees within two years and Ph.D.s within five years. Extensions could be granted on an individual basis. There was also limited provision for subsequent post-doctoral research.

Visa restrictions. By simplifying passport regulations for visiting scholars and making them more difficult for others, the Chinese authorities can now ensure that virtually all state-sponsored students go to the United States on the more restrictive "J" visas for visiting scholars. Upon completion of their studies, U.S. rules require such visa holders to return to their home countries for at least two years before being eligible to work in the United States.

Visa extensions. In the past, visiting scholar "J" visas could be extended by the United States at the request of the host university. Now all such requests are forwarded to the SEDC, and the

---

SEDC was authorized to send 3,000 students overseas in 1988 on behalf of the central government. Of that number, 20 percent, or about 600, were to be sent to the United States. In addition, between 3,000 and 4,000 students, also publicly funded, were to be sent to the United States by local, city, and provincial organizations. Officials insisted that these figures for the central and the local publicly funded students represented no change either proportionally or in absolute numbers by comparison with recent years.

[34] See, for example, Zhuang Yan, "Zhongguo liuxue renyuan gongzuo toushi."

U.S. Embassy in Beijing will not grant an extension without the
Commission's approval.

Work prerequisites. Chinese graduates are supposed to work for
a specified period at home before going abroad for further study.
M.A. degree holders, for example, are supposed to work for two
years.

Contracts and fines. In 1987, a new practice was introduced requiring written agreement between those going abroad and their
Chinese employers. The agreements are supposed to specify ob-
ligations on both sides, including what the employer needs and
what the student will study. Some of these contracts apparently
also required guarantors, the posting of bonds, and compensa-
tion if the student failed to return on schedule.[35]

As of early 1988, only the visa regulations were being uniformly
applied. Nevertheless, most of these regulations were cited in the
Chinese students' open letter to Li Peng, released no doubt to coincide with the spring meetings of the NPC, where academic
delegates were planning to publicize their demands for a bigger education budget. The most widely quoted of Ding Shisun's April 4 remarks concerned the overseas study problem. "Don't blame students abroad for not returning home," he said. "The real problem
is whether or not they are respected in their work." He declared
himself opposed to the new restrictions being imposed upon them,
including the "thousand and one ways" of trying to bring them
back. He argued that, under present conditions, the real problem
was not bringing them home but what to do with those who returned. To illustrate his point, he told of a new Ph.D. who gave up
a US$ 40,000-a-year job abroad to return to Beijing University.
With great difficulty, they found housing for him and a laboratory
to work in plus an associate professor's title that carried a basic
monthly salary of 122 rmb (US$ 33).[36]

---

[35] This list is taken from the unpublished background briefing paper written for
the Institute of International Education (Henderson and Shive, "Diversity and
Dynamism in International Education): Henderson and Shive were directors of the
IIE's Southeast Asia and China offices in Hong Kong and Guangzhou, respectively.
The IIE is an American nonprofit organization that administers international education programs for government and private industry. My thanks to the authors for
permission to cite their briefing paper.

[36] *Zhongguo qingnian bao,* April 5, 1988.

Later in Hong Kong, Ding Shisun reiterated this point. "I don't want to solve that problem," he said with reference to promoting the return of students abroad. "Let it solve itself. Get the country in better shape, and I believe that some, although not all, of them will come back of their own accord. If policies on the role of intellectuals and science are correct and if living and working conditions are a bit better, they will come back." He speculated that it would take five to ten years for these conditions to be met. He confirmed, moreover, that this was one point on which the SEDC had in the interim agreed to compromise, noting, for example, that official statements had stopped mentioning the specific time limits for study abroad. He said that this was an indication that such limits would be enforced more "flexibly" than initially intended.[37]

Despite all the lessons that recent Chinese history had to teach on this score, sources agree that no one associated with the decision even tried to calculate the potential consequences of opening the door and pushing tens of thousands of people through it forthwith. Once those consequences began to multiply in the mid-1980s, the authorities were left essentially with only two alternatives: (1) allow large numbers to remain abroad, thereby negating the original purpose for which they were encouraged to leave, or (2) try to reintegrate them into a system where conditions and standards could not begin to match those in accordance with which the students had been trained abroad.

A third alternative, advocated by some international advisors as the only viable short-term solution and under consideration in early 1989, was to create new separate research facilities and work units in China itself. These facilities would be designed specifically to accommodate the expertise and expectations of the graduates returning from abroad. A variation of this third alternative is the compromise ad hoc solution of special concessions in individual cases, as worked out by Ding Shisun and others as well. But he declined to comment on the political or social costs of luring students

---

[37] Professor Ding's spring 1988 comments were widely rumored to have created important enemies for him. He nevertheless confirmed and reiterated, during interviews with the Hong Kong press the following October, all the earlier statements attributed to him, seemingly unperturbed by the well-placed rumors, which even suggested that his successor as president of Beijing University had already been selected. Prof. Ding remained in that position throughout the spring 1989 democracy movement, which originated on his campus. His resignation was announced the following August (*Ming Pao*, Aug. 19, 1989; *Renmin ribao*, Aug. 24, 1989).

back from overseas by offering them immediate promotions such as an associate professor's title that otherwise would require at least ten years' seniority to achieve. Inevitably, someone else did, however. Although it was not state policy, noted one delegate derisively at the spring 1988 meetings, in practice institutions had already worked out a three-tier remuneration scale. Chinese-Americans received the best of everything; Chinese who had earned degrees abroad were in second place; and those trained at home were last in line—while the old pre-1949 priorities and prejudices were being reconstituted in the process.[38] Thus, both advocates and critics of using Western standards to recreate in China a Western-oriented academic subculture have become actors in a historical drama that apparently has many sequences yet to run.

Postscript, 1989: Students Protest

It would be convenient to argue that the multiple crises of 1988 were responsible for the outburst of student protest in 1989. It is, of course, possible that campus tensions might have been defused enough to preempt the explosion had one or more of the following conditions not existed in 1988. That is, (1) if tertiary enrollments had not been allowed to increase faster than the ability of the economy to absorb them, or if training, expectations, and opportunities had at least been more realistically matched; (2) if inflation had not escalated out of control; (3) if the economic austerity measures had therefore not been deemed necessary, further reducing employment opportunities; (4) if profiteering and influence peddling did not govern access to so many of life's benefits, including the immediate prospects of college graduates; (5) if the Education Commission had had the foresight not to escalate simultaneously the student finance and work assignment reforms as well as the measures to promote return among students overseas—all at a time when professional opportunities were still few, mobility limited, and academic salaries so low that moonlighting had become the only official solution; and finally (6) if anyone had been able to express confidence that solutions could be found, that economic rectification would work, and that the authorities had the ability to lead the country out of the impasse into which their reforms had propelled it.

It is possible, in other words, that conditions in 1988 caused the events of 1989. But the link between the cause and effect is certain-

---

[38] *China Daily,* April 13, 1988.

ly not sufficient and probably not even necessary. This is because, by 1989, the imperatives driving the student protest movement had already taken on a life of their own. They were no longer tied solely or directly to the above issues of campus-related economic and educational reforms, although these had initially helped activate them. The tradition of Chinese student activism is such that once genuinely mobilized, it creates its own momentum and then perpetuates itself as each phase builds upon the last to prepare conditions for the next. New issues and demands are added to old, and the movement can continue indefinitely, that is, so long as any of the demands remain unmet and the object of the protest cannot or will not control or coopt it.

Essentially, the imperatives underlying the current generation of student protest were already in place by the end of fall semester, 1985. They then set in motion a chain of events that culminated a year later in Hu Yaobang's resignation as Party leader and from there led directly to Tiananmen Square, 1989. Of all the clashing interests that the reforms have aroused, therefore, none has been more damaging to the Deng Xiaoping administration than the upsurge of student resentment during the autumn of 1985.

The catalyst, in September 1985, was Japan's trading practices and other irritants in the Sino-Japanese relationship. But the protest turned quickly inward, against a range of negative consequences arising from the economic reforms. The most important issues were high prices, widespread corruption, and the special privileges enjoyed by the families of high-level officials, who appear to benefit more than others from the new opportunities to engage in trade and travel. The students also began demanding the unhindered right to protest such negative consequences as they saw fit, once it became apparent that the authorities were trying to stop them. Meanwhile, the entire national Party apparatus was mobilized to do just that, when everyone realized that the students were not only articulating widespread urban discontent over the same issues, but were also trying to coordinate a nationwide unofficial demonstration to coincide with the fiftieth anniversary of the anti-Japanese December 9 Movement.

Between mid-October and December 1985, virtually every provincial and city Party secretary in the country visited every leading university and personally listened to students' complaints. Their concerns were essentially the same everywhere: the rising cost of food and books, inflation generally, unreliable supplies of nonstaple foods, poor living conditions, job assignments, corruption, bad Party work style, as well as the original questions about Japan, foreign trade, and the economic implications of the new open-door policies. Everywhere, too, the Party secretaries delivered the same message: people should not conclude that the economic reforms were leading overall to negative results. The reforms were of primary importance, the negative aspects secondary, and it was wrong to blame the former for the latter.[39]

This unprecedented exercise in direct "heart-to-heart" exchanges between students and provincial Party secretaries, plus subtle pressures and not-so-subtle threats, did succeed in preempting the nationwide protest students were planning for December 9. But with no substantive solution possible, the administration switched gears during the first half of 1986, reviving Deng Xiaoping's 1980 argument that political/administrative reforms were actually the prerequisite for success in the economic sphere. The economic problems, it was argued, arose not from lapses in the implementation of economic reform but from a failure to implement fully its political counterpart. Earlier themes from the "reforms of 1980" reappeared during the summer. These were especially the separation of Party from government and administration, decentralization, socialist democracy, and popular participation. Universities in particular were again included in the campaign, which dominated political study during the fall semester, 1986.

Anhui Province was apparently selected as the pacesetter. A national political theory seminar was held there in October to discuss political reform as a precondition for further economic progress. A provincial meeting of Anhui university Party secretaries had already met in August to discuss how the new campaign should be developed. The meeting focused on two basic problems to be solved within institutions of higher learning, namely, the separation of Party and university management, and popular participation to include both teachers and students in university administration.[40] The administration's aims and motives seemed clear. The *People's Daily* ran a five-part series in October and November on democratic management at Anhui's University of Science and Technology.

---

[39] The analysis of the 1985 and 1986 student protests presented here is elaborated in Suzanne Pepper, "Deng Xiaoping's Political and Economic Reforms: China's Students Protest," Feb. 24, 1987, *UFSI Reports* (Universities Field Staff International, Indianapolis, Ind.), no. 30 (1986), Asia.

[40] *Anhui ribao* (Hefei), Aug. 24, 1986; Xinhua, English, Oct. 21, 1986, in *SWB,* FE/8398/BII/10, Oct. 24, 1986.

The university appeared to have been chosen as the new model and one of the university's vice-presidents, Fang Lizhi, was among the campaign's most outspoken proponents.[41]

Perhaps most significant of all Deng Xiaoping's comments supporting these themes during the fall was the one carried on the front page of the *People's Daily* on December 7, *after* off-campus student protests had already begun in Hefei over the election procedures of local people's congress deputies. Paramount leader Deng proclaimed by headline that in carrying out political reform "daring and determination should come first, prudence second." Obviously, the movement for democratic reform had backing at the highest level.

What is less clear is whether the revived political reform campaign was seen by its high-level backers simply as a diversionary tactic to buy time and distract everyone from their economic complaints in the hope that these would soon pass, or whether the leaders genuinely saw political reform as the solution for their economic problems. In any event, the suppressed student activism of the previous year, the approach of the December 9 anniversary date, and the new official calls for popular participation, plus the continuing economic grievances, proved a combustible mix. Off-campus student protests spread rapidly from Hefei to several other cities during December, culminating in Shanghai and Nanjing with huge mass street demonstrations that extended well beyond the student population.

This round of student protest was also easily controlled, however. Given the official support apparent at the start, and local tolerance everywhere as the demonstrations developed, it was generally assumed at the time that these were protests with a high-level political purpose. Only after they threatened to escalate out of control did the central authorities step in and order the students back to campus. Why Hu Yaobang and not Deng Xiaoping was forced to take responsibility for the December 1986 protests has yet to be revealed. Hu resigned as Party leader in January; Fang Lizhi was expelled from the party and dismissed from his university position; and an "anti–bourgeois liberalization" backlash subsequently gave new life to the "conservative" opposition. Li Peng became its compromise candidate for premier in late 1987, and Zhao Ziyang moved over to replace Hu as Party general secretary.

---

[41] *Renmin ribao,* Oct. 22, 26, and 31, 1986; Nov. 4 and 14, 1986.

Meanwhile, the conditions for the next phase of the student movement were being similarly realigned. Democracy and political reform had exchanged places with the predominantly economic grievances of 1985 to become the chief focus of student attention. In this sense, Deng and others who initially advocated political reform as a device to help surmount their economic difficulties were successful—except that in the process they lost control of the agenda.

As has happened many times in past CCP-led mass movements, when leaders mobilize the masses and the latter respond, different participants and local activists interpret the same message from the center differently. Some are more likely than others to follow their own inclinations, some inevitably go to excess, and so on. As far as the center is concerned, such mavericks are useful especially in a movement's early stages and can usually be brought into line later. They only become a threat to the extent that they cannot be controlled and have acquired a mass following of their own in the process. Accordingly, it was Fang Lizhi's critical interpretation of "bourgeois" democracy, rather than Deng Xiaoping's "anti-bureaucratic" socialist variation, that caught the imagination of the student crowd. And in this way, also, both Hu Yaobang and Fang Lizhi, who lost his Party membership but not his voice, acquired a political significance in official disgrace that they had not enjoyed before.[42]

---

[42] An analysis of the political ideas underlying the student protest movement is, of course, beyond the scope of this monograph. Those ideas were, however, more complex than the above paragraph suggests by concentrating on the movement's leadership. Inherent in the popular response, for example, was an undercurrent of Maoist mass-line or "work unit" democracy that was obviously different from both the Western and Deng Xiaoping's anti-bureaucratic conceptions. Thus while student demonstrators were occupying Tiananmen Square in May, one middle-aged, middle-ranking Beijing cadre remarked to a friend during a visit to Shenzhen that "Mao would have sent someone out to talk to them." The cadre went on to explain that workers and cadres alike in her industrial system felt they had much less opportunity to "participate" within that system now than in the 1970s, when meetings were called for every problem and people could raise opinions that today would result in their dismissal.

A cadre in Gansu Province said much the same thing to a visiting American academic in June, although the context was rural rather than urban. At least in the past the leaders had to go to the villages and call meetings, said the cadre, unlike the present when they just drive by without even getting out of their cars.

Such political comparisons are related to another that developed in response to the multiple economic and educational crises of 1988 and could be heard even among university intellectuals. Or, as a recent Zhongshan University graduate reflected

Thus the students let the economic crises of 1988 essentially pass them by, with only a brief flurry of wall posters and their small shoeshine protest to mark the spring 1988 NPC meetings. There is no way of knowing whether, as some Chinese officials argued, the students had now accepted the negative economic consequences of the reforms or whether, in the absence of the political issue, economic grievances would have continued to loom as large as in 1985. What seems most likely, however, is that the economic and political concerns simply merged to create the general collapse of confidence that overtook the administration in 1988.

In addition, with the downfall of Hu Yaobang, the current generation of student protest became linked directly to the dynamic of disagreement among top Party leaders over reform strategy. This in effect compromised the students' ability to respond to economic grievances of any kind in 1988, because to do so would have aided the cause of their "conservative" opponents and by implication further weakened the position of their remaining supporter, Zhao Ziyang. Zhao, as the leading promoter of the economic reforms for a decade, was placed increasingly on the defensive by the problems of 1988. Conservative Party leaders appeared to dominate the economic rectification program announced in the fall. Using conservative measures to deal with the crises, they strengthened their own political position in the process while Zhao's reformers seemed suddenly bereft of effective alternatives.

In any event, just as conservative CCP leaders were exploiting the economic disarray to their own political advantage, so dissident intellectuals were also using the ensuing confidence crisis to promote their cause. They spoke out increasingly during the winter of 1988–89 most notably on political issues, human rights, and amnesty for political prisoners. The multiple symbolism of 1989 became the focal point for the new political reform offensive. The year marked the seventieth anniversary of China's most important student protest on May 4, 1919; the fortieth anniversary of the founding of the People's Republic; and the tenth anniversary of the "Democracy Wall" movement that helped bring Deng Xiaoping back to power in the late 1970s. If a starting point needs to be identified, it would probably be activist Ren Wanding's public

---

while discussing those crises with journalist friends in Hong Kong, "Maybe Mao's policies were better for China after all." The waves of "nostalgia" for the Maoist past, reported both before and after June 4, 1989, derive from such reflections and comparisons.

reaffirmation of the demands for which he was imprisoned in 1979. Ren broke a ten-year silence in November 1988 to renew his call for "people's democracy, human rights, social justice and reform."[43] Next came Fang Lizhi's open letter to Deng Xiaoping in January, proposing a general amnesty for all political prisoners to mark the fortieth anniversary of the People's Republic. This demand was subsequently taken up by prominent intellectuals both in China and abroad.[44]

Concurrently, there developed a little-publicized demand to recategorize intellectuals as a separate class or stratum. The post-1976 confirmation of their status as "intellectual laborers" was treated at the time as a "liberating" gesture intended to remove the political stigmata attached to them during the 1966–76 decade especially, by placing them on par with the working class. But dissatisfaction had grown over that gesture because it implied a subordinate status. This dissatisfaction paralleled resentment over the ongoing devaluation of the intellectuals' economic standing in an increasingly materialistic environment. The latter sense of grievance was heightened by the unfulfilled promise from the mid-1980s to grant white-collar workers substantial pay increases in order to enhance their economic position specifically by comparison with their blue-collar counterparts. Thus a new demand developed during 1988–89 for an official separate identity signifying the intellectuals' distinctive contribution within the social division of labor.[45]

---

[43] *South China Morning Post,* Nov. 23 and 29, 1988. The latter issue contains a translation of the essay written by Ren Wanding and circulated to the Western press at this time.

[44] See, for example, *South China Morning Post,* Jan. 10, Feb. 23 and 26, 1989.

[45] See, for example, He Tao, "Xu chongshen zhishifenzi shi yige duli jieceng" (Intellectuals Must Be Reaffirmed as an Independent Stratum), *Shehui kexue bao* (Social Sciences Information) (Shanghai), no. 143 (1989). This article is also discussed in *China Daily,* Mar. 15, 1989, and *Zhejiang ribao,* Mar. 21, 1989. The demand for a separate class status was the most forceful expression of the intellectuals' revived sense of purpose and independence that became evident during 1988–89. Deng Xiaoping himself contributed to this demand and was reported in November 1988 to have said that "science and technology are number one among the productive forces, and intellectuals should be elevated from the old ninth category to first place." (According to a report featured in *Shanghai keji bao* [Shanghai Science and Technology], Feb. 10, 1989; for a carefully argued rebuttal of Deng's statement, see *Renmin ribao,* Mar. 31, 1989.)

Among Western writers, Beijing correspondent for the *South China Morning Post,* Marlowe Hood, probably provided the most consistent record of the complex intellectual currents that arose at this time including the self-conscious demand for a dis-

On the one hand, then, Chinese intellectuals' political demands placed them within the mainstream of dissent and reform rising concurrently in other Communist-led countries. But on the other hand, the demand for a separate class identity seemed doubly incongruous amid the calls for freedom and democracy. The incongruities lay, firstly, in the logic of a class-based antagonism deliberately perpetuated; and secondly, in the modern restoration of an ancient special status, which the demand also seemed to anticipate.

By March, Beijing students responding to the surging spirit of dissent within the intellectual community as a whole were reportedly "counting the days" to May 4 when they planned to hold their own commemorative activities independent of the official celebrations. The students also planned to base their themes on the old May Fourth-era demands for "democracy" and "science." Fang Lizhi had recently identified these as a challenge to the CCP's leadership, calling the new demands for democracy and science "a new source for hope among Chinese intellectuals" in place of the "thoroughly discredited" socialism of the Lenin-Stalin-Mao variety.[46] The official themes approved in late February by the CCP Secretariat for the anniversary celebrations were patriotism, reform, and a pioneering spirit.[47]

---

tinct class identity (see for example his articles in the *Post*: Nov. 3, 1988, Feb. 23 and 26, 1989, Mar. 5, 1989, April 25, 1989, May 13, 1989; and passim for the winter and spring of 1988–89; the May 13 reference is a full-page report on the Bolinas, California, conference "China 1989: Quest for Identity," attended by several prominent Chinese intellectuals).

The intellectuals' revived awareness of themselves as a social elite (*jingying*) took a variety of forms ranging from a newly articulated desire for intellectual independence; to the more conventional Chinese sense of social responsibility in critical times; and beyond that to the demand for recognition as an "independent force," both dissident and otherwise, essential for political and social progress. Debates and disagreements over specific points flourished, one benchmark being the autumn 1988 "Academic Symposium on the Question of Intellectuals," at Beidaihe (*Shijie jingji daobao* [World Economic Herald] [Shanghai] Sept. 12, 1988, p. 13; and *Guangming ribao*, Sept. 8, 1988). On the non-dissident role for intellectuals, see the arguments surrounding the controversial "new authoritarianism" theory (for example, *Shijie jingji daobao*, Mar. 13, 1989, p. 11). Among the many Chinese sources that publicized these developing currents during 1988–89 were: *Shijie jingji daobao*; *Shehui kexue bao*; *Jingjixue zhoubao* (Economics Weekly) (Beijing); *Lilun xinxi bao* (Theoretical Information News) (Beijing); *Lianhe shibao* (United Times) (Shanghai).

[46] See, for example, Fang Lizhi, "China's Despair and China's Hope," *New York Review of Books*, Feb. 2, 1989, p. 3. After its publication in the United States, parts of this essay were reportedly posted on the Beijing University campus.

[47] *South China Morning Post*, Feb. 26, 1989; March 7, 1989.

Even if specific goals were not yet precisely formulated, prepara-
tions for the next phase of the student movement were thus essentially in place when Hu Yaobang died suddenly in mid-April. The
students were back at the starting line and ready to move out again,
taking up where the December 1986 democracy protests had left
off. Hu Yaobang provided the perfect, if unanticipated, link. As
the protest movement developed during the first week after his
passing, specific demands began to take shape. Among the first formulation was a set of seven, drafted by representatives of students
from nineteen Beijing colleges and universities on April 23: (1)
reassess Hu Yaobang's merits and demerits; (2) allow the people to
run newspapers; (3) increase educational funding and raise the pay
of intellectuals; (4) reevaluate the 1986 student movement and the
opposition to bourgeois liberalization; (5) make public the truth of
the April 20, 1989, incident (when police allegedly beat student
demonstrators); (6) oppose corruption, oppose bureaucratism, and
severely punish official profiteering; (7) report truthfully all the
events from the death of Hu Yaobang to the student demonstrations in Tiananmen Square.[48]

Later demands would include more pointed references to
inflation, the special privileges of cadres, Swiss bank accounts, and
so on, but the leading concerns throughout were political. The
specific campus-related issues that had dominated higher education
news in 1988 were relegated in 1989 to a supporting role at best.
And by the time the Party plenum finally met in June, the ten-year
development plan for education had been swept off the agenda by a
"student tide that grew into an upheaval and from an upheaval into

---

[48] *Ming Pao*, April 24, 1989. Once the student protests actually began in mid-
April, the Hong Kong Chinese-language press provided more detailed reports than
their English-language competitors, or at least the selection of the latter seen in Hong
Kong. Clippings from several Chinese-language Hong Kong papers during April and
May 1989 are now on file at the Universities Service Centre section of the main library, Chinese University of Hong Kong. During the days immediately after the
June 3-4 military crackdown, however, Hong Kong editors threw caution to the
winds and seemingly printed every report, confirmed or otherwise, that reached their
desks. During the summer, after emotions had calmed somewhat but before
memories began to fade, sixty-four Hong Kong journalists who had covered the protest movement in Beijing for Hong Kong publications rewrote some of their most
important stories and published them jointly (Liushisiming xianggang jizhe, *Renmin
buhui wangji: bajiu minyun shilu* [The People Will Not Forget: A Record of the
1989 Democracy Movement] [Hong Kong: Xianggang jizhe xiehui, 1989]).

a counter-revolutionary rebellion" involving students and city residents throughout the country.[49]

Education reform itself had slipped once again on everyone's list of priorities, this time an unintended but also unprotected victim caught up in the dynamic of China's reform politics. Yet this too follows a time-honored twentieth-century Chinese tradition whereby education is inevitably vulnerable to the imperatives of its larger political environment, but compromised also by the interests of its own intellectual clientele.

---

[49] From an address by Jiang Zemin (Zhao Ziyang's successor as CCP general secretary) at a Beijing forum of university leaders (*Renmin ribao,* July 15, 1989).

CHAPTER EIGHT

Conclusion

The reader, having progressed to this point, might well conclude that the Chinese finally escaped the confines of their Confucian past at the turn of the century, only to be trapped in a perpetual search for the ideal reform model. Meanwhile, the society as a whole remains seemingly unreconstructed after the collapse of the old order. But the ancient habit of seeking ideal reference points in past precedents lingers on as the search continues for a consensus over functional substitutes to replace the old unified hierarchy of power, learning, and authority. Except that the most relevant past now has a shorter time span and includes twentieth-century China's search for authoritative precedents in the experience of foreign countries as well. In education, as in other sectors, both the achievements and the destructive impulses of China's modern development seem to derive from this as yet unfulfilled search for ideal solutions, together with the precedents adopted and rejected in the process.

For Mao, the reference points became the CCP's rural Yan'an experience; the Russian revolution in several phases of its development; and, specifically for education, the various components of the old reformers' critique of the established system. For Deng Xiaoping by the late 1970s, the precedents were China's pre–Cultural Revolution past; the West and especially the United States as its most successful representative; and, for education, the regularity of the established system. To the power holder goes the privilege of selecting the precedents and trying to establish the new orthodoxy, an effort that seems to have become as elusive in the present as the mythical Confucian ideals were for the past.

Such a conclusion is difficult to avoid when, for example, key points from the 1931 League of Nations report criticizing China's regular education system are held up for comparison beside that system's post-1976 successor: preferential access to the best schools from primary upwards for children of well-connected parents; admission to the best primary schools governed by tests to select the intellectually and physically superior; student-teacher ratios at all levels among the most inefficient in the world and teachers with the lightest work loads; the need for a dependable taxation system to ensure adequate primary school financing; the need for secondary schooling that combines college-preparatory and work-oriented functions without dividing into two separate systems; the "dazzling" influence of the American success story; the inexplicable attachment to the credit system; college teachers reading lectures out of textbooks; the elitist traditions of schools and learning and their isolation from "the masses"; and a belief in the autonomous powers of science and technology. That these features of China's society and its education system should prove so enduring is all the more noteworthy given the massive assaults that have been leveled against them during the past fifty years and the changed constellation of interests that now sustain them as a result.

The reform mentality was apparently created by the overdue decision to break the monopoly of Confucian learning. The rush to embrace its Western equivalent was soon tempered with questions about its applicability in the Chinese context. That reassessment initially grew from a complex self-critical reaction that set in among intellectuals themselves after May 4, 1919. They were reacting partly against the new Western learning, which they themselves were importing, and partly from the perspective of that learning against continuing features of Chinese tradition, which they also were perpetuating.

In the argument that developed, the new education was portrayed as a "hybrid," a "head with no base," and the "worst of both worlds." The specific points as they emerged in the 1920s were the creation by the new Western learning of an urban-oriented elite divorced from the realities of Chinese society, the mechanical adherence to Western educational models, and the formalistic nature of these models when transplanted in Chinese soil. The intellectuals' aversion to manual labor, their aspiration to become officials, and their separation from the masses and the countryside all featured in this early critique, which had adherents at points all along the political spectrum. Yet despite the common denominator of agreement, the education system as a whole defied reform. This failure was traceable in part to the ambivalence and conflicting interests of the intellectuals themselves, even though the larger environment of politics and war usually emerged as the immediate cause of defeat for most of the individual reform projects in the pre-1949 era.

The Communist Party appeared to accept the logic of the reformers' concerns and, unlike the Guomindang, seemed intent on incorporating their goals into its new national education policy. But several changes naturally occurred when disparate sketches were transferred onto a national canvas and integrated with the imperatives of a newly victorious Marxist revolution as well. In the end, the new political parameters drawn around the reformers' goals, once they were applied on a national scale, would create conditions as detrimental to their realization as those that had earlier confounded the individual reform experiments.

Initially lacking the self-confidence to proceed alone, the Communist Party turned to the Soviet Union as model and guide. This decision immediately violated the first principle of the inherited critique. Nor would the issue of mechanical foreign borrowing be allowed to die, given the excesses to which the exercise was pushed in the early 1950s. In addition, the Soviet model of that time could provide few solutions for any other of the critique's most basic concerns. Equally important, the regimented academic "Stalin model" that the Chinese transplanted was itself under attack in the Soviet Union at the same time for offending against some of the same principles at issue in the Chinese context. A final complication was that the Stalin model required an educated elite, left alone to pursue the specialized tasks required for economic development. But this had been achieved in the Soviet Union only after a new generation of "proletarian intellectuals" had been promoted and integrated within the system following the radical early phases of the Russian revolution. The Chinese educated elite, by contrast, remained essentially unchanged but for the continuing diminution of its political influence and its further transformation from generalist to modern specialist by the 1950s reorganization of the tertiary sector.

Hence, the first "cultural revolution" in 1958 combined both the imperatives of Khrushchev's reforms then underway in the Soviet Union and the as yet unrealized promise of the Chinese revolution itself. When that first attempt failed, Mao went on to reaffirm its goals in 1966. It is likely, therefore, that the similarities between Mao's two cultural revolutions and two similar radical episodes in the history of the Soviet Union are not purely coincidental. But their Chinese equivalents were different from past exercises in foreign borrowing since they were more accurately an attempt to adapt the experience of the Soviet revolution to the long-acknowledged demands of Chinese critics and revolutionaries. This process of integration began under Mao's leadership in Yan'an and culminated in the 1966–76 Cultural Revolution. During that decade, Mao tried to restructure the entire education system on the basis of the "irregular" antielitist, work-oriented norms that had in Yan'an been applied to the rural sector alone. The earlier objection to an urban-oriented intellectual elite, isolated from the society its expertise was supposed to serve, finally achieved satisfaction in a national effort based on the old reformers' ideals, albeit reformulated within the context of cultural revolution and class struggle.

The key features of this experience—once the Red Guard phase had passed in the late 1960s—can be summarized as follows. Quantitative growth at the mass level became a primary goal, promoted in the form of a shortened ten-year system of universal elementary and secondary schooling. As a result, both elementary and secondary enrollments reached their highest levels ever by the end of the 1966–76 decade. Along with quantitative expansion, the content and quality of education were also equalized. The increasingly clear and stratified distinctions that had developed in the wake of the Great Leap Forward were special targets. Cultural Revolution policies aimed to break up the entire bifurcated structure by requiring everyone to attend their nearest neighborhood school through the secondary level. The concern for relevance was addressed by adapting a more practical and vocationalized curriculum for all. This strategy also concerned itself directly with the social implications of education that offered clearly different kinds of education for different kinds of students (urban and rural, working class and white-collar) and aimed to reduce those distinctions. Everyone's children were to receive a similar kind of work-oriented schooling.

These same principles were also applied at the tertiary level, where teaching and study plans were essentially cut in half. The goal of trying to pursue international or advanced Western standards in content and quality at this level was deliberately abandoned and replaced by the "appropriate technology" alternative. The underlying argument was that China, as a poor country, could not afford to acquire the highest achievements of Western science and technology, nor were these appropriate for China's needs given the overall level of development. When actually implemented in terms of the drastically curtailed curricula, of course, this objective raised a further question about the extent to which an underdeveloped country could afford to do *without* advanced training and technology altogether.

The Cultural Revolution strategy also abolished the unified college entrance exams, emphasizing instead class and political backgrounds as prerequisites for college admission. Another prerequisite was the two-year work requirement, tied to the expectation that after graduation, students were supposed to return to the locality and sector where they had previously been working (although this principle was often honored only in the breach). Socially, young people were rewarded for their work experience by being reclassified as workers or peasants, regardless of their family origins. Thus, the claim that the Cultural Revolution strategy enabled workers and peasants to attend college appeared somewhat fraudulent because many "worker-peasant-soldier" college students during the early 1970s were actually of the reclassified variety. The assumption was that, just as the regular pre-1966 education system could corrupt any working-class student who might gain access to it, so urban, white-collar youth transferred into a working-class environment could similarly be changed by that experience. This assumption had always underlain the Party's orientation toward intellectuals, as expressed in the dual aim of trying to instill proletarian values in the existing intellectual elite, while educating workers and peasants to become "proletarian intellectuals." The latter goal was promoted by the Cultural Revolution emphasis on universalizing secondary education and establishing complete middle schools even in the rural communes.

This strategy, in other words, represented radical education reform tied to social revolution enforced nationwide for everyone. The masses were cast as beneficiaries and the existing educated elite as the target. The structures that trained them were leveled, the leadership within them overturned, and the elites themselves sent out for proletarian reeducation.

One of the strategic errors inherent in this "line" was the damage done to higher education. Another was to have tried to enforce it via the all encompassing two-line struggle. This last, in retrospect, ensured that Mao's line and everything associated with it could prevail only so long as he was able to retain power. When power was lost at his death, all the enemies Mao had created along the way united in repudiating both his line and those who had helped him implement it. Conversely, the post-Mao reforms in education must also be assessed within this political context because they represent both the alternative strategy for socialist development and an explicit political repudiation of the Cultural Revolution experiment as well.

Deng Xiaoping's solution accordingly was to reverse his predecessors' priorities on almost every point, ending both social revolution and radical education reform. Repudiated in the process were the issues inherited from the old pre-1949 critique related to foreign borrowing, intellectual elites, and urban-rural disparities.

The basic goal of universalizing elementary education was retained, but the delivery system was evidently weakened with the dissolution of the collective economic base that sustained it in the rural areas. The new strategy set as its goal the achievement of advanced international standards, based on the belief that science and technology are keys to the West's economic superiority. The education system was then restructured to produce the talent that would achieve those aims. Human and material resources were reconcentrated in the tertiary and college-preparatory sectors. The system was also restructured to exploit and reinforce the existing social divisions of labor. Because only a minority can aspire to higher learning, the keypoint college-preparatory stream was deliberately restricted in size and selection concentrated among the existing urban elites. Vocational education was promoted as the most relevant alternative for everyone else, to prepare them both practically and psychologically for the world of work they will enter upon leaving school. This logic was also responsible for the sharp quantitative reduction enforced at the secondary level, on the grounds that the Cultural Revolution's mass enrollments were unnecessary given China's level of development.

One of Deng Xiaoping's strategic errors thus followed inevitably from playing out the logic of the two-line struggle. Most significant for education, in this respect, was the refusal to distinguish either analytically or in practice between the class-based communist revolution and the antiestablishment critique of the education system that Mao had joined together. As a result, the "forces of regularization" reestablished themselves with the full support of the new administration in order to serve its modernization goals. In the process, the basic ideas and assumptions of Chinese educators about how to run modern schools in order to produce a quality product reemerged virtually unchanged from those of half a century earlier. The only thing missing seemed to be the old antiestablishment critique itself, which was banished from the realm of public discourse along with the leftist excesses of the Maoist era.

Education policy makers have consequently found themselves with "so many problems we never anticipated" and liabilities that have now been registered at every level: primary, secondary, and tertiary.[1] Just as Mao apparently overestimated his power to break the regular system, so the professional educators working under Deng Xiaoping's authority have discovered the truth of Wang Meng's warning. The old "leftist" arguments together with the interests and concerns they reflect can be neither eliminated nor ignored, at least not yet. This is not just because they have taken on an ideological life of their own, but because they are still tied to essentially the same divisions within twentieth-century Chinese society that inspired them in the first place. These are especially the distinctions between elites and masses, between city and countryside, and between the outward-looking coastal areas and the inward-oriented hinterland. Like a complex of enduring fault lines, these divisions represent the as yet unreconciled interests within Chinese society as a whole, along which the search for a new, modern consensus to replace the old has repeatedly broken. But at the same time, those divisions and interests have become an important force contributing to the dynamic of the development process itself.

The most significant interests that developed around the Cultural Revolution educational strategy were those represented by the mass enrollments at the elementary and secondary levels, reinforced by a unitary structure that offered a similar kind of vocationally oriented education for all. Hence the reimposition of clear-cut vocational tracks and elitist academic streams, together with the reduced enrollments, gives contemporary relevance to the old arguments. These live on in the undercurrent of pressure and criticism that continued throughout the 1980s.

Clearly on the defensive, central decision makers responded in the mid-1980s by promulgating a compulsory nine-year (elementary and junior secondary) education decree, as yet unenforced; by allowing a limited increase in secondary enrollments; and by agreeing "in principle" to eliminate keypoint schools at the elementary and junior middle levels. For higher education, the consequences of producing too many college graduates all drawn from the same urban keypoint middle school stream was not acknowledged until the end of the decade. Viable solutions will mean not only luring back the thousands from that stream who graduated into successful student careers overseas, but inducing those educated at home to work

---

[1] The quote is from the SEDC spokesman interviewed in Beijing in December 1988.

in the "basic-level" units for which neither their training nor their expectations are appropriate.

Given the endemic nature of the concerns underlying these issues, Deng Xiaoping's reform administration would evidently have been better advised to integrate them into its strategy from the start. Certainly, respecting the lessons of history rather than (continually erasing them and then) having to rediscover them the hard way would have reduced the costs to the nation and its young people. During the 1980s, these costs have been registered in terms of new illiterates in the countryside; demoralized urban youth without jobs, schools, or futures; and a new generation of college graduates with aspirations that cannot be fulfilled, while the needs of society for trained personnel go unmet.

In a further ironic parallel with the Maoist past, a second strategic error apparent in the education sector by the late 1980s concerned the damage being done specifically at the tertiary level. Unlike the 1966–76 era, the intention in the 1980s was neither deliberate nor politically motivated—at least not until the spring of 1989. But neither is the damage entirely the unintended consequence of inflation, corruption, and other problems afflicting the economy as a whole. The administration not only left the education system unprotected from these adverse consequences of its market-oriented reforms, but even pushed forward with their direct application to institutions of higher learning at a time when those consequences were at their height. The sequence of events is all the more surprising in that higher education was initially a favored sector, so important for Deng Xiaoping's modernization goals in the late 1970s that it justified restructuring the entire education system to concentrate resources at the tertiary level and within the college-preparatory keypoint stream. Perhaps the growing awareness of dislocations within that part of the system influenced the increasingly cavalier approach towards it. But the announcement of further student finance and job assignment reforms in 1988—when inflation-eroded university budgets and academic incomes were already major campus concerns—had an impact so immediate that it even led to reduced applications at the senior high school level for the 1988–89 academic year.

After June 4, 1989, of course, China's institutions of higher learning were locked irreversibly into the larger contradictions between economic and political reform that finally overtook the Deng Xiaoping administration at the end of its first decade in power. But applying the lessons of recent history, such an end should probably have been anticipated since education has, both intentionally and otherwise, been so regularly eclipsed by other priorities. In addition, however, the "error" of tying the old education concerns to the ongoing political power struggle is also being deliberately repeated. This is occurring as the next phase of the cycle begins under the leadership of a "new" Deng Xiaoping administration dominated, after June 4, by the CCP's conservative leaders. They, like most everyone else, have obviously chosen to ignore the admonition against playing out the logic of the "line struggle," issued in 1987 by Wang Meng, whose appointment as Minister of Culture they terminated forthwith.

First, the new leadership has emphatically rejected the intellectuals' irredentist demand for a separate social identity and their bid for greater political influence. The message issued in countless official statements is that "the working class is the leading force of our country," that "the alliance between workers and peasants is the foundation of political power," and that "intellectuals are a part of the working class."[2]

With the battle thus joined, the associated rhetoric inevitably combines the official line denouncing the "counter-revolutionary rebellion" and the intellectual elitism responsible for it with antidotes that might be interpreted as a Maoist revival but which are also inherited from a much older tradition. Some people understand neither China nor foreign countries and "mechanically copy Western things," admonished a *People's Daily* writer. "Some people think of themselves as society's 'elite' (*jingying*), feel much superior to the laboring people, and are neither willing to work hard on the front line of production at the basic levels, nor to merge with the masses and learn through practice."[3]

Except for the ubiquitous political study and a year of military training for Beijing University freshmen, few concrete measures aimed at translating the rhetoric into reality within the education sector could be confirmed in practice by early 1990. But the meas-

---

[2] See, for example, *Renmin ribao,* July 15, 1989, Aug. 4, 17, 27, and 29, 1989, Sept. 10, 1989, Oct. 12, 1989; and Li Tieying (minister in charge of the SEDC), "Gaodeng jiaoyu bixu jianchi shehuizhuyi fangxiang" (Higher Education Must Adhere to the Socialist Direction), address to the National Higher Education Work Conference, July 15, 1989, in *Qiushi* (Seeking Truth) (Beijing), no. 16 (1989), pp. 4–8. The interpretation of the statements quoted as a specific rejection of the demand for a separate social identity is my own.

[3] *Renmin ribao,* Aug. 12, 1989.

ures announced centered on the already revived theme of society's needs and grass-roots application. The freshman class nationwide was formally reduced in number by about 30,000. The enrollment plan for 1989, prepared before the spring protests began, had been fixed at 640,000. The reduction to just over 600,000 was announced in July. Most seriously affected were the country's leading institutions, that is, the 36 key universities led directly by the SEDC, which together absorbed half the cut. The other half was to be shared about equally between the 300 additional centrally administered institutions and the 700 run by lower level governments. These two categories were ordered to reduce admissions by 7,000 to 8,000 freshmen respectively.[4]

Although the two-way selection procedure remained in effect, the majority of graduating seniors had to accept state job assignments as announced in early 1989, due to the difficulties students encountered in finding jobs that matched their aspirations. The majority inevitably had to accept placement "at the basic levels." The past practice of assigning students directly to national organizations was wrong, declared Premier Li Peng. College graduates must first be "tempered in practice."[5] More than 80 percent of the 1989 graduating seniors were accordingly assigned to work in "localities" and only 17 percent to central or national-level work units. Between 80 and 90 percent of the graduates from provincial colleges were assigned to prefectures, counties, or below.[6]

Similarly a new requirement for graduate study is one or two years of practical experience in basic-level work units.[7] In addition, all college graduates assigned to Party and government organization at or above the provincial level between 1985 and 1988 inclusive are being required to take leaves-of-absence for two or three years in order to gain practical, grass-roots experience. In the future, such organizations will have to recruit staff from among college

---

[4] *Wenhuibao,* Hong Kong, July 22, 1989. Beijing University, where the protests began, bore the brunt of these measures. Not only did its new students have to spend their entire freshman year at the Shijiazhuang military academy, but their numbers were reduced from a planned 2,000 to about 700. The military academy experiment was officially declared a success and extended to include other leading universities in 1990.

[5] *Renmin ribao,* Sept. 10, 1989.

[6] *Renmin ribao,* Sept. 26, 1989; *Zhongguo jiaoyu bao,* Sept. 26, 1989; *China Daily,* Aug. 3 and Sept. 27, 1989.

[7] According to *China Daily,* Aug. 12, 1989, citing a SEDC circular; and *Zhongguo qingnian bao,* Sept. 14, 1989, citing a SEDC decision.

graduates so tempered.[8] Finally, the SEDC has abandoned its more flexible posture of late 1988 to reaffirm most of the guidelines and restrictions announced earlier that year aimed at controlling overseas study.[9]

The SEDC defended all of these measures in its first formal post–June 4 policy summation and in subsequent statements. CCP leadership had grown lax, claimed Education Minister Li Tieying in the December summation. The new aim was to strengthen Party building and political education. "In principle," the immediate post–Cultural Revolution leadership formula of "university president responsibility under the leadership of the CCP committee" should be revived, he said, to enhance the authority of the latter by comparison with the former in a direct reversal of 1980s practice. Political criteria should be similarly revived in assessing qualifications for student enrollment, job placement, staff promotions, and overseas study.[10]

Li Tieying also cited the recent laxity in enrollment work. The 1988 planned intake of 640,000 had actually been exceeded by 100,000, he claimed. He did not mention that the expedient of enrolling outside the plan had been used by schools to earn extra income since they are allowed to keep the fees paid by such extra self-financed students. But henceforth, he said, enrollment must adhere strictly to the state plans, and he defended the 1989 reduced intake as necessary to counteract recent excesses. The growth of tertiary institutions was also to be curtailed. He noted that in 1984 and 1985 alone, some 200 new schools had opened. The SEDC

---

[8] According to a leftwing Hong Kong newspaper (*Wenhuibao,* Aug. 22, 1989) and subsequently confirmed in a telephone interview with a SEDC spokesman in Beijing (*Hong Kong Standard,* Aug. 23, 1989).

[9] *Renmin ribao,* July 27, 1989, and Sept. 10, 1989; *China Daily,* Oct. 9, 1989; Wang Zhigang and Mei Minhui, "Guojia jiaowei fuzhuren He Dongchang tan: Zhongguo jiaoyu kaifang yu liuxuesheng zhengce" (SEDC Vice-minister He Dongchang on: China's Policy of Educational Openness and Overseas Study), *Liaowang zhoukan* (Outlook Weekly) (Beijing), overseas ed., no. 34 (Aug. 21, 1989), pp. 15–16; and citing new draft guideline "principles" in a State Council document, *New York Times,* Oct. 18, 1989, and *Hong Kong Standard,* Oct. 20, 1989.

[10] Li Tieying's report to the National People's Congress Standing Committee, Dec. 23, 1989, in *Renmin ribao,* Jan. 3, 1990. The aim of reviving Party leadership over universities by placing the presidential responsibility system beneath it was reiterated at a spring conference on Party building in tertiary institutions. The conference also advocated reviving the tradition of central and local Party leaders *outside* the education sector exercising an active supervisory role over institutions of higher learning (e.g., *Renmin ribao,* April 13 and 17, 1990).

would no longer permit the establishment of new tertiary level institutions nor approve requests to upgrade, as from junior to regular college status. Those unable to meet stipulated standards should be improved, reorganized, or if necessary merged. Students for their part should adjust their expectations downward "to the basic levels, the villages, the border regions, and bitter occupations." Qualified college graduates "should obey the state's requirements and the state should be responsible for assigning them appropriate work."[11] When the admissions plan of 620,000 was announced for 1990, a SEDC spokesman said that intake would be reduced or curtailed "in those schools where political education work is weak and in specialties where the aim of study is unclear," as well as in specialties for which job openings were limited and in schools undergoing reorganization. The practice of accepting fully self-financed students was said to be still in the "experimental" stage and such students were not to exceed 3 percent of all those admitted. Recognized alternatives for unsuccessful candidates included the television university and correspondence courses.[12] Education Commission Vice Minister He Dongchang also revealed that henceforth keypoint elementary and middle schools would no longer be regarded as an appropriate form of education and that other methods of promoting students in the lower grades were under consideration.[13]

In all of these ways, then, the recently rediscovered concerns about adapting higher education more appropriately to China's needs have been reinterpreted by the post–June 4 leadership not just as a social responsibility, or as part of a time-honored twentieth-century Chinese controversy, but also as a form of punishment to be imposed collectively on the country's intellectual elite. Thus, Ding Shisun would probably approve the reduced tertiary enrollments and school mergers—but not as retribution against those where political education was weak and certainly not at the cost of the presidential responsibility system which allowed him to

---

[11] Li Tieying in *Renmin ribao*, Jan. 3, 1990. According to figures subsequently issued by the State Statistical Bureau in its annual communiqué, only 597,000 freshmen were actually admitted into regular tertiary level programs in 1989, said to be 10.8 percent less than the year preceding (*Renmin ribao*, Feb. 21, 1990).

[12] *Renmin ribao*, March 7, 1990.

[13] He Dongchang's comments were made at a meeting on "joyful education" organized by the Education Commission in May (*Yangzi wanbao* [Yangtze River Evening News], Nanjing, May 24, 1990). The *People's Daily* account of this Beijing meeting did not include He Dongchang's statement on keypoint schools (*Renmin ribao*, May 24, 1990).

publicize his demands in the first place. The keypoint college preparatory stream has enjoyed a controversial existence at best throughout the 1980s, and many of its critics would surely applaud its demise—were the government's motives not also inspired by the likely political aim of trying to undercut the pretensions and aspirations built into the college preparatory stream from elementary school upward.

Solutions are, in other words, being deliberately redefined as part of a leftist backlash against the urban-based Western-oriented wing of China's political and intellectual establishment. However necessary, then, if actually implemented in the manner announced during 1989–90, such solutions will undoubtedly be eclipsed by yet another backlash against them—when the balance of political forces shifts once more and the logic of the two-line struggle proceeds to its next conclusion. In the process, we will be able to watch as yet another typical episode unfolds in the history of China's educational development—foiled again by the political imperatives surrounding it.

Presumably, these imperatives will wind down, and their destructive impulses will also moderate over time. Eventually, it may be possible to objectify social interests and select reasonable policy alternatives from both sides of the left-right political divide. Successes in economic development might even render irrelevant contradictions such as those between college graduates' aspirations and society's needs. As the last decade of the century begins, however, such eventualities seem more like utopian visions of the century to come than a realistic conclusion for the one ending.

In the meantime, China's search for ideal models must continue even as the most recent precedents sought in the example of international communism disintegrate. If China's modern development continues to follow the now familiar pattern, its present leaders will not be able to stand indefinitely against what Chinese intellectuals were, by early 1990, already describing as the new "international tide" of communism discredited in Eastern Europe and the Soviet Union. If that tide prevails, new Chinese leaders will draw inspiration from it and seek new precedents within it. But if in this way old patterns and interests continue to interact with the new, then the latter must inevitably address the still unresolved issues that have given impetus to China's educational development for most of the twentieth century.

Selected Readings on Chinese Education

Alitto, Guy S. *The Last Confucian: Liang Shu-ming and the Chinese Dilemma of Modernity.* Berkeley and Los Angeles: University of California Press, 1979.

Barendsen, Robert D. *Half-work Half-study Schools in Communist China.* Washington, D.C.: U.S. Department of Health, Education, and Welfare, 1964.

Bernstein, Thomas P. *Up to the Mountains and Down to the Villages: The Transfer of Youth from Urban to Rural China.* New Haven: Yale University Press, 1977.

Borthwick, Sally. *Education and Social Change in China: The Beginnings of the Modern Era.* Stanford, Calif.: Hoover Institution Press, Stanford University, 1983.

Bullock, Mary Brown. *An American Transplant: The Rockefeller Foundation and Peking Union Medical College.* Berkeley and Los Angeles: University of California Press, 1980.

Chen, Theodore Hsi-en. *Chinese Education Since 1949.* New York: Pergamon Press, 1981.

———. *The Maoist Educational Revolution.* New York: Praeger, 1974.

Chinese Education. A quarterly journal of translations edited by Stanley Rosen. Armonk, N.Y.: M. E. Sharpe.

Cleverley, John. *The Schooling of China.* London: George Allen and Unwin, 1985.

Hawkins, John N., ed. *Education and Social Change in the People's Republic of China.* New York: Praeger, 1983.

Hayhoe, Ruth. *China's Universities and the Open Door.* Armonk, N.Y.: M. E. Sharpe, 1989.

Hayhoe, Ruth, ed. *Contemporary Chinese Education.* London: Croom Helm, 1984.

Hayhoe, Ruth, and Marianne Bastid, eds. *China's Education and the Industrialized World.* Armonk, N.Y.: M. E. Sharpe, 1987.

Kallgren, Joyce K., and Denis Fred Simon, eds. *Educational Exchanges: Essays on the Sino-American Experience.* Research Papers and Policy

Studies, no. 21. Berkeley: Institute of East Asian Studies, University of California, 1987.

Keenan, Barry. *The Dewey Experiment in China: Educational Reform and Political Power in the Early Republic.* Cambridge: Harvard University Press, 1977.

Kwong, Julia. *Cultural Revolution in China's Schools, May 1966–April 1969.* Stanford, Calif.: Hoover Institution Press, 1988.

Lampton, David, et al. *A Relationship Restored: Trends in U.S.-China Educational Exchanges, 1978–1984.* Washington, D.C.: National Academy Press, 1986.

Orleans, Leo A. *Chinese Students in America: Policies, Issues, and Numbers.* Washington, D.C.: National Academy Press, 1988.

_____. *Professional Manpower and Education in Communist China.* Washington, D.C.: National Science Foundation, 1960.

Price, Ronald Francis. *Education in Modern China,* second ed. London: Routledge and Kegan Paul, 1979.

_____. *Marx and Education in Russia and China.* London: Croom Helm, 1977.

Rawski, Evelyn Sakakida. *Education and Popular Literacy in Ch'ing China.* Ann Arbor: University of Michigan Press, 1979.

Rosen, Stanley. *Red Guard Factionalism and the Cultural Revolution in Guangzhou.* Boulder, Colo.: Westview Press, 1982.

Shirk, Susan *Competitive Comrades.* Berkeley and Los Angeles: University of California Press, 1982.

Taylor, Robert. *China's Intellectual Dilemma: Politics and University Enrollment, 1949–1978.* Vancouver: University of British Columbia Press, 1981.

Thomson, James C., Jr. *While China Faced West: American Reformers in Nationalist China, 1928–1937.* Cambridge: Harvard University Press, 1969.

Unger, Jonathan. *Education Under Mao.* New York: Columbia University Press, 1982.

West, Philip. *Yenching University and Sino-Western Relations, 1916–1952.* Cambridge: Harvard University Press, 1976.

White, Gordon. *Party and Professionals: The Political Role of Teachers in Contemporary China.* Armonk, N.Y.: M. E. Sharpe, 1981.

INSTITUTE OF EAST ASIAN STUDIES PUBLICATIONS SERIES

CHINA RESEARCH MONOGRAPHS (CRM)

6. David D. Barrett. *Dixie Mission: The United States Army Observer Group in Yenan, 1944*, 1970 ($4.00)
17. Frederic Wakeman, Jr., Editor. *Ming and Qing Historical Studies in the People's Republic of China*, 1981 ($10.00)
21. James H. Cole. *The People Versus the Taipings: Bao Lisheng's "Righteous Army of Dongan,"* 1981 ($7.00)
22. Dan C. Sanford. *The Future Association of Taiwan with the People's Republic of China*, 1982 ($8.00)
23. A. James Gregor with Maria Hsia Chang and Andrew B. Zimmerman. *Ideology and Development: Sun Yat-sen and the Economic History of Taiwan*, 1982 ($8.00)
24. Pao-min Chang. *Beijing, Hanoi, and the Overseas Chinese*, 1982 ($7.00)
25. Rudolf G. Wagner. *Reenacting the Heavenly Vision: The Role of Religion in the Taiping Rebellion*, 1984 ($12.00)
27. John N. Hart. *The Making of an Army "Old China Hand": A Memoir of Colonel David D. Barrett*, 1985 ($12.00)
28. Steven A. Leibo. *Transferring Technology to China: Prosper Giquel and the Self-strengthening Movement*, 1985 ($15.00)
29. David Bachman. *Chen Yun and the Chinese Political System*, 1985 ($15.00)
30. Maria Hsia Chang. *The Chinese Blue Shirt Society: Fascism and Developmental Nationalism*, 1985 ($15.00)
31. Robert Y. Eng. *Economic Imperialism in China: Silk Production and Exports, 1861–1932*, 1986 ($15.00)
33. Yue Daiyun. *Intellectuals in Chinese Fiction*, 1988 ($10.00)
34. Constance Squires Meaney. *Stability and the Industrial Elite in China and the Soviet Union*, 1988 ($15.00)
35. Yitzhak Shichor. *East Wind over Arabia: Origins and Implications of the Sino-Saudi Missile Deal*, 1989 ($7.00)
36. Suzanne Pepper. *China's Education Reform in the 1980s: Policies, Issues, and Historical Perspectives*, 1990 ($12.00)

KOREA RESEARCH MONOGRAPHS (KRM)

9. Helen Hardacre. *The Religion of Japan's Korean Minority: The Preservation of Ethnic Identity*, 1985 ($12.00)
10. Fred C. Bohm and Robert R. Swartout, Jr., Editors. *Naval Surgeon in Yi Korea: The Journal of George W. Woods*, 1984 ($12.00)
11. Robert A. Scalapino and Hongkoo Lee, Editors. *North Korea in a Regional and Global Context*, 1986 ($20.00)
12. Laurel Kendall and Griffin Dix, Editors. *Religion and Ritual in Korean Society*, 1987 ($15.00)
13. Vipan Chandra. *Imperialism, Resistance, and Reform in Late Nineteenth-Century Korea: Enlightenment and the Independence Club*, 1988 ($17.00)
14. Seok Choong Song. *Explorations in Korean Syntax and Semantics*, 1988 ($20.00)
15. Robert A. Scalapino and Dalchoong Kim, Editors. *Asian Communism: Continuity and Transition*, 1988 ($20.00)

JAPAN RESEARCH MONOGRAPHS (JRM)

6. Masumi Junnosuke. *Postwar Politics in Japan, 1945–1955*, 1985 ($25.00)
7. Teruo Gotoda. *The Local Politics of Kyoto*, 1985 ($15.00)
8. Yung H. Park. *Bureaucrats and Ministers in Contemporary Japanese Government*, 1986 ($15.00)
9. Victoria V. Vernon. *Daughters of the Moon: Wish, Will, and Social Constraint in Fiction by Modern Japanese Women*, 1988 ($12.00)
10. Steve Rabson, Translator. *Okinawa: Two Postwar Novellas by Ōshiro Tatsuhiro and Higashi Mineo*, 1989 ($10.00). Introduction and afterword by Steve Rabson.